Pronoun Envy

Pronoun Envy

Literary Uses of Linguistic Gender

Anna Livia

June '08
Happy father's Day
Daddy!
Love as always,
Pippa

OXFORD

UNIVERSITY PRESS

2001

OXFORD
UNIVERSITY PRESS

Oxford   New York
Athens   Auckland   Bangkok   Bogatá   Buenos Aires   Calcutta
Cape Town   Chennai   Dar es Salaam   Delhi   Florence   Hong Kong   Istanbul
Karachi   Kuala Lumpur   Madrid   Melbourne   Mexico City   Mumbai
Nairobi   Paris   São Paulo   Shanghai   Singapore   Taipei   Tokyo   Toronto   Warsaw

and associated companies in
Berlin   Ibadan

Copyright © 2001 by Anna Livia

Published by Oxford University Press, Inc.
198 Madison Avenue, New York, New York 10016

Oxford is a registered trademark of Oxford University Press

Library of Congress Cataloguing-in-Publication Data
Livia, Anna.
Pronoun envy : literary uses of linguistic gender / Anna Livia.
p. cm.—(Studies in language and gender)
Includes bibliographical references and index.
ISBN 0-19-513852-X (cloth)—ISBN 0-19-513853-8 (pbk.)
1. English language—Gender.   2. English language—Grammar, Comparative—French.
3. French language—Grammar, Comparative—English.   4. Nonsexist language in literature.
5. English language—Pronoun.   6. French language—Pronoun.   7. French language—Gender.
8. Sexism in literature.   9. Sexism in language.   I. Title.   II. Series.
PE1211 .L58 2000
306.44—dc21   00-021515

1 3 5 7 9 8 6 4 2

Printed in the United States of America
on acid-free paper

To Jeannie, Emma, and Asher

Acknowledgments

I would like to take this opportunity to thank some of the people who helped me carry out my research and complete this book, which started off life as my doctoral dissertation at University of California at Berkeley. Preeminent among these is Suzanne Fleischman, my mentor at U.C. Berkeley, who imparted to me her fascination with the linguistic analysis of literary texts and encouraged me to explore the rocky domain of linguistic gender. Without her finely calibrated sense of logic and consequence and her built-in bullshit detector, this book would have lacked the detail and structure it now has. Kira Hall, my friend and colleague, also lent a sharp and willing ear to my ruminations about gender and binary thinking. Robin Lakoff provided, over a series of lunch dates, both a sounding board for my ideas and an acute commentary on contemporary representations of femininity and masculinity. Others who have helped strengthen the original manuscript include the three anonymous Oxford reviewers, to whom I am very grateful. Their thoughtful questions and suggestions allowed me to see how what I had written might sound to outside ears. The Research Board at the University of Illinois granted me valuable research time in which to expand my arguments into new areas. I would also like to thank other friends and colleagues who offered more tangential support in the form of enthusiasm for the project or for my scholarship in general: Douglas Kibbee, Karen and Alain Fresco, Armine Mortimer, Julian Boyd, Ann Smock, and Nina Wakeford. My series editor at Oxford, Mary Bucholtz, was unfailingly supportive and perceptive, and I owe it to her that the manuscript made its way through the review process and into these covers.

An excerpt from an earlier version of chapter 2 appeared as "The Riddle of the Sphinx: Creating Genderless Characters in French" in Mary Bucholtz, Anita Liang, and Laurel Sutton, eds., *Cultural Performances:* Proceedings of the Third Berkeley Women and Language Group (Berkeley: Berkeley Women and Language Group, 1996), 421–33. An excerpt from an earlier version of chapter 5 appeared as "Fear of Sewers: Who Sees This, Who Thinks This? Who Says This?" in Natasha Warner et al., eds., *Gender and Belief Systems: Proceedings of the Fourth Berkeley Women and Language Conference, April 19, 20, and 21, 1996,* (Berkeley: Berkeley Women and Language Group, 1996), 439–46. An excerpt from an earlier version of chapter 6 appeared as "'She Sired Six Children': Pronominal Gender Play in English," in Mary Bucholtz, A. C. Liang, and Laurel A. Sutton, eds., *Reinventing Identities: The Gendered Self in Discourse* (New York: Oxford University Press, 1999), 332–47. An excerpt from an earlier version of chapter 7 appeared as "Disloyal to Maculinity," in Anna Livia and Kira Hall, eds., *Queerly Phrased: Language, Gender, and Sexuality* (New York: Oxford University Press, 1997), 349–68.

Permissions: Chapter 2: Editions Bernard Grasset has kindly given permission to reproduce extracts from *Sphinx* by Anne Garréta in chapter 2 of this work. Chapter 3: Little, Brown and Company (UK) has kindly given permission to reproduce extracts from *Love Child* by Maureen Duffy in chapter 3 of this work (excluding USA). Jonathan Clowes Ltd. has kindly given permission to reprint extracts from *Love Child* by Maureen Duffy in chapter 3 of this work in the USA. Chapter 5: Les Editions de Minuit has kindly given permission to reproduce extracts from *L'Opoponax* by Monique Wittig in chapter 5 of this work. Chapter 6: Katherine Arnold has kindly given permission to reproduce extracts from *The Cook and the Carpenter* in chapter 6 of this work.

Contents

Pronoun Envy

1

"Un homme sur deux est une femme"

Introduction—Pronoun Envy and Phallogocentrism

Pronoun Envy

In November 1971, women students at Harvard Divinity School protested that the masculine *He* should not be used in reference to God, nor should masculine pronouns be used to refer to people in general. Each time someone in the lecture room used the masculine pronoun or a masculine generic such as *man* or *mankind* when speaking of humanity at large, the women blew paper kazoos to express their disapproval. The matter was reported to the *Harvard Crimson* (the college in-house magazine). Calvert Watkins, chair of the Harvard linguistics department, responded with a letter cosigned by seventeen colleagues, including the departmental secretary. They assured readers that what was really at issue was not masculist tyranny, but the question of markedness. Since the masculine is the unmarked term of the masculine/feminine dyad, it has both generic and specific use. "There is," Watkins et al. informed readers, "no need for anxiety or pronoun envy" (*Harvard Crimson*, 26 November 1971, 17).[1] Yet pronoun envy there has certainly been these last twenty-five years, if we are to take the phrase to signify the desire for gender parity in language. Pronoun envy motivates more than two decades of feminist writing, writing that makes linguistic issues central to the text—experimenting with new forms, rejuvenating old and little-used forms, or simply eliminating linguistic gender for animate referents. Watkins et al.'s remark that the use of *he* as a generic is merely a question of markedness was either extraordinarily disingenuous or extraordinarily obtuse, for the hierarchy the marked/unmarked relationship sets up in ideologically loaded pairs such as white/black, male/female, or old/young is deeply problematic.

Nor has reaction to pronoun envy been restricted to Anglophone communities. In an article provocatively entitled "Priez Dieu, elle vous exaucera" (Pray to God, She Will Grant Your Prayers),[2] first published in *F Magazine* in January 1978, the French feminist novelist Benoîte Groult reports on the creation of Femmes et hommes dans l'église (Women and Men in the Church) (Groult 1981, 125–28). This is an international group of Catholics and Protestants based in Brussels whose aim is to put an end to sexism in the church in all its forms. One of their projects was to rewrite the liturgy so that, for example, as the women divinity students at Harvard had demanded seven years earlier, it no longer employed falsely generic masculine pronouns. If God was not perceived as masculine, the statement "Priez Dieu, elle vous exaucera" would no longer be shocking in its use of the feminine pronoun. Groult's article opens with a slogan from the Mouvement de Libération des Femmes (MLF; French women's liberation movement), "Cinquante pour cent des hommes sont des femmes" (Fifty percent of men are women), explaining that the Christian brothers were beginning to apply this revelation to the church, where 50 percent of brothers turn out to be sisters. The quotation that heads this introduction, "Un homme sur deux est une femme" (One man in two is a woman), is another MLF slogan that was chanted at the Tomb of the Unknown Soldier during an MLF march in August 1970. Could the famous unknown *soldat* (m.) turn out to be a *soldate* (f.)? Or should the epicene (common-gender) term *militaire* be used to avoid the question?

Like its precursor, penis envy, "pronoun envy" is a wonderfully dismissive label, putting an end to debate by declaring the premise ludicrous. Women do not possess a penis; in the popular perception, it is the very fact of this lack that makes us women. To envy a man his penis is foolish, fruitless, and pathological. To envy men the generic use of the masculine pronoun, then, is equally pathological and equally doomed to frustration and failure. Watkins et al. graciously observe that there is no need for female divinity students to experience this futile desire, since it is not the pronouns themselves but the Indo-European system of markedness that is at issue. This maneuver shifts the blame from one element in the language to the system itself. Far from supporting structural changes or radical realignment, however, the *Crimson* correspondents declare: "The fact that the masculine is the unmarked gender in English . . . is unlikely to be an impediment to any change in the patterns of the sexual division of labor toward which our society may wish to evolve" (*Harvard Crimson*, 16 November 1971, 17). No sociological evidence is offered to support this claim, apart from the assertion that the feminine is unmarked in the language of the Tunica Indians.[3] *Rarissimi* examples of role reversal do little to appease the injured, though they seem to satisfy their producers.

The observation that linguistic structure is biased in favor of the masculine and to the detriment of the feminine, so cavalierly dismissed among these Anglophones as motivated by "pronoun envy," is accorded, among Francophones, the title *phallogocentrisme*, which, though grander and Greeker, is equally Freudian. The term was coined by Jacques Derrida following his rereadings of the works of Sigmund Freud and Jacques Lacan (Derrida 1975; see also Spivak 1976). Phallogocentrism indicates in philosophical outlook, if not in practical intent, that the centrality of the phallus to signifying practice is aberrant and that the system needs critical attention—critical attention implying not suggestions for reform, but a focus on the object under discussion. Derrida quotes Lacan's observation that "le phallus est le signifiant privilégié" (the phallus is the privileged signifier) ("La signification du phallus," in *Les Ecrits*, 692; quoted in Derrida 1975, 132) and recognizes "le phallogocentrisme comme androcentrisme" (phallogocentrism as androcentrism) (Derrida 1975, 132). Or, in Namascar Shaktini's more transparent prose, "[o]n peut décrire le phallogocentrisme comme la tradition qui constitue un système signifiant organisé autour du genre" (one can describe phallogocentrism as the tradition that constitutes a signifying system around gender) (Shaktini 1985, 66). The system revolves not simply around gender, I would add, but specifically around gender difference, and indeed a hierarchy of difference. Unlike the English phrase *pronoun envy*, which suggests that the protester is misguided, the term *phallogocentrism* recognizes both that gender is a central, indeed the central, component of language (as conceived by structuralist linguistics) and that it is organized around the mark of masculinity.[4]

In this work I investigate feminist and other expressions of pronoun envy, or opposition to phallogocentrism, in written texts in English and French. I concentrate on those texts that in some way problematize the traditional functioning of the linguistic gender system. The constitution of the corpus of texts under investigation may itself seem controversial to readers more used to a high level of thematic or stylistic continuity. I have assembled a body of data from the written language that demonstrates the working of gender in modern French and English, both in their canonical and in their more marked usages. I concentrate on French and English because it is in these languages that the most daring experimental works have been produced. The focus is on written texts rather than the spoken language because many morphological indicators of gender in French are only apparent in the written form. The works examined are rather different from one another in genre, ideology, and time period. In form, they include novels, prose poems, and personal testimonies. In political outlook, they variously express a militant feminist separatism, a belief in sociosexual androgyny, and a reinvestment in the traditional sex roles, as well as a parody of those roles. In time period, while most originate in the last quarter of the twentieth century, a few date from the early years of the century, and one from the nineteenth century.

Pronominal Quarrels

The pronominal system, and its workings and origins, has been a subject of fascination and some political debate among European thinkers since the sixteenth century. While most speakers, most of the time, are content to use language to convey their message, at times of social strife many turn to linguistic distinctions to provide validation for their political beliefs. During periods of political upheaval, language is often seen (erroneously) as a source of natural, timeless laws, and proponents of conservatism will quote these laws as models for a well-ordered society. More radical elements will often counter by a demand for linguistic change. Some of the earliest European examples of this ideological move come from discussions of chapters of the Bible. The biblical accounts of the creation of Eve and the tower of Babel have proved rich mines for both feminist and antifeminist arguments over the centuries as the two sides pick apart the exact wording of Genesis, in its different translations, to prove that either Eve or Adam was created first. The masculist tendency sees the origin of language as parallel to the origin of the sexes, resulting in descriptions of male and female language in which the female is subordinate to the male in all things (Baron 1986, 11–20).

The English men James Burnet (Lord Monboddo) and Rowland Jones both wrote influential accounts of the origins of language in the late eighteenth century: Monboddo's six-volume *Of the Origin and Progress of Language* was first published in 1773, Jones's *The Origin of Language and Nations* in 1764. The late eighteenth century was a period of questioning throughout Europe, a time of malaise that would culminate in the American War of Independence (1775–1783) and the French Revolution (1789). While Monboddo and Jones were discussing the origins of language in England, Diderot and his fellow *encyclopédistes* were hard at work on the seventeen volumes of the *Encyclopédie ou dictionnaire raisonnée des sciences* (1751–72), a mammoth intellectual attempt to tame and bring order to a changing world by encoding and containing it in definition and description. At the same time, Jean-Jacques Rousseau was busy producing his own meditation on the origins of language and its relation to the social contract in *Discours sur l'origine de l'inégalité* (1754) and *Du Contrat social* (1762).

As concerns pronouns specifically, Jones discusses the use of the letter *i*, which is also the number *1*, to represent Adam, the first man, and the first person pronoun. "The first person pronoun signifies man as an indefinite line placed alone or by himself at the centre of things" (Baron 1986, 15). The second person pronoun is based on the creation of Eve from Adam and represented by the letter *u*, or two *i*s joined together. Other eighteenth-century writers, including Robert Baker, Michael Maittaire, and John Horne Tooke, theorize about the origin and motivation of the third person singular pronouns in English (*he*, *she*, and *it*), deriving them from various Old English sources including *he* from *haetan* (to call), and *she* from *swag* (to sway, keep). All three assume that the pronoun *he* was originally epicene and only recently gained its masculine meaning. The supposed epicene origin of *he* is taken as justification for its use with referents whose gender is unknown. In fact, the Old English system of masculine *he*, feminine *heo*, and neuter *hit* already encoded both gender and high animacy. (According to the hierarchical ordering of noun phrases by which sentient referents like human beings are placed higher than lifeless objects like rocks or abstract ideas).

French has traditionally been considered, in the English folk-linguistic view, soft, feminine, even effeminate. It is the language of love, the language in which the serpent spoke to Eve (Baron 1986, 58) according to the seventeenth century Swedish writer Anders Kempe, who describes God speaking Swedish, Adam, Danish, and Eve, French. For the French, on the other hand, their language is based on reason and logic. "La syntaxe française est incorruptible. . . . Tout ce qui n'est pas clair, n'est pas français" (French syntax is incorruptible. . . . Whatever is not clear, is not French), as Antoine de Rivarol claimed in an oft-quoted lecture, *De l'universalité de la langue française*, in 1784. Descartes's "Je pense donc je suis" (or "Cogito ergo sum," in its original Latin) is still quoted today as proof of the national propensity for rational thought. Inherent in the view that French syntax is incorruptible is the belief that it should therefore be defended from the onslaught of modern usage. The French language represents the best of France, the quintessence of the French spirit, and must not be allowed to change, for change will lead to linguistic impurity and incomprehension, paralleled by social turbulence and depravity. The following declaration of Voltaire encapsulates the eighteenth-century French abhorrence of linguistic change:

> Il me semble que lorsqu'on a eu dans un siècle un nombre suffisant de bons écrivains devenus classiques, il n'est plus guère permis d'employer d'autres expressions que les leurs, et qu'il faut leur donner le même sens, ou bien dans peu de temps, le siècle présent n'entendrait plus le siècle passé.

> (It seems to me that when one has had a sufficient number of good writers in one century whose works have become classics, it is scarcely permitted to use other expressions than theirs, and that one must give them the same meaning, or else in a short time, the present century will no longer be able to understand the previous one. (quoted in Lodge 1993, 181)

Voltaire's reference to the work of "good writers," rather than, say, eloquent orators, is not casual. The championing of the rationality and purity of the French language runs parallel with the belief that the written form represents the purest form of the language. Written texts can be preserved and enshrined in a way that, before the advent of tape recorders, was impossible for the spoken language. Written language is also more conservative and slower to change.

Because of the Renaissance interest in preserving Latin texts and its passion for tracing back to Latin every element in the romance languages, the Latin origin of the third person pronouns in French has not been obscured to the same extent as the Old English origin of English pronouns. The French subject pronouns *il* and *elle* originate in the nominative forms of the Latin demonstrative pronouns: *il < ILLE, elle < ILLA*. The French object pronouns *le* and *la* originate in the accusative forms of the Latin demonstrative pronouns: *le < ILLUM, la < ILLAM* (see also Rickard 1989, 69–70, and Harris 1978, 99–122, for an account of the history of the morphology of personal pronouns from Latin to modern French). There are, consequently, fewer early fanciful accounts of the origin of French personal pronouns. Discussion of the gender inequality built into the system does not begin until the nineteenth century. Instead, French writers as early as the sixteenth-century essayist Michel de Montaigne in his account of a trip to Italy (1580–81) play with gendered third person pronouns to express the androgyny, homosexuality, or transsexuality of the referent (this point is expanded in chapter 7). During the French Revolution, it was the second person pronoun that found itself the target of reformers. The polite *vous* was outlawed in favor of the egalitarian *tu* in the belief that linguistic change should parallel and help enforce social change. (A similar pronominal change was imposed in Italy under Mussolini: Fascist ideology required that citizens use the egalitarian *tu* form for the second person singular in place of the customary polite third person form, *lei*.)

As this discussion shows, it is particularly in times of social turbulence that different constituencies turn to language to prove their points or demand change. Indeed, as Deborah Cameron demonstrates in *Verbal Hygiene*, the urge to improve or clean up language is "as basic to the use of language as vowels are to its phonetic structure" (1995, 1). Dennis Baron has shown, with a wealth of examples, that the gender bias inherent in the use of *he* as a generic has been a hot issue since the middle of the nineteenth century (1986, 205–9). Interest increases with the rise of the movement for women's liberation and equal rights. The texts discusssed in this study mostly come from the latter half of the twentieth century, a period when feminist activity and the consequent antifeminist backlash have been at their peak.

Linguistic Analysis of Literary Texts

While text-based linguistics is by now well established, the linguistic analysis of literary works usually focuses on the micro level of text construction, leaving such "literary" concerns as plot, character, theme, and moral or ideological point to literary theorists. I do not mean to imply a strict segregation between the two realms; there are, of course, important areas of overlap, especially in the fields of narrativity and stylistics. In general, however, lower-case *discourse*, involving an examination of such textual features as tense, aspect, deictics, and focalization or information packaging (to name but a few), is considered the province of linguistics. The wider-societal upper-case *Discourse* is deemed more suited to disciplines such as history, rhetoric, or literary criticism, which look at the interplay between texts and culture. In this work, I am concerned not only with the micro (linguistic) level, but also with the macro (ideological) level. Since, as well as having interesting linguistic realizations, gender is an important cultural phenomenon, it would seem wilfully perverse to disregard the stated intentions of the feminist and other authors studied here by confining myself to linguistic analysis proper.

Over the last twenty years (during which period the majority of the texts examined here were published) a substantial amount of research has been carried out both in the linguistic field of language and gender and in the literary field of feminist fiction. There has, however, been little overlap between the two domains of feminist research. Linguistic scholars have paid scant attention to feminist literary texts (there is of course a whole body of criticism devoted to more mainstream work). For their part, literary critics rarely use the tools of linguistics to examine feminist fiction, and as we will see in chapters 4 and 5, those literary scholars who have attempted this feat do not always manifest a robust grasp of the discipline. I therefore examine both the linguistic complexities of the texts and their effect on such features as character development and moral or ideological purpose.

As I have already noted, since the seventeenth century both the French public and the French government have assumed that the written word is the purest and most correct form of the language, the standard by which the spoken word is to be judged. Indeed, the academician Vaugelas declares *bon usage* (good usage) to be the speech of the majority of the royal court and that of the most highly esteemed authors of the day. Since France became a republic there has been no royal court, leaving the work of esteemed authors as sole arbiter of grammar and style. English has not been subject to nearly the same level of codification and protection as French. There is, after all, no Haut Comité de défense et d'expansion de la langue (High Committee for the Defense and Expansion of the Language) in England or the United States to rival the French committee created in 1966 by de Gaulle (renamed the Délégation générale à la langue française in 1989) (Judge 1993, 7–27). Nevertheless, English speakers often behave as though they too believed that the written word should dictate the grammatical and stylistic rules of the spoken language. "He speaks in full paragraphs" and "she talks like a book" are usually words of praise suggesting that the speaker in question has successfully emulated the written model.

Anyone who has transcribed even a five-minute segment of naturally occurring conversation knows that "talking like a book" is both an unachievable and a highly undesirable goal. Spoken language chunks information into easily comprehensible segments. Speakers give each other signals as to when they are about to finish their turn, when others may interrupt, and when they are about to launch into a long narrative and wish to hold the floor for an extended period. These devices, which involve intricate and sophisticated repetition, checking back, and self-correction, are unnecessary in written texts but vital to the smooth running of spoken discourse.

(See Labov and Waletsky 1967, Labov 1972, Labov and Fanshel 1977, Goodwin 1990, and Schiffrin 1994 for detailed discussions of conversation and discourse analysis). Beginning linguistics students are continually told that they need to collect spontaneously produced and attested examples from native speakers in realistic contexts and that the constructed dialogue of literary texts is invalid for any claim they might wish to make about the spoken language. For sociolinguists, at least, the distinction between written and spoken language no longer needs to be argued. It is recognized within the discipline that the two often behave like separate but related systems, each with its own syntax, semantics, lexicon, and pragmatics. Points at which the spoken language differs from the written should be treated not as mistakes but as evidence of a different set of rules.

For literary scholars, in contrast, the written word tends to take precedence over spoken interactions, and the differences between the two systems are not so salient. Many English teachers believe that reading good books will help their students speak well and, conversely, that illiterate students speak badly. While literary scholars may wonder why it is helpful to use linguistic tools to analyze written texts, sociolinguists may ask how it is useful to linguistics to study literary language. This is not, of course, the first work that is linguistic in methodology and literary in content. Deborah Tannen and Robin Lakoff often use literary examples to support and illustrate their points about spoken interactions between men and women. Their coauthored article on Bergman's *Scenes from a Marriage* (reprinted in Tannen 1994) discusses communicative competence and pragmatic structures with reference to the character's spoken interaction, for example. The characters in this fictionalized representation of reality act out scenes that are larger than life, distilled to produce intense focus on the topic at hand, with intervening material filtered out. This distillation of experience is, indeed, one of the main functions of art. (See also Romaine 1999, chapter 11, on "Writing Feminist Futures.")

In *Pronoun Envy* I examine literary texts in order to see how far the gender system can be pushed in English and French. This is not to say that claims I make about the functioning of these texts will automatically map onto the spoken idiom, nor will they necessarily prove true of other world languages. The writers studied here experiment with gender in ways that would be almost unreplicable in spoken discourse. They test the reader's comprehension, demonstrating both the flexibility and the limits of the gender system. They also test the imagination, so that what is produced is not a blueprint for linguistic change but a challenge. Can a text with these modifications continue to function on any level?

Linguistic analysis provides a set of formal procedures that are more adept at getting at how a text is woven together than are by the more traditional literary tools of theme, character, plot, and story line. Good readers develop instincts about the way a text works, about how one author's style differs from another's, and these insights are extremely valuable, but the application of linguistics, with its insistence on relationships at the micro level of noun and pronoun, of the verb phrase and its arguments, can identify repetitive patterns that show how different devices work and, conversely, what happens to the structure of the text when literary experiments are introduced.

Linguistic Determinism and Literary Texts

As seen in the earlier discussion of the parallels forged between social change and linguistic reform, revolutionary movements tend to promote linguistic change, while the more conservative elements in society resist it in the name of preserving transcendent values. Contemporary feminist interest in the search for epicene third person pronouns and the avoidance of gender markers stems from the same basic belief that the language one speaks directly affects one's worldview. Since many of the writers whose work is considered here were strongly influenced by the hypothesis of linguistic determinism, it will be useful to look briefly at the axiom or ideology known as the Sapir-Whorf hypothesis.[5]

In its strong version, linguistic determinism, this hypothesis posits that the language one speaks determines one's perceptions of reality. In its weak version, linguistic relativity, it asserts that one's native language exerts a powerful influence over one's perceptions of reality. The difference is one of degree. The concept of linguistic relativity is most clearly formulated in Sapir's statements repudiating earlier beliefs in a correlation between linguistic morphology and cultural development:

> It is quite an illusion to imagine that one adjusts to reality essentially without the use of language and that language is merely an incidental means for solving specific problems of communication and reflection. The fact of the matter is that the "real world" is to a large extent unconsciously built on the language habits of the group. (Sapir 1929; quoted in Mülhäusler and Harré 1990, 3).

If one accepts any version of the hypothesis that the possibilities and exigencies of a language necessarily have an impact on the way speakers of that language perceive the world, then one must accept that linguistic structure is a central part of the formation of consciousness. In Edward Sapir's words, "Such categories as . . . gender . . . are systematically elaborated in language and are not so much discovered in experience as imposed upon it because of the tyrannical hold that linguistic form has upon our orientation in the world" ([1929] 1970, 68–9). We are born into a linguistic community whose language we learn as infants, inheriting the categories it uses, perceiving the distinctions it makes, and placing greater value on those distinctions because they are encoded in language than on others for which we have no words, or that are unimportant in the grammatical system. Language is constantly under construction, and this construction is of necessity a community event, though the community may not always be a community of equals.

The most widespread, popularized interpretation of the hypothesis of linguistic determinism is the belief that Eskimos (apparently meaning the

Inuit, Yupik, or indeed Athabascan peoples) have 100 words for snow. This statement is intended to indicate that they are able to make distinctions among the many different types of snow that speakers of other languages cannot make or even perceive. This idea is, of course, related to the French belief in phallogocentrism, or the centrality to the signifying practice of the word and the power of naming (see note 4). Fortunately, the "great Eskimo vocabulary hoax" has received both academic and popular rebuttal, the former by Laura Martin (in an *American Anthropologist* research note 1986), the latter by Geoffrey Pullum (1991). This rebuttal centers around two points, one purely linguistic, the other cognitive and psychological. The linguistic rebuttal goes as follows: Eskimo languages in general have rich, highly productive derivational morphology by which one stem may accrete large numbers of suffixes and prefixes; it is therefore more accurate to say that the morphology of Eskimo languages enables speakers to include many details about the snow in one construction, where English or French would use discrete lexical items. The cognitive-psychological rebuttal goes as follows: it is natural for communities to be concerned with and have a rich vocabulary for significant items in their immediate environment; the lack of such a rich vocabulary does not prevent members of other communities from perceiving the same distinctions, however.

The Danish novelist Peter Høeg's best-selling mystery *Miss Smilla's Feeling for Snow* (1992; made into a movie with the title under which it was published in the United States, *Smilla's Sense of Snow*) revolves around its heroine's ability to read the snow in its many different forms, a talent she has inherited from her Inuit mother and perfected during her childhood in Greenland. Attempts have been made by the English translator to preserve both the Inuit words and the English versions—for instance, *it kangirluarhuq*, big blocks of freshwater ice (300), and *it qanik*, fine powder snow (102)—presumably to demonstrate that aided by the syntax of one's native tongue, one can perceive distinctions in water density and formation that remain invisible to nonnative speakers.

While we might not accept that it is Smilla's command of Inuit, rather than her keen eye and familiarity with ice, that allows her to interpet snowy footprints and walk across Copenhagen harbor on almost submerged ice floes, we would probably agree that her language emphasizes distinctions that mostly seem irrelevant to other linguistic communities. This concept of linguistic relativism is also useful in looking at gender. "The world is presented in a kaleidoscope flux of impressions which has to be organized by our minds—this means largely by the linguistic systems in our minds" (Whorf 1956b, 213). This interpretation allows for the influence of other, nonlinguistic, semiotic factors, while attributing an important place to language and the categories it sets up. Essential to this hypothesis is the belief that because different languages have different structures that create different sets of oppositions, members of one linguistic community will not experience the world in the same way as members of another. It follows that we cannot examine power relations, and the creation of individual, gendered subjects, without knowing what positions are constructed by a language and what other roles the same linguistic devices may fill. This is the philosophical outlook of most of the authors whose work is studied here.

It should be noted that because most contemporary language scholars subscribe to versions of linguistic relativity, discussions of linguistic determinism are becoming obsolete among linguists. This does not mean that notions of linguistic determinism have disappeared entirely from the popular realm. Authors such as George Orwell have been very influential in popularizing the notion that language can control its users. In the less popular, more academic realm, feminist debates about identity politics versus constructionism frequently border on determinism. While proponents of identity politics are often dismissed as essentialist—that is, as believing that sexual identity is an essential part of one's makeup, independent of social environment—social constructionists may be criticized for overemphasizing the role of language in forming identity. Any suggestion that language is in some way more active or agentive than its users smacks of linguistic determinism. Judith Butler, for example, writes of discourse that it "inserts itself in . . . linguistic life," while individual language users (or, to use her terms, "culturally intelligible subjects") are "the resulting effects of . . . discourse" (1990, 145). If speaking subjects are reduced to the role of patient, or effect, while language takes the role of agent, then we must imagine language as creating the speaker.

Are we to assume that Butler's statement is intended paradoxically, suggesting an agonistic relation, as in "slavery creates freedom" and "heterosexuality creates homosexuality" (i.e., the terms "slavery" and "heterosexuality" can only be fully understood in contradistinction to their semantic opposites, "freedom" and "homosexuality"); or a metonymic relation, as in "guns create shooters" (i.e., although people manufacture guns and shoot them, without guns there would be no shooters)? Or must we assume a return to a structuralist concept of the constitutive and defining power of the institution? Butler herself clarifies this point: "[a]s a process, signification harbors within itself . . . agency" (1990, 145). If agency is located within the process of signification—that is, the process by which signifiers refer to signifieds—then it is divorced from the speaker who activates the system. As one reads *Gender Trouble*, Butler's pioneering work on gender, with its provocative subtitle *The Subversion of Identity*, one carries with one a picture of Charlie Chaplin in *Modern Times*, disappearing into the enormous cogs and wheels of an out-of-control conveyor belt he has inadvertently activated. Language, as conceived by Butler, is such a piece of machinery. "All signification takes place within the orbit of the compulsion to repeat," she argues, adding that "agency is to be located within the possibility of a variation on that repetition" (1990, 145). One of the projects of this book is to look at the "variations on repetition" provided by a range of authors in a corpus of experimental texts that use the cogs and wheels of language to go beyond the pathetic vision of the little tramp caught in the machine to discover speakers who consciously position themselves along the masculine-feminine continuum, using the possibilities offered by the gender system to their own ends.

Formal and Semantic Gender

The term "gender" has cultural, sexual, biological, and morphological meanings. Butler is primarily concerned with cultural gender, or the social rules associated with women and men. Greville Corbett (1991) describes gender as a linguistic category affecting the noun. He distinguishes between two major types of gender systems: semantic and formal. Semantic gender systems are understood to reflect "natural gender" as an extralinguistic feature related to bodily anatomy or sex. Semantic gender systems classify nouns referring to male humans and animals under the masculine gender, while nouns referring to female humans and animals are classified under the female gender. Inanimate referents may be felt to have "metaphorical" gender, or they may be assigned to a neuter gender category. Formal gender systems, in contrast, depend not on referential categories such as sex, but on the morphology (form) or phonology (sound) of the noun itself. Latin, for example, has grammatical gender formalized in its declension system. Nouns ending in *-a* (*mensa*, table; *puella*, girl; *agricola*, farmer) are typically feminine, while nouns ending in *-us* (*populus*, people; *senatus*, senate; *virus*, slime) are typically masculine, independent of their meaning.

English has only semantic gender. Thus masculine pronouns *he*, *him*, and *his* anaphorize (refer back to) semantically masculine nouns, that is, humans and animals perceived as culturally male. The feminine pronouns *she*, *her*, and *hers* anaphorize semantically feminine nouns. French, in contrast, has both semantic and formal gender. The masculine pronoun *il* anaphorizes a grammatically masculine noun. *Il arrive* may refer to the arrival of Uncle Eric (both formally and semantically masculine); *le vent* (the wind—formally masculine and semantically neutral); or, indeed, *Madame le capitaine* (a woman military captain—formally masculine but semantically feminine). *Elle arrive* may refer to the arrival of Aunt Florence (both formally and semantically feminine), *la bourrasque* (the gust of wind—formally feminine and semantically neutral), or *la sentinelle* (the sentryman—formally feminine but semantically masculine). This difference between English and French is particularly remarkable when we consider the possessive adjectives *his*, *her* and *son*, *sa*. *His* and *her* take the same semantic gender as the possessor. *His aunt* refers to the aunt of a semantically masculine relation (Eric's aunt, Stephen's aunt). *Her father* refers to the father of a semantically feminine relation (Florence's aunt, Julie's aunt). In contrast, *sa tante* tells us nothing whatever of the cultural gender of the relation; the feminine *sa* is used because the noun *tante* has grammatically feminine gender. Similarly, in the expression *son père* the masculine adjective is used because *père* is grammatically masculine; we cannot tell what cultural gender the father's relation has, and it could equally well be a son or a daughter. (See Pauwels 1998, 36–43, for further discussion of semantic and formal gender in European languages.)

It will be appreciated, then, that manipulation of the linguistic gender systems of English and French entails very different processes and occasions very different results. The two categories, semantic gender and formal gender, are not, however, entirely discrete. In the event of a clash between the two systems, semantic gender will tend to take precedence over formal gender. French traditionalists insist that *professeur* (teacher) is grammatically masculine, but generation after generation of French schoolchildren faced with a woman teacher persist in speaking of "le professeur . . . elle," using a feminine pronoun to anaphorize a masculine noun. In metaphorical reference, cultural gender is often alluded to, despite the fact that the noun itself refers to a semantically neutral entity. Pauwels quotes this telling example from Anne-Marie Houdebine-Gravaud (1988):

> On parle en France de la Tour Eiffel comme symbole de Paris, et ce mois-ci (mars 1989 [sic]) elle est souvent citée sur les ondes: la vieille dame va fêter son centenaire. La vieille dame? la métaphore sexuelle a été produite par le genre. (Pauwels 1998, 40)

> In France we consider the Eiffel Tower to be the symbol of Paris and this month (March 1989) she is the talk of the media: the old lady is about to celebrate her one hundredth birthday. The old lady? The sexual metaphor is occasioned by the gender of the noun.

Clearly, French ears hear not merely a grammatical requirement in the gender of nouns but also culturally salient information.

Sex and gender, as we have seen, are not the same thing. Gender is both a formal linguistic system involving nouns (requiring, in French, the grammatical agreement of pronouns, adjectives, and past participles) and a semantic system that refers to the cultural classification of human beings, their actions, and their attributes. A definitional slippage often occurs between semantic gender and sex. It is generally accepted by both literary critics and sociolinguists that gender (in its nongrammatical sense) is a cultural construct with different manifestations at different periods and in different contexts. Consensus over the category *sex* is harder to obtain, however. Many linguists see sex as an extralinguistic category, that is, a biological phenomenon that predates language or any attempt at classification in a semiological or culturally meaningful system, entailing the possession of XX or XY chromosomes and differently formed and functioning reproductive organs. In contrast, literary critics, following Butler's *Gender Trouble* (1990), are more likely to see sex, like gender, as problematic and culturally defined and to contest the possibility of an extralinguistic category, since in their view categories are imposed in and by language.

Butler argues, for example, "Bodies cannot be said to have a signifiable existence prior to the mark of their gender" (1990, 8); and again, further on, "the mark of gender appears to 'qualify' bodies as human bodies: the moment in which an infant becomes humanized is when the question 'is it a boy or a girl' is answered" (1990, 111); and "any theory of the culturally constructed body . . . ought to question 'the body' as a construct of suspect generality when it is figured as prior to discourse" (1990, 129). These three statements, though similar, are not fundamentally the same. To say that "the body" is necessarily a discursive category is not the same as saying it has no existence until it has a gender. Since we cannot refer to or even conceptualize the body without a signifying system of some kind, we may readily accept that "the body" cannot be an extralinguistic category. However, "the body " and "the sexed body" are not the same concepts. The question "Is it a boy or a girl?" is culturally both urgent and imperative. The answer will provide the appropriate pronouns to be used in reference to the baby, but we can speak about the baby without recourse to "he" or "she." As we will see in the texts analyzed here, it is perfectly possible both to conceptualize, and to write about, an unsexed, problematically sexed, transsexed, or alternately sexed human body.

Nor is it only in the realm of literature and the imaginary that such feats of cognition can occur. Women who lose a wanted fetus prior to the seventeenth or eighteenth week, when sexual attributes may be discerned on an ultrasound, grieve the loss of a tiny human being. Whether the fetus is medically or legally human at sixteen weeks of gestation is irrelevant to the grief experienced. Women who miscarry tell moving stories of the foods they ate during pregnancy that they believed their babies liked: "my baby loved peanuts"; "my baby liked steak, that was its favorite food." They refer to the fetus as "my baby"—obviously perceived as fully human—even though the baby's sex is unknown and never will be known, even though the neutral, low-animate pronoun "it" is used to anaphorize this referent. In this work, then, we will consider *sex* a semantic category referring to biological features of the human body, while we reserve the term *gender* (in its nongrammatical sense) for the culturally significant performance of masculinity and femininity.

A series of experiments carried out in the late 1980s shows that there is some validity to the notion that differences in the encoding of formal gender will cause native speakers to perceive semantic gender in different ways (Tukia and Tukia 1987). Researchers studied groups of children aged between sixteen months (a year and a quarter) and forty-two months (three and a half years) from English-speaking, Hebrew-speaking, Swedish-speaking, and Finnish-speaking communities in the United States, Israel, and Finland (both Swedes and Finns were from Finland). The languages in question range from "neutral" with respect to gender marking (Finnish does not encode gender in its pronominal system) to "medium" (English and Swedish encode gender distinctions only in the third person singular) to "high" (Hebrew encodes gender throughout both pronominal and numerical paradigms). The children were tested to see at what age they were able to recognize their own gender. The results are highly suggestive. Between twenty-four and thirty-four months, the Hebrew-speaking children had a much better knowledge of their sexual identity than did those from the other linguistic communities. They began to lose this superiority after their third year of life, however. While 100 percent of Swedish and American children were able to recognize their own sex by the age of thirty-seven to forty-two months, only 78 percent of Hebrew-speaking children could do this (1987, 26). These results indicate that while grammaticalized distinctions may influence early learning, cultural cues quickly compensate in socially charged areas such as gender. Feminists concerned about the tyranny of grammatical gender may feel both justified and reassured: justified, because if children speaking a highly gendered language such as Hebrew are quicker to identify their own sex, then it would seem that they are being prompted by the grammar to perceive sexual distinctions as highly relevant and important; reassured, because if children speaking less gendered languages such as Swedish and English catch up with and even surpass the Hebrew speakers within three to five months, then culture too plays an important part in gender assimilation.

Sexuisemblance *or Semantic Gender*

Sexuisemblance and the related adjective *sexuisemblantiel* are terms invented by Damourette and Pichon (1911–27—a work that abounds in such neologisms) to express the notion that nominal gender has semantic motivation.

> La sexuisemblance existe en français. . . . Le problème essentiel, le problème sémantique, est de savoir ce qu'est pour le psychisme du locuteur français, la sexuisemblance, pourquoi son langage comporte du masculin et du féminin et ne comporte pas d'autre classement général. (§306)

> Sexuisemblance exists in French. . . . The essential problem, the semantic problem is to know what sexuisemblance means in the psyche of the French speaker, why his language has masculine and feminine and not other general classes.

The authors assert that feminine nouns in French designate referents that are small, weak, or passive, while the referents of masculine nouns are big, strong, or active. In support of this theory, they produce an imaginative, colorful, but ultimately specious argument to the effect that, for example, machines that depend on another, stronger machine for their ability to function are feminine, while those which generate their own power are masculine.

> Un moteur communique la puissance et l'action à toutes les machines sans force propre qui lui obéissent; ces machines, la balayeuse, la perceuse, la moissionneuse, . . . ne peuvent rien sans lui. (§320)

> An engine$_m$ communicates power and action to all the machines$_f$ without strength of their own which obey it; these machines$_f$, the carpet sweeper$_f$, the drill$_f$, the harvester$_f$, can do nothing without it$_m$. (See note 6 for explanation of subscripts $_f$ and $_m$.)

These grammatically feminine machines are contrasted with the proud masculinity of the *viseur* (viewfinder), "appareil libre, dont il faut savoir se servir, et qui semble, à chaque action nouvelle, participer de la liberté de l'homme qui le manie" (an independent tool, which one needs to know how to use, and which seems, with each new movement, to participate in the freedom of the man who uses it) Damourette and Pichon 1911–27, §306. This parlor game is amusing as long as one bears in mind that the mere mention of the grammatically feminine but dynamically autonomous *automobile* or *locomotive*, on the one hand, and the grammatically masculine but dependent *carburateur* or *wagon*, on the other, reduces its validity to nought.

Old-fashioned grammarians are not the only ones who have imputed semantic motivation to linguistic gender assignment. The idea has been taken up most notably by the French feminist psychoanalyst Luce Irigaray (1987, 1990), directrice de recherches at the influential Centre national de la recherche scientifique française, although she does not use the term *sexuisemblance*. She states that in French, nouns with feminine grammatical gender tend to have referents to which low value is attached. *La lune* (the moon) and *les étoiles* (the stars) are feminine and unimportant, while *la terre* (the earth) is divided up as men's property (87, 121), Irigaray claims. Elsewhere she writes of the hidden sex of words, noting that masculine nouns have referents that are larger or more socially prestigious than related feminine nouns. As examples, she offers *fauteuil*$_m$ and *chaise*$_f$ (armchair and chair); *château*$_m$ and *maison*$_f$ (castle and house); *ordinateur*$_m$ and *machine à écrire*$_f$ (computer and typewriter); *avion*$_m$ and *auto*$_f$ (airplane and car); and *Boeing*$_m$, *Caravelle*$_f$, and the super-aircraft, *le Concorde*$_m$ (1990, 83–91). While this pattern may be of psychological significance in the French unconscience (I do not profess to any knowledge in this realm), it does not extend beyond a contrast between individual lexical items. If one adds other terms from the same semantic field, one obtains rather different results. *Un appartement*$_m$ is smaller than *une maison*$_f$; *un logis*$_m$ (dwelling) is less sumptuous than *une résidence*$_f$ or *une demeure*$_f$ (an abode), and *un cabinet*$_m$ (toilet) is less pretigious than *une cabine*$_f$ (cabin).

Medieval grammarians, in particular the Modists, also connected masculine gender with activity, feminine gender with passivity. Martin of Dacia explains the gender difference between the Latin *lapis* (stone), masculine, and *petra* (rock), feminine, saying that *lapis* derives from the active phrase *laedens pedem* (injuring the foot), whereas *petra* derives from the passive *pede trita* (worn or trodden by the foot) (Baron 1986, 93–94)

In a debate on the Linguist Network, an e-mail newsgroup serving academics involved in linguistics, one contributor uses the lack of a clear gender or sex distinction to humorous effect, demonstrating that specious arguments die hard:

> Hebrew is a dire villain. Not only most of its pronouns are "sexy," but so are its numerals! Further, its grammar encourages disgraceful promiscuity: male nouns take female numerals and vice versa. So does Arabic, by the way, but, if memory serves, Arab grammarians restored a semblance of morals by call-

ing male numerals female, female numerals male, and having the female of the species wear a chador, and the male a beard, or at least a moustache. (Jacques Guy, Linguist Network, 14 Oct. 1993)

While this example, with its flying leaps from gender to sex to morality to promiscuity to the wearing of the chador, is particularly striking, the technique involved has a long and respectable history in literary style. In its conflation of gender and human generation it is reminiscent of eighteenth-century ideas equating grammatical gender with the human sex organs. Johann Gottfried Herder, for example, sees linguistic gender as a means of reproducing sexual distinctions between men and women: "The attribution of sex through language (is) . . . an interest of mankind, and the genitals of speech are, as it were, the means of its propagation" ([1772] 1996, 134; quoted in Baron 1986, 91). For further discussion of this type of mentalist explanation for nominal gender assignment, see Yaguello 1987, 101–5 and Baron 1986, 93–97.

Novels That Play with Pronominal Gender

Since the second wave of feminism began in the late 1960s, linguistic issues have been subjected to intense scrutiny by feminist theorists. Participating in the discussion of language and gender and the relationship between language and worldview, a discussion that crosses national and linguistic boundaries to span Western Europe and North America, fiction writers have experimented with innovative solutions to the problem of creating a feminine subject position in languages that encode the masculine as unmarked, generic, and universal. These literary experiments have focused on language at the syntactic, semantic, lexical, and discourse levels, but whatever technique is employed to expose, expel, or expatiate upon the gender bias in language, behind the experiment lurks a belief in a modified version of the Sapir-Whorf hypothesis. The attraction in such a hypothesis for feminists, intent on drafting a blueprint for a better world, is obvious. It presumes that grammaticalized gender systems enforce a view of the world as inherently gendered and that the system naturalizes the categorization of human beings as either masculine or feminine, obliging the speaker to focus on the distinctions between males and females rather than on their similarities. If one believes that linguistic structure is causing a continuum to be perceived as two sharp polarities and that natural, biological differences have taken on a symbolic significance that attributes power to one group while disempowering the other, then it is logical to wish to alter or jettison grammatical gender markers.

Out of the feminism of the 1960s and 1970s in both England and France came an appeal for nonsexist language that focused on, among other things, third person pronouns. Pronominal repetition of gender information appeared at best redundant, at worst a constant reminder of the hierarchy of power between the sexes, especially at a time when statements like "le masculin l'emporte sur le feminin," (the male embraces the female), found in popular grammar books—referring to the use of the male pronoun for referents of unknown gender—frequently went unchallenged. Many fictional works were written during this period that either used existing pronouns in new ways or created common-gender pronouns in order to downplay, eradicate, or reverse the traditional grammatical insistence on gender. Such texts include three fictional works by Monique Wittig, *L'Opoponax* (The Opoponax) (1964), *Les Guérillères* (The Women Warriors) (1969), and *Le Corps lesbien* (The Lesbian Body) (1973); June Arnold's *The Cook and the Carpenter* (1973); and Marge Piercy's *Woman on the Edge of Time* (1976). Michèle Causse's *Voyages de la grande naine en Androssie* (The Big Dwarf's Adventures in Androssie) (1993) follows Wittig in its creation of neologistic feminine pronouns.

While the novels of the 1960s and 1970s were written to express ideas of female separatism or sexual egalitarianism, the 1980s and 1990s saw an ideological development toward the concept of gender as a system of positions and performance, accretions and repetition, with no necessary or binding link to the physical configuration of the body. Androgyny became popular in both fashion and fiction. Anne Garréta's *Sphinx* (1986), which avoids giving any grammatical clue as to the gender of the two main protagonists, was greeted as a work unique in this respect by French critics. This reception does something of a disservice to the novel, which has strong ideological and grammatical links to the Anglophone feminist novels of the 1970s that set out to counterbalance the inequities of the gender system by creating epicene neologisms. Nor is *Sphinx* the only novel written in a romance language that avoids gender marking: the Uruguayan Cristina Perez-Rossi's *Solitario de Amor* (Loves Solitude) was published in 1987. Elisabeth Vonarburg's *Chronique du pays des mères* (Chronicle of the Mothers' Country) (1992) reverses the usual hierarchy by according the feminine unmarked status. In English, there is by now a large body of fiction featuring genderless characters, including Brigid Brophy's *In Transit* (1969); Maureen Duffy's *Love Child* (1971); Sarah Caudwell's mysteries *Thus Was Adonis Murdered* (1981), *The Shortest Way to Hades* (1984), and *The Sirens Sang of Murder* (1988); and Jeanette Winterson's *Written on the Body* (1992). These novels were in fact preceded in the early years of the century by two science fiction–fantasy novels: David Lindsay's *Voyage to Arcturus* (1920) and Natalie Clifford Barney's *The One Who Is Legion*, or *A. D.'s After-Life* (1930).

In table 1.1, I have provided a list of literary works written between 1868 and 1999 that experiment with or challenge the linguistic gender system, particularly in the pronominal paradigm. This list is not intended to be exhaustive. It simply indicates the nature of the texts to be studied here, underlining the fact that we are dealing with an established literary and linguistic phenomenon, not a collection of one-off items. These works come from all over Western Europe, including England, France, Norway, Germany, and Spain, as well as the United States and Canada, and were

Table 1.1 Literary Works that Play with Pronominal Gender

Genre	Date	Title	Author	Residence
Tran	1868	*Mes Souvenirs*	Herculine Barbin	France
Sci/Fan	1920	*Voyage to Arcturus*	David Lindsay	England
Tran	1928	*Orlando*	Virginia Woolf	England
Tran	1930	*L'Ange et les pervers*	Lucie Delarue-Mardrus	France/ United States
Tran	1930	*The One Who Is Legion, or A. D.'s After-Life,*	Natalie Clifford Barney	France/ United States
Les	1964	*L'Opoponax*	Monique Wittig	France
Les	1969	*Les Guérillères*	Monique Wittig	France
Tran	1969	*In Transit*	Brigid Brophy	England/ Ireland
Sci/Fan	1969	*The Left Hand of Darkness*	Ursula K. Le Guin	United States
Les	1971	*Love Child*	Maureen Duffy	England
Sci/Fan	1971	*The Kin of Ata Are Waiting for You*	Dorothy Bryant	United States
Les	1973	*Le Corps lesbien*	Monique Wittig	France
Les	1973	*The Cook and the Carpenter*	June Arnold	United States
Sci/Fan	1976	*Woman on the Edge of Time*	Marge Piercy	United States
Sci/Fan	1977	*Egalias døtre*	Gerd Brantenberg	Norway
Mys	1981	*Thus Was Adonis Murdered*	Sarah Caudwell	England
Sci/Fan	1981	*Auf der Reise nach Avalun*	Inka Künkel	Germany
Mys	1984	*The Shortest Way to Hades*	Sarah Caudwell	England
Les	1986	*Sphinx*	Anne Garréta	France
Les	1987	*Solitario de amor*	Cristina Perez-Rossi	Uruguay/ Spain
Mys	1988	*The Sirens Sang of Murder*	Sarah Caudwell	England
Les	1992	*Written on the Body*	Jeanette Winterson	England
Sci/Fan	1992	*Chronique du pays des mères*	Elisabeth Vonarburg	Quebec
Les	1993	*Voyages de la grande naine en Androssie*	Michèle Causse	Quebec/ France
Tran	1994	*Appelez-moi Gina*	Georgine Noël	Belgium/ France
Tran	1999	*Bruised Fruit*	Anna Livia	England/ United States

Note: Les: A Lesbian novel (9); Sci/Fan Science fiction or fantasy (7); Tran Transsexual/ hermaphrodite work (7); Mys Mystery (3); Total = 26.

written in English, French, Norwegian, German, and Spanish. They represent four principal literary genres: science fiction and fantasy, detective fiction, lesbian romances, and works featuring transsexual or hermaphrodite characters.

It is not surprising that these particular genres have been chosen for experiments with gender; in their way, each is peculiarly appropriate, though their pronominal strategies are rather different in each case. Science fiction brings us visions of new planets and new societies full of possibilities merely glimpsed on Earth; as such, it is an excellent genre in which to try out gender codes radically different from the ones with which we are familiar. Authors can create egalitarian societies and invent pronouns that refer to their asexual, ambisexual, polysexual, or pansexual characters. In science fiction novels, therefore, neologistic pronouns are much more common than gender avoidance. Detective fiction revolves around finding the clues to a puzzle, a quest in which the reader too is involved. Psychological mysteries require reader and detective alike to employ everything they know about the world, including stereotypes and cultural commonplaces, to find the murderer. The gender of one of the main protagonists may be a piece of the puzzle that is withheld, forcing readers to employ their arsenal of assumptions to uncover it. In detective fiction, the author tries to avoid using gender-specific terms but without calling attention to this strategy. Pronouns and gendered lexical items are therefore eradicated, and neologistic pronouns are not created to replace them. In lesbian novels, authors may avoid gender-specific terms, as with detective fiction, but their textual strategy is often to call attention to this feat, requiring readers to work extra hard to repair the gap. Withholding information about the sex of partners in a love story may allow the author to describe lesbian lovers without being "flagrant." Instead of simply leaving the gender slot blank, as is the wont of mystery writers, authors of lesbian romances may employ little-used and even archaic resources of the linguistic system to avoid revealing the gender of a protagonist. The archaisms themselves call out that something is different, altered, other. In works describing transsexual characters, in contrast, the description of an intersexed or alternately sexed body disturbs the usual rules of prononimal reference. Authors of such texts typically use a variety of means to refer to the transsexual character, including alternating masculine and feminine pronouns, the first person plural, and the third person indefinite "one."

Although it is relatively easy to classify novels as belonging to the science fiction or mystery genres, the categories of lesbian and transsexual writing often overlap. I classify as transsexual works that feature characters of ambiguous or changing sex and in which the pronominal anomalies are caused by the need to refer to these figures. I classify as lesbian works that recount a love story between two (or more) women in which the gender of at least one of the characters is not made manifest by the usual pronominal means, but for which there exists some other textual evidence. Arguably, *Orlando* could be classified a lesbian love story, since it recounts the (imaginary) life of Vita Sackville-West and her relationship with the author, Virginia Woolf. For my purposes, however, I will call it a transsexual novel, because the pronouns used to refer to Orlando, the eponymous hero/ine, rather than being epicene or absent (as is more typically the case with lesbian romances), change from masculine to feminine as Orlando's sex changes. Similarly, *The One Who Is Legion*, or *A. D.'s After-Life* could be classified a lesbian love story since it tells of the death of a young person who in many ways resembles Renée Vivien, the author's dead lover; but, again, because of the ambiguous gender of this figure and the pronouns used to refer to him/her, I include it with the transsexual texts.

The chapters that follow are organized according to the linguistic characteristics of the text. I start with an examination of novels in which gender is not indicated by the usual linguistic means. Since these texts are the most marked, they tell us by their very difference much about the usual workings of gender. In chapter 2, I discuss the French novel *Sphinx*, in which neither the gender of the first person narrator nor that of the narrator's beloved is indicated grammatically. In chapter 3, I look at five English novels—*Written on the Body*, *Thus Was Adonis Murdered*, *Love Child*, *In Transit*, and *The One Who Is Legion*—that all feature genderless narrators and, in many cases, genderless third person characters as well. In chapters 4 and 5, I turn to an examination of Wittig's three novels, *L'Opoponax*, *Les Guérillères*, and *Le Corps lesbien*. Wittig invents feminine forms for grammatically masculine nouns as well as exhumes archaic feminines; this systematic feminization of the lexicon is the subject of chapter 4. In chapter 5, Wittig's use of the epicene pronoun *on* in *L'Opoponax* will be discussed in detail, as well as *elles*, the pronominal vehicle for *Les Guérillères*, and *j/e*, a neologism invented for *Le Corps lesbien*. From there, I move on to a study of Anglophone novels featuring neologistic pronouns. *The Left Hand of Darkness*, *Woman on the Edge of Time*, and *The Cook and the Carpenter* are the principal texts studied in chapter 6. In chapter 7, I turn to a rather different line of inquiry involving fictional works that feature characters whose gender or sexual identity is itself at issue. In this chapter, I examine *Appelez-moi Gina* (Call me Gina) (1994) by Georgine Noël, a male-to-female transsexual; the autobiography "Mes Souvenirs" in *Herculine Barbin dite Alexina B.* (1868); and two hermaphroditic novels *L'Ange et les pervers* (The Angel and the Perverts) by Lucie Delarue-Mardrus (1930), and my own *Bruised Fruit* (1999). These last texts are of particular interest because of the contrast they provide with the feminist gender play examined in earlier chapters and the questions they ask of biological and cultural gender. While feminists believe that the linguistic gender system plays an active role in the derogation of women, accounts by and about these sexually liminal figures show that the system is unable to incorporate them into its gender binary, posing the question of whether gender is, in fact, a binary.

Gender Marking

Before undertaking an analysis of specific texts, it is useful to look at the function of linguistic gender in French and English and consider the findings of the various studies conducted into the decline or increase of gender marking. In this way, the use contemporary authors have made of the gender system can be placed in its linguistic context. As we have seen, linguistic gender marking is far more widespread and systemic in French than in English, where it is semantic in motivation and may be observed mostly in the third person singular of the pronominal paradigm, as well as in some

marked semantic pairs and lexical items. However, as the rest of this book
sets out to demonstrate, the contrasting pairs *he* and *she*, *his* and *her*, and
his and *hers* bear a heavy functional load. Even French, considered a highly
gendered language because it has both semantic and formal gender, is losing many of the markers previously considered a vital part of its structure.

    In the early years of the century, the French grammarians Jacques
Damourette and Edouard Pichon claimed, "Loin d'être en régression, les
flexions sexuisemblantielles paraissent en progrès" (far from declining in
use, gendered suffixes seem to be on the increase), declaring that, "la langue
moderne forme chaque jour de nouveaux féminins" (modern use creates
new feminine forms each day) (1911–1927, §274). They list a number of
terms that had been used in the eighteenth century and were making a comeback in the work of early-twentieth-century writers. We cannot accept
Damourette and Pichon's opinion as to the resurgence of feminine terms
in French uncritically, however. The authors observe that "la langue de la
conversation courante, pour peu qu'elle ait besoin d'une précision de sexe,
forge des vocables" (the language of informal conversation, whenever it
has the slightest need to specify sex, invents new words) (§275), offering
dentistesse (woman dentist), *philosophesse* (woman philosopher), *ministresse*
(woman minister), *vautouresse* (female vulture), *phoquesse* (female seal), and
louesse (she-wolf) as examples. All this list of terms indicates, as far as linguistic
gender in French is concerned, is that *-esse* may be added to almost any animate noun to refer to the female counterpart of the unmodified noun, and
that it was a highly productive morpheme in the early years of this century.
It does not prove that what Damourette and Pichon call *la sexuisemblance*
is actually on the increase (or that it was on the increase in the 1920s).
Clearly, distinctions between masculine and feminine entities may be made
lexically in modern French by the use of suffixes such as *-esse*, and *-elle* (see
Damourette and Pichon 1911–27, §273–277 for further lists of masculine
and feminine forms; see also Yaguello 1988, 115–39, and Niedzwiecki 1994,
131–231, for an overview of affixes specifying the femininity of the referent and their connotations). The fact that such distinctions may be made
easily does not prove that they are made either frequently or systematically.

    It would not be hard to create female versions in English for the terms
listed above. The suffixes *-ess*, *-ix*, and *-ette* can be called into service in parallel fashion: *authoress*, *poetess*, *sculptress*, *actress*, *aviatrix*, *majorette*, and
rockette are well attested. However, as early as 1976, American linguists have
been at pains to point out the "semantic derogation of women" inherent
in many of the terms used to indicate that an activity is carried out by a
woman (Schulz 1976). Robin Lakoff observed in her pioneering work
Language and Woman's Place that reference to *a woman sculptor* is sex
biased because, as she explains, "since there is no term ** male sculptor*, the
discrepancy suggests that such activity is normal for a man but not for a
woman" (1975, 23). Dennis Baron painstakingly lists a plethora of sex-
marked terms cited in English dictionaries between 1537 and 1980 (1986,
112–36). This lively chapter is headed by a quotation from Augustin Calmet

(1729): "She shall be called *man-ess*, because she was taken out of man." In both French and English, the means for designating the gender of an agent are far from lacking; the question is whether and how they are actually used.

The feminization of traditionally invariable terms in popular spoken French such as *voyou/voyoute* (hooligan), *loubar/loubarde* (punk), and *debout/deboute* (standing up, a deadverbal adjective) is well attested. When it is necessary to specify that a particular friend is female, one frequently hears *mon ami-e* (my friend_f),[6] pronounced so that the second word is trisyllabic, a yod plus schwa or /œ/, to indicate that the feminine form is intended and resuscitating an archaic pronunciation. Once this pronunciation has been introduced into the conversation, a male friend will be distinguished by the suffixing of *homme* (man) as in *mon ami homme*. This follows the common pattern that after a marked term has been used in a discourse, the unmarked term may lose its "neutral" sense and require special marking as well.[7] Such practices, though widespread, show by their emphatic, contrastive, or humorous nature that they go against the more common trend.

Current linguistic research does not support Damourette and Pichon's belief that gendered inflexions are on the increase. Many studies have been carried out to date on gender concord in spoken French (Bauche 1928, Brunot and Bruneau 1933, Durand 1936, Wagner 1968, Kneip 1985, Audibert-Gibier 1988, and Blanche-Benveniste 1990), and all show an overall decline in observance of the traditional rules of grammatical concord. Reasons for this decline differ according to the theorist and the type of study conducted. I will give only a summary of the most significant findings here.

Marguerite Durand notes an increasing tendency to make past participles and post-copular adjectives (known as *attributs* in French and *predicate adjectives* in English) invariable (1936, 23–3, 65–108, 293–96). Thus, for example, in popular spoken French, *grand* in post-copular position is invariable: *la chaise est grand* (the chair is big), whereas in prenominal position it agrees with the gender of the noun it qualifies: *la grande chaise* (the big chair). Durand gives a list of morphological, syntactic, phonological, and semantic environments that are most conducive to invariability. The further the adjective is from the noun it qualifies, the more likely it is to be invariable, as may be seen in the following: "il y a deux choses que j'ai oubliés de dire qui sont importants" (there are two things_f I've forgotten_m to say which are important_m) (66). In this example, the grammatically masculine adjective *importants* is separated from the grammatically feminine noun *choses* by two subordinate clauses and therefore does not agree with the gender of the noun it qualifies. The past participle "oubliés" appears in its masculine plural form, demonstrating that no agreement has been made with the antecedent feminine noun "choses."

The data Durand collected include examples where the anaphoric pronoun is also invariable: "ma main **il** est pas assez fort" (my hand_f it_m is not strong_m enough); "mes poires, **ils** sont tombés toutes véreux" (my pears$_f$, they$_m$ have fallen down all$_f$ full$_m$ of worms). Although both *main* and *poires* are grammatically feminine, the masculine pronoun is used to anaphorize them. For Durand's respondents, the pronoun becomes invariable when it immediately follows the noun, suggesting that the closer the tie between noun and pronoun, the less need is felt for grammatical agreement.

The behavior of the noun-pronoun bond runs counter to what we have seen above concerning the behavior of post-copular and prenominal adjectives. The further the adjective is from the noun, the less likely it is to agree; but the further the pronoun is from the noun, the more likely it is to agree. We could hypothesize that the noun-pronoun bond may still benefit from some grammatical linking, since the pronoun may be carried over the course of several utterances without further mention of the noun it anaphorizes. Since adjectives tend not to be carried beyond the sentence boundary, we could hypothesize that the continued agreement of prenominal adjectives may be explained by the fact that the noun and adjective form a single unit in the speaker's mind. This would indicate that French is moving toward a state more like that of English with respect to gender marking: in the pronominal system gender is still a powerfully cohesive device, whereas in the rest of the linguistic structure it is tending to disappear.

The findings of Durand are consistent with the agreement hierarchy established by Corbett.

> The Agreement Hierarchy
> attributive < predicate < relative pronoun < personal pronoun
> As we move rightward along the hierarchy, the likelihood of semantic agreement will increase monotonically (that is, with no intervening decrease). (1991, 226)

Corbett offers four examples from French that demonstrate this hierarchy in relation to the grammatically feminine but semantically masculine nouns of address *sa sainteté* (his holiness) and *sa majesté* (his majesty):

1. Sa Sainteté n'est pas si ombrageuse de s'en formaliser.

   His$_f$ holiness$_f$ is not so touchy$_f$ as to take offense.

2. Sa Sainteté, avec laquelle je viens de parler . . .

   His$_f$ holiness$_f$ with whom$_f$ I have just been speaking.

3. Votre Majesté partira quand elle voudra.

   Your Majesty$_f$ will leave when he (literally she) wishes.

4. Sa Majesté fut inquiète et de nouveau il envoya La Varenne à son Ministre.

   His$_f$ Majesty$_f$ was uneasy$_f$ and once again he sent la Varenne to his minister.

The possessive adjective *Sa*, the predicate modifier *ombrageuse*, and the relative pronoun *laquelle* are all in the feminine form. In contrast, the personal pronoun appears in the feminine form in example 3 but in the masculine form in example 4.

Some theorists have suggested that the main function of formal gender in romance languages is to demonstrate syntactic cohesion: "des classificateurs tels que masculin, féminin, neutre servent à marquer la cohésion syntaxique plus que l'expression des rôles sexuels" (classifiers like masculine, feminine, neuter mark syntactic cohesion rather than expressing sex roles) (Tukia and Tukia 1988, 27). Yet in modern French it is word order that is primarily responsible for demonstrating which qualifiers modify which nouns; gender inflections repeat information that is already provided syntactically. The further a qualifier is from the noun it modifies, the more need there would theoretically be for such additional marking. Yet we know from Durand's study that it is precisely in the case of the more remote qualifiers that gender distinctions are dropped in favor of invariability. The example sentence Tukia and Tukia give to support their claim is extraordinarily contrived: "cette belle table est plus neuve que ce beau petit bureau est ancien" (this$_f$ beautiful$_f$ table$_f$ is newer$_f$ than this$_m$ beautiful$_m$ little$_m$ desk$_m$ is old$_m$) (27). Apart from the difficulty of imagining a context in which such a sentence could be felicitously uttered, the morphological cohesion produced depends on a contrast between grammatically feminine and grammatically masculine items. This works for a comparison between *une table* and *un bureau*, or *une chaise* (a chair$_f$) and *un fauteuil* (an armchair$_m$); it would not work for *un bureau* (an office$_m$) and *un cabinet* (a doctor's office$_m$) or *une chaise*$_f$ and *une bergère*$_f$ (an easy chair), not to mention the many thousands of other possible comparisons between same-gendered French nouns.

As Durand's research demonstrates, gender concord is on the decline in spoken French, and even anaphoric pronouns may, in certain circumstances, neutralize the masculine-feminine distinction. In the written language, a more formal and therefore more fixed system, gender distinctions persist, and the traditional rules for concord are adhered to. We should bear in mind, then, that we are dealing with a phenomenon that is of much greater importance in the written medium. Feminists who decry the grammatical obligation to think in terms of gender may be reassured by the fact that in the oral medium the traditional rules for concord are increasingly being ignored. Pronominal gender distinctions are still made (with the exceptions noted above), and as we will see, it is particularly in the pronominal realm that experiments and innovations have been made in feminist fiction. It should be said, however, that the writing system almost always lags behind the spoken language. Popular spoken French frequently offers a preview of future changes in the written language.

In English, the question of gender concord affects only the noun-pronoun bond; there is no obligation, nor indeed capacity, to make adjectives and past participles agree with the noun they qualify. Masculine generic *he* and its replacement by plural nouns and plural pronouns or by *he* or *she* remain a subject of debate concerning the written language. Indeed, Oxford University Press's own *Guidelines for Authors* section on "Gender-Neutral, Bias-Free Language" (15–16) makes the following recommendation: "When discussing people in general, do not use one gender-specific pronoun; use 'he or she' or change to plural if appropriate: When a child goes to school, he or she . . . ; When children go to school they. . . ." Many writers find "he or she" clumsy and prefer not to pluralize the noun, however. Jennifer Coates, in her contribution to *Queerly Phrased* (1997) (co-authored with Mary Ellen Jordan), insisted, despite strong opposition from editors at Oxford, that she wished to use singular "they" to anaphorize unspecified antecedents. As editors of the book, Kira Hall and I were obliged to state formally that we were prepared to accept responsibility for any complaints made about this usage. Thus singular "they," as in "No one in their right mind would marry anyone after just a month" (Coates and Jordan 1997, 218), slipped into a scholarly work published by a proudly traditional press that sees itself, and is seen by others, as a pillar of correct usage. The spoken language does not share the qualms exhibited by the Oxford editors; speakers of all social classes commonly use singular "they" for unspecified antecedents. As many scholars have shown (Bodine 1975, Baron 1986, Frank and Treichler 1989), singular "they" not only has a long history of widespread use as a generic pronoun in speech, it has also persisted in writing "despite the persistent actions of prescriptive grammarians to eliminate its use" (Pauwels 1998, 132).

When we turn to an examination of texts concerning characters whose own gender identity or sexual orientation is considered marginal, we will observe a form of hypercorrection. Gender concord, neglected in unmarked situations, may be reintroduced to emphasize an ambiguous or oppositional identity. Many writers play on the ambiguities of gender and animacy. Literary devices such as personification and the pathetic fallacy depend on a slippage between these categories for their effect. The insistent use of gendered pronouns, or of pronouns referring to the gender opposite that of the referent, are devices used in both English and French literary works.

Reanalysis

It seems from these literary uses of gender that far from being an unnecessary evil, the system is in many ways a useful resource, able to encode far more than information about sex or the connections between nouns and their modifiers. In my examination of the current functioning of the French gender system, I will use the concept of reanalysis, a term used in historical linguistics to refer to "the process by which a form comes to be treated in a different way grammatically from the way in which it was treated by speakers" of an earlier state of the language (Crowley 1992, 148). We have seen that linguistic gender in French has both semantic and formal readings and that these readings sometimes clash. Reanalysis occurs typically when a form is structurally ambiguous—that is, when it can have more than one interpretation. One of these interpretations comes to dominate and then takes over completely. Since semantic gender tends to take precedence over formal gender in French, we might say that the gender system has begun to be reanalyzed as a semantic category. In English, gender is already a purely semantic category, but it can also function to show community membership in sexually liminal communities. (See also Corbett 1991, 137–43, for an account of how gender agreement is gained and lost.)

Redundancy, or the conveying of the same piece of information more than once, is an important element in this process of reanalysis. If the main function of gendered pronouns in English and French is to convey the cultural gender of the noun anaphorized, it is evident that this information becomes redundant at the second, let alone third, fourth, or fifth appearance of the pronoun. In French, in which a five-word sentence may encode gender four times—in the singular determiner, qualifying adjective, and past participle as well as lexically in the noun, as in *la vieille femme est assise* (the$_f$ old$_f$ woman$_f$ is sitting down$_f$)—the likelihood of redundancy is even higher.

In his work on redundancy, Roger Lass (1990) uses the concept of *exaptation*, a term he has imported into linguistics from the natural sciences. Lass quotes the work of the evolutionary biologists Stephen Jay Gould and Elisabeth Urba, who coined the term to explain certain developmental features of the archaeopteryx. This dinosaur was feathered but at first flightless, the feathers serving to keep it warm. When it no longer needed feathers to serve that function but had evolved a skeletal structure that would support flight, the feathers *exapted* from their earlier thermoregulatory function to a new, aerodynamic one.

Gould and Urba (1982) report that large amounts of redundant DNA are stored in the cells of many organisms in the form of duplicate genes. As much as a quarter of the amount of total genetic material of fruit flies and human beings is a duplication of other genes. The surplus DNA is of enormous evolutionary importance since it provides the locus for change. There is, of course, no perfect parallel between the structure of DNA and that of linguistic material, but, as Roman Jakobson has pointed out, redundancy serves an essential function in language too. Discussing the sound shape of speech, Jakobson observes that redundant features "serve to support and enhance the distinctive features" (Jakobson and Waugh 1987, 39). Because the same piece of information is encoded two (or more) times in an utterance, the hearer has more chances to recognize the salient distinctions. According to Lass, there are three possible futures for redundant linguistic material: it may be jettisoned; it may be kept as "non-functional residue"; or it may exapt. We might quarrel with the view that duplicated material is nonfunctional—a view prefigured in the title of Lass's article "How to Do Things with Junk"—but the question of the uses of redundant material is an important one.

A central question of this book, then, is to what extent the pronominal gender system in both English and French can be said to be in the process of reanalysis (or exaptation). Are gender markers being pressed into new service, or are they being jettisoned as "junk"? Gender (as opposed to sex) started out in Proto-Indo-European as a classification system for nouns with similar phonological properties (Fodor 1959, 212–13).[8] Although the urge to find a semantic basis for linguistic gender continues apparently unsatiated, it is generally accepted among linguists that for inanimate referents, nominal gender is an arbitrary, now largely redundant morphological system serving to mark concord between determiners, adjectives, past participles, and pronouns and the nouns they qualify.

While grammatical gender may be gradually disappearing from the spoken language, as we will see, in literary texts it is being put to interesting and innovative uses. Do the varied uses of gender seen in the literary works examined here amount to reanalysis? Has the gender system exceeded its morphosyntactic and semantic bounds to extend into the realm of discourse pragmatics? Do the trappings of gender cross intersentential boundaries to effect the cohesion of the text as a whole? These are important questions, given the many guidelines and handbooks on nonsexist language published in both English and French in recent years. As well as suggestions for the feminization of individual lexical items, terms of address, and job titles, which can be changed without causing a fundamental alteration in the functioning of the system, these guidelines frequently make proposals for the replacement of the pseudo-generic *il* or *he*, a morphosyntactic change that, I argue, has consequences beyond the individual clause boundary. As we will see in the analyses that follow, gender cannot be discussed in isolation from other textual features such as cohesion, empathy, and focalization, features that affect the text as a whole, not merely discrete elements within it.

In the next chapter I move from a discussion of theoretical and ideological issues such as pronoun envy and the politicization of language, linguistic determinism, and gender marking to the study of a text that demonstrates by its own functioning how these issues are played out concretely. In chapter 2, I offer an in-depth linguistic analysis of *Sphinx*, by Anne Garréta, and the devices she uses to avoid mentioning the gender of the two protagonists. This analysis serves both as a study of the textual structure of *Sphinx* itself and also, more broadly, as an introduction to the linguistic tools that will be deployed throughout the rest of *Pronoun Envy*.

Rather than overload the introduction with technical terms, it will be more efficient and ultimately more satisfying to let the reader absorb them as they come up in the different texts studied.

2

"Sexes mêlés je ne sus plus rien distinguer"

Nongendered Characters in French

In 1986 the French writer Anne Garréta created a minor literary sensation with her novel *Sphinx.* The novel was greeted as a tour de force by French critics for its complete avoidance of gender markers in connection with the two main characters. We begin our examination of the functioning of gender in French with an analysis of this novel because of its extremely marked nature. The absence of the expected gender markers demonstrates, by its effect on many different structures in the text, how these markers usually function. We focus on the techniques available in French for gender avoidance—repetition of the proper name, synecdochic lexical substitution, and deverbal nouns—and examine not only how they function, but also how their use affects other devices, demonstrating the corollary effects of pronoun avoidance on such phenomena as cohesion and empathy.

In an interview with the *Le Monde* critic Josiane Savigneau (4 April 1986), Garréta explained her belief in the new androgyny as represented by such pop icons as Michael Jackson and the artist formerly known as Prince.

> On assiste depuis quelque temps à une avancée. Des gens comme Michael Jackson ou Prince en sont les symboles. Les rôles deviennent de moins en moins séparés. Le fait d'avoir en face de soi une femme ou un homme n'a plus la même importance. J'ai voulu dans ce roman, tirer les conséquences de ce qui s'est passé durant ces dernières années.

> For some time we have been witnessing a social evolution. People like Michael Jackson or Prince are its symbols. Roles are becoming less and less separate.

The fact of having a man or a woman before you no longer has the same importance. In this novel I wanted to draw out the consequences of what has happened in these last few years.

Gender roles are no longer important, Garréta insists, pointing to her novel as proof. The text is, she says, "a trap," set to expose reader assumptions about gender roles, even when these are not supported by the usual grammatical structures. But if the trap works, if every reader of *Sphinx* needs to adopt a working hypothesis about the gender of the narrator and the beloved based on social or cultural clues in the absence of grammatical ones, precisely who has been caught in the trap? What can *Sphinx* tell us about the workings of the linguistic gender system?

In a romance language like French, in which every noun has grammatical gender and where that gender will govern the concord of all related determiners and adjectives, where many verbal constructions composed of an auxiliary and a main verb will also exhibit concord, and where third person singular pronouns have different forms according to the gender of the antecedent noun, the creation of two genderless characters is quite a feat. Garréta shrugs, however, "Once you have identified all the prototypical situations in which gender is marked in French, there's nothing easier than to skirt the difficulty" (personal communication, 18 November 1993).[1] Anyone could, with a few precautions, avoid the mark of gender. In an unpublished paper entitled "To Hell With Gender?" Garréta uses the metaphors of an obstacle course, a hunt, and an escape from disease to describe the gender system. She writes of "falling prey to genderedness" and observes that "relief came in the form of possessive adjectives," which, in French, match the gender of the object possessed, not the possessor, as in English. Garréta points out the "treacherous past participles," "possible betrayers of gender," and the "many sleepless nights spent searching for that last little minute mark of gender that might have escaped me" in contrast with "those marvelously convenient (invariable) adjectives" (1989, 9–11). Clearly, Garréta considers the gender system at best a nuisance and at worst a kind of tyranny.

Garréta argues that since the category of gender enforces a division of referents into masculine and feminine, and since the feminine is the marked form, the very existence of the linguistic gender system automatically constitutes women as inferior to men and excludes them from the realm of the universal (1989, 14). In this she echoes statements made by feminist thinkers as diverse as Mary Daly (1979), Monique Wittig (1986), and Luce Irigaray (1990):

> Women are silenced/split by the babble of grammatical usage. Subliminal and subtle Self-splitting is achieved by the very pronouns we are trained to use to designate Ourselves. (Daly 1978, 18–19)

> Gender is the linguistic index of the political opposition between the sexes and of the domination of women . . . it is the unique lexical symbol that refers to an oppressed group. No other has left its trace within language to such

a degree that to eradicate it would not only modify language at the lexical level but would upset the nature of the structure itself. (Wittig 1986, 64, 72)

Une libération sexuelle ne peut se réaliser sans changement des lois de la langue relatives aux genres. (Irigaray 1990, 459)

No sexual liberation can come about without a change in the linguistic laws relating to gender.

This mode of thought goes back to the weak version of the Sapir-Whorf hypothesis, that the language one speaks affects one's perceptions of the world. Garréta identifies the writings of Roman Jakobson, particularly his work on translation, as an important part of her intellectual background. His work, along with that of Roland Barthes and Emile Benveniste, was one of the motivating factors for writing *Sphinx* (personal communication, 18 November 1993). However, Jakobson argues against the strong version of Sapir-Whorf. He refutes Whorf's claim that "facts are unlike to speakers whose language background provides for unlike formulation of them" (Whorf 1956c, 235) with the declaration that "[a]ll cognitive experience . . . is conveyable in any existing language. . . . No lack of grammatical devices in the language translated into makes impossible a literal translation of the entire conceptual information contained in the original" (1971, 264). Jakobson clarifies his objection by explaining that "languages differ essentially in what they *must* convey and not in what they *can* convey" (264). It is this distinction between necessity and possibility—between a positive force toward and a lack of constraint against—that provides the key to Garréta's vision of her work. Writing of Jakobson's observation that the preexisting categories of language oblige speakers to give certain items of information, Garréta remarks, "And gender seems to be one of these coercive, inescapable categories. Many feminists have felt concerned about what Barthes used to call 'this fascist propensity of language'" (unpublished essay, 1989). The traditional view is that French necessarily conveys gender at the level of morphosyntax; the existence of Garréta's *Sphinx* would demonstrate that in fact the provision of gender information is merely a possibility, not an obligation. If so, gender must be considered a stylistic rather than a grammatical device, and style implies choice on the part of the writer or speaker. If a writer can be said to have chosen to provide information about gender, he or she can be asked to explain the motivation for this, or motivation may be sought in the text itself. Garréta is thus turning the tables on the reviewers and readers who persistently ask why she has avoided gender markers and what the true sex of her protagonists is. Why do these readers seek gender information so persistently? is her implicit demand.

Further to her discussion of the sexist nature of language structure, Garréta remarks, "If everyone agrees that the function of genders is mainly a syntactic one, that is, it helps mark the relationship words in a sentence entertain" (i.e., which determiners, adjectives, pronouns, etc. relate to which nouns), "the question remains whether this classification according to genders is purely arbitrary" (unpublished essay). She then goes on to discuss the concept of *sexuisemblance*, or the semantic motivation for the gender of nouns in French, outlined in chapter 1. It is the first part of her sentence that is of interest here, with its assumption that the principal function of gender is syntactic. The writing of *Sphinx* would prove, presumably, that other linguistic elements such as word order carry out this syntactic function, and therefore, in Garréta's thinking, it is the ideological force of the gender system, that is, the suppression of women, that motivates its continued existence in French.[2] According to this logic, a gender-neutral novel featuring androgynous characters would contribute to the erosion of sex-based oppression. However, the necessity for sexual distinctions is so deeply engrained in our society, with sexual dimorphism manifested in almost every cultural product from speech to shampoo, that, as the feminist theorist Marilyn Frye asserts, "If one were to succeed in removing sex-marking from one's behavior altogether, one's behavior would be so odd as to precipitate immediate crises of intelligibility and strenuous moral, religious or aesthetic objections from others. Everything one did would seem strange" (1983, 21).

Is there, then, a "crisis of intelligibility" in *Sphinx*? Or does the concept of markedness come to its aid despite its own best efforts? Since the feminine is the marked term of the masculine-feminine dyad, the term that conveys more specific information and is narrower in scope than the unmarked term (Waugh 1982), in the absence of any specific information with regard to gender identity, will the reader not tend to assume masculine protagonists are involved? In many ways the unmarked term resembles the default option on a computer menu: it is what you get without having to make any adjustments yourself, the option most people will use most of the time. It is important to note, however, that one can change the options. Or, to phrase this in terms of markedness theory, a "plus interpretation" of an unmarked term is possible, given sufficient context. In other words, if the marked term is *woman* and the unmarked term *man*, it is possible for *man* to refer to a woman. More significantly, a minus interpretation of the marked term is also possible: *woman* can also refer to a man. If this were not the case, not only *Sphinx* but any attempt to alter language practice and conceptual patterns would be doomed to failure. Faced with politically correct language that avoids any mention of gender, many people now assume a woman is involved because the masculine would be incorrect and the feminine overspecified (i.e., giving supplementary but irrelevant information). In this view, a chairperson is assumed to be a woman rather than a man.

Cooperative Readers

Before we examine *Sphinx* for such signs of intelligibility as textual coherence and cohesion, it is useful to look at some reader expectations of fiction. Although Paul Grice formulated his rules of conversation for dyadic spoken interaction, his analysis of the role of implicature is of central importance in understanding the workings of fiction. Grice's conversational principle states that you "make your conversational contribution such as is required, at the stage at which it occurs, by the accepted purpose or direction of the talk exchange in which you are engaged" (1990b, 151–52). The essential components of this principle are the four maxims of quantity, quality, relevance, and manner, which state that one should say only what one believes to be sufficient, true, relevant, and clear. Readers assume that the author will abide by the cooperative principles prevailing in the textual genre at hand.

Different fictional genres flout the maxims in different ways. The requirements of suspense in a detective story, for example, cause the maxim of quantity to be flouted, since the author cannot give us all the information we want at the beginning of the novel. It is, in fact, our very desire for that information (whodunit?) and the author's refusal to give it to us that create suspense. *Sphinx,* in its brooding *roman noir* style, sometimes seems to parody the hard-boiled mystery genre made famous by writers like Raymond Chandler and Dashiell Hammett. Novels that turn around a duplicitous narrator flout the maxim of quality, since readers believe the narrator above all others. Interpretation of the maxims must be contextual: novels work with and within the conventions of their time, place, genre, and ideology at the same time as they create and sustain that ideology or genre. Each genre works against a background of maxim-governed behavior to which it adds its own particular literary conventions. When readers perceive that the maxims are being flouted, they look for the reason for that flouting, for what it implies. They will apply this implicature to their understanding of the text and thus impose coherence and meaning on it.

Plot Summary: Sphinx

This novel recounts the love story between the unnamed narrator Je and A***, object of the narrator's desire. Je is a young white theology student living in Paris, while A*** is a black American dancer from New York City who works in a Parisian cabaret. The two meet and fall in love. When the cabaret disc jockey dies of an overdose, Je abandons his/her theological studies and takes the job. Later, A*** falls off the stage, breaks her/his neck, and dies. After A***'s death, Je goes to New York to meet A***'s mother, then returns to Europe grief-stricken and in shock. S/he wanders through the streets of Amsterdam only to be set upon by thugs, robbed, beaten, and thrown bleeding into a canal. The narrator describes A***'s body in loving, sensual detail, yet nowhere in this 230-page novel is there any grammatical clue as to the gender of the two protagonists.

As Frye so articulately observes, sex is the first thing we want to know about a person or fictional character. Faced with epicene proper names such as Dominique, Laurence, or Frédéric[3] in French, or Chris, Robin, or Morgan in English, we look further on in the text for pronouns and, in French, adjectival or participial endings to disambiguate. When readers realize that in *Sphinx*, narrator and beloved alike lack the usual marks of formal gender, they will ask why this is, assuming it to be a deliberate tactic on the part of the author, not a mere quirk of style. The situation with regard to other sociocultural variables, such as race or physical ability, for example, is very different. If a new character is introduced by a white author and no mention is made of their race, they are assumed to be white, since white is the unmarked term. Unless mention is made of disability, they will further be assumed to be able-bodied. In many narratives, the reader may never be told the race of a protagonist. The author may not consider this essential information but, more important for the present study, the morphosyntax of French (and indeed English) does not require that race or ability be encoded in the same way as gender. Whether or not the author considers gender an important variable, the structure of the language makes it required information. The same is not true of race. The narrator's beloved is described as black and American, in contrast to the narrator, who is white and French. While these differences have an enormous social impact on the couple and on the way they are treated by others, they are not encoded at the morphosyntactic level.

Faced with the genderless riddle of *Sphinx*, readers come up with a number of working hypotheses to explain its avoidance of gender; they are compelled by their own participation in the text to create at least one hypothesis. It is not possible to read with an attitude of gender neutrality; in order to imagine the characters, one needs to clothe them in the attributes of one sex or the other. Although there are no linguistic clues, there may be cultural indications of the sex of the narrator. Je has the strength to lift a dead body already weighted down with a heavy piece of masonry and the freedom to walk unhindered through the most obscure back street of Paris after midnight; he or she is patted on the shoulder by a mafioso in a bar and given advice on sexual conquest. Furthermore, the narrator enters the men's toilet in the company of the club owner and a priest without calling attention to this act. When we put these facts together, it begins to sound as though the narrator is a man. The narrator's retreat to Solesmes contributes to the ambiguity, for this could refer to the town of Solesmes, to the Abbaye Sainte Cécile, a female convent, or to the Benedictine monastery. However, given the narrator's theological studies, the implication here is that Solesmes is not simply the town itself. Since Solesmes is far more famous for its monastery, which dates back to the Middle Ages, than for its convent, which is of more recent date, the unmarked meaning of a retreat to Solesmes is a retreat to the monastery.

None of this provides conclusive proof that the narrator is a man. Indeed, as the author states, "I refrained (from letting) my characters engage in activities that would have unequivocally attributed them a specific sexual identity. None of them became pregnant, for instance" (Garréta 1989, 13). According to Grice's rules of conversation, cooperative readers will assume an equally cooperative author: if the reader needs to know gender—and I have argued that this is one of the first things he or she will look for—then the author will provide the means to ascertain this. If there are indications that the narrator is a man, perhaps the author wishes to point out how strong sex-role stereotyping is by showing that we can tell whether someone is male or female by what they do in the world—in other words, that linguistic cues are redundant. If most theology students are male, if most dancers are female, perhaps we need look no further to solve the enigma. Taking a slightly broader perspective, the reader may examine the genre itself (or the *intertext*) for information and conclude that since the atmosphere of *Sphinx* emulates the *roman noir*, the absence of gender markers is a clue in itself. Following this line of inquiry, perhaps the gender roles themselves come from a marked set and we should read *Sphinx* as a lesbian novel. This is, indeed, the reading I have always given it.

The suggestions outlined here are intended only to indicate the implicational process and do not exhaust the possibilities. Different readers will come up with different explanations, but all cooperative readers will take it upon themselves to make the text cohere, changing their working hypothesis as the text reveals new clues. The title of the novel itself is an enigma. While in classical Greek mythology a sphinx is a female monster with the head and breasts of a woman, the body of a lion, and the wings of an eagle, in Egyptian mythology it is a male monster with the head of a man and the body of a lion. Garréta complains wryly, "I have been asked numerous times to 'reveal' the 'true' gender of narrator and character (i.e., if there's something missing it must be hidden)" (personal communication, 18 November 1993). In this she echoes Michel Foucault: "Do we truly need a true sex? [Western societies] have obstinately brought into play this question of a 'true sex' in an order of things where one might have imagined that all that counted was the reality of the body and the intensity of its pleasures" (Foucault 1980, vii). This exasperation with the exigencies of our entry into language, with the "fascist propensity" of language, is understandable, but the answer to Foucault's question, insofar as the reader of *Sphinx* is concerned, is yes—the narrator and A*** truly need a true sex because we need to know how to refer to them. The reality of the human body, as currently constituted, is that it is either male or female (except for rare exceptions, discussed in chapter 7, and on science-fictional worlds such as Le Guin's Gethen, discussed in chapter 6). It does not make sense to behave as though we are living in a nongendered utopia because we may desire one.

It is not because common sense tells them everyone has a gender that readers and critics alike seek incessantly for clues to the gender of *Sphinx*'s protagonists. (Common sense might tell them equally that everyone has a body, either fit or disabled, and that everyone has a race.) It is because language lays out its speakers' expectations in its grammar: there is a category for gender that must be filled. Garréta's procedure is to avoid those linguistic categories that encode gender. That no other French author has ventured to repeat the experiment and that Garréta's subsequent novels, *Pour en finir*

avec le genre humain (To put an end to human gender/the human race)
(1987) and *Ciels liquides* (Liquid Skies) (1990), return to the traditional
gender markers demonstrate how rare and complicated gender avoidance is.
The resulting text is highly marked, and because of this markedness, it calls
attention to the strategies used to create it. Garréta cannot eliminate the
gender system from the language at large, and it is in the context of the whole
structure of the French language that her novel will be read. This is not to
say that the novel itself is a failure. On the contrary, *Sphinx* has been extremely
successful: widely read, widely reviewed, and widely praised.

Cohesion

Let us turn now to an examination of the linguistic "tricks" Garréta uses to
avoid mention of gender—repetition of the proper name, lexical substitution, and use of deverbal noun phrases—to see how they affect the reading
of the text. Since gender is no longer necessary to demonstrate syntactic
relations, what other functions does it serve? I will argue that the gender
system is so entrenched in French that one cannot avoid it without creating other difficulties. Prince and Michael Jackson may strike the reader as
effeminate in dress and body language, but both are nonetheless referred
to as *he*. (Though not, of course, in languages that do not encode gender
grammatically, such as Finnish or American Sign Language. I am not concerned with linguistic universals, but with French and English.)

While readers seek coherence on the level of the text as a whole—hy-
pothesizing as to why the gender of the two most important characters is
not revealed—they work simultaneously to find cohesion at the micro level,
and indeed the two levels are intricately connected. A novel that seems incoherent in some important particular (lack of gender continuity for the
two main characters, for example) requires the reader to create coherence
where the author has refused it. Tanya Reinhart divides the concept of
coherence into two: *explicit* and *implicit* (1980, 163). Implicit coherence,
according to Reinhart, is "explicitly incoherent." This may seem at first sight
like a contradiction in terms, but Reinhart explains that implicit coherence
requires "the application of special procedures to impose coherence." She
gives an example taken from Hrushovski: "He opened the door. A few pieces
of clothing were strewn about. He caught the fish in his net." In Hrushovski's
example, the reader has to work hard to invent a world in which opening a
door, seeing clothing lying around, and catching a fish may all take place
in the same place. When told that someone is opening a door, we assume
they are entering a room or building, that is, a place where we do not expect anyone to be fishing. However, if we rotate our angle of vision 180
degrees, we might conceptualize the person as leaving a wooden cabin and
walking on a beach toward the water, in which case seeing clothes strewn
about and catching fish are easily compatible.

Reinhart further divides explicit coherence into *cohesion*, which is the
set of formal grammatical devices that marks a text as one unified whole

and separates it from other texts or from other episodes in the same text; *consistency*, or semantic coherence; and *relevance*, whereby disparate elements may be connected to the same underlying discourse theme. Cohesion has, in turn, been further subdivided by Halliday and Hasan, and we will examine their taxonomy below. Table 2.1 presents Reinhart's divisions graphically.

Reinhart offers the explicit connectors "it's like" and "that's why" as examples of consistency, or semantic coherence. These semantic connectors are printed in boldface in the following exchanges:

2.1.   A: Well unless you're a member, if yer a member of TM people do, ah simply because simply because it's such a fucking high price to get in there, it's like thirty-five dollars
         B: **it's like** water polo
         A: Why, is it expensive? (Reinhart 1980, 165).

In example 2.1, B produces an explicit semantic connector—"it's like"—linking water polo to TM (transcendental meditation). A, assuming B is acting cooperatively, searches around and suggests that water polo too is expensive. In fact, B is a researcher conducting an experiment on speakers' reactions to incoherent turns. The findings of this experiment show that most speakers will endeavor to create cohesive links to apparently incoherent utterances, repairing discrepancies themselves.

2.2.   Schizophrenic patient: I was living at home. But my father is dead now . . .
      That's why you can say he probably decided to smoke a pipe.
      [The interviewer was smoking a pipe.] (Reinhart 1980, 164).

In this exchange between a schizophrenic patient and her doctor, the patient uses the explicit semantic connector "that's why" to make a link between the doctor's pipe smoking and her father. Despite the semantic

Table 2.1   Coherence and Cohesion

Coherence	(1) Implicit: explicitly incoherent, i.e., reader has to work to imagine a world in which apparently disparate events may occur in the same place.
	(2) Explicit: elements consist of
Explicit Cohesion	(1) Relevance: disparate elements are connected to the same underlying theme
	(2) Consistency: semantic coherence created by the presence of explicit semantic connectors ("it's like", "that's why")
	(3) Cohesion: the set of formal grammatical devices that mark a text as one unified whole and separate it from other texts

Source: Graphic representation of Reinhart 1980.

connector, this link is hard to repair, since the patient has just mentioned that her father is dead. It is the use of this connector that, precisely because it fails to connect, produces the effect of dislocation typical of schizophrenic speech.

Relevance works as a device for creating textual cohesion by assuming a link between disparate elements to the same underlying theme. To demonstrate this, we will turn once more to the discourse of schizophrenics. William Labov and David Fanshel, in their work on therapeutic discourse, give the following example, in which A is a psychiatrist and B the patient:

2.3.   A: What is your name?
         B: Well, let's say you might have thought you had something from
             before, but you haven't got it any more.
         A: I'm going to call you Dean. (Labov and Fanshel 1977, 76)

Labov and Fanshel's analysis of this interaction is that B's response is incoherent, since it does not answer A's question. The psychiatrist's question has narrow focus, admitting only a limited set of possible answers: "Dean," "My name is Dean," "Dean Bloggs," "Mr. Bloggs," "My parents call me Dean but I prefer Donny," and so on. However, if we imagine an underlying discourse theme of forgetting and losing vital parts of oneself (which may be the theme in B's mind), then B's reply is relevant to A's question: that's a good example of one of those things I feel like I don't have any more. With this reading, it is A's response to B—"I'm going to call you Dean"—that is incohesive, since, for B at least, the topic was not B's name but things that B has lost. As you can see by my own response to example 2.3, the impulse to repair apparently incoherent speech, even that of schizophrenics, is very strong. (For lengthier examples of schizophrenic discourse, see Sheehan 1983 and Ribeiro 1994.)

Defining *cohesion*, Halliday and Hasan state: "where the interpretation of any item in the discourse requires making reference to some other item in the discourse, there is cohesion" (1976, 11). The closer the link between coreferential elements in a sentence or sequence of discourse, the greater the cohesion created. The tightness of the link creates a hierarchy amongst the different devices. Semantic coherence produces a more closely knit text than relevance, and grammatical coherence produces a tighter bond than semantic coherence, although all cohesive devices will almost certainly be present in the same text and may even be used to link the same elements. Table 2.2 represents Halliday and Hasan's findings concerning the relative strength of the cohesive link created, in descending order from least to most cohesive. Reinhart's "consistency" covers much the same ground as their "semantic cohesion."

The functioning of these cohesive devices will be demonstrated by reference to examples from *Sphinx*. We will start with relevance and semantic coherence, which are both relatively straightforward, before moving on to the different types of grammatical coherence.

Table 2.2 Strength of Cohesive Link

Relevance
Semantic coherence (consistency)
Grammatical coherence
Proper name repetition
Reference
Lexical substitution
Pronominal reference/anaphor
Ellipsis

Source: After Halliday and Hasan 1976.

Relevance

In *Sphinx*, an important underlying discourse theme is that of the love affair between the narrator and A***. Anything that adds to the reader's understanding of either of the two protagonists will therefore be relevant, but unless the mention is bound by some grammatically cohesive element, the effect will be one of random details strung together. Faced with details about other characters, described without recourse to grammatical cohesion or semantic coherence, readers will assume these details must somehow be relevant to the protagonist.

2.4.   Dans un monte-charge on enfournait un Noir hurlant et écumant sur une civière. Entre deux portes une femme attendait. . . . Je me souviens d'avoir noté qu'elle portait un bonnet de laine et que ses bas, tombant sur des savates déformées, étaient filés. (201–2)

     A black man on a stretcher, who was yelling and foaming at the mouth, was being loaded into a goods elevator. Between two doors, a woman stood waiting. I remember noticing that she was wearing a woolly hat and that her stockings, which hung down over broken-down shoes, were laddered.

In example 2.4, no explicit connection is made between the black man, the waiting woman, and the narrator, save that the narrator remembers seeing the woman. Processing this information, the reader assumes that the other two characters are unimportant in themselves and only relevant insofar as they reflect the narrator's mood of despair after her/his lover has died.

Semantic Coherence

Semantic coherence is exhibited in example 2.5 in which *c'était comme* (it was like) explicitly connects the two sentences:

2.5.   Je lui promis de revenir le lendemain matin dès neuf heures et l'embrassai avant de la quitter. C'était comme un arrachement. (200)

> I promised to come back next morning at nine and kissed her before leav-
> ing. It was like being torn away.

There is no ambiguity about the connection the author is making between the two sentences in example 2.5. The narrator states explicitly that leaving A***'s sick mother in the hospital was like being torn away.

Grammatical Coherence: Proper Name Repetition

Proper name repetition produces the least cohesive link of the devices for creating grammatical coherence. When a proper name is repeated without intervening material, it may be assumed to refer to another person with the same name, or to point to something extraordinary about the sequence of actions performed by that person.

2.6.   A***$_i$ m'entretint longtemps de choses diverses. . . . Nous étions ivres et
       A***$_i$ plus que moi. (111)

       A***$_i$ talked to me about various things. . . . We were drunk and A***$_i$
       more so than I.[4]

A second mention of the same person would most commonly appear in pronominal form, as in example 2.9, but if one uses a third person pronoun instead of a proper name in French (or indeed English), one is obliged to provide gender information.

Grammatical Coherence: Reference

Reference, which employs parallel noun phrases to designate the same referent, is more cohesive than repetition of the proper name but still provides a fairly weak textual link.

2.7.   Je me rendis . . . aux conférences que donnait . . . le Père ***$_i$, jésuite
       espagnol. . . . Le Padre***$_i$ professait . . . une foi. (28–29)

       I went to . . . the lectures given . . . by Père***$_i$, a Spanish Jesuit. . . . The
       Padre***$_i$ professed his faith.

In example 2.7 both *le Père****** and *le Padre****** refer to the same person. The first designator conveys only that the man in question is a priest, while the second provides the extra information that he is Spanish. Although the latter is an expansion on the former, they are not closely linked, since either is comprehensible by itself.

Grammatical Coherence: Lexical Substitution

Lexical substitution, in which, for example, a noun phrase is used as a synonym for the proper name, creates a stronger link than proper name repetition or simple reference. Since both the first noun phrase introduced in a given discursive unit and the second phrase, which picks out the same referent, may stand by themselves, the tie between them is not as strong as with anaphoric or elliptic reference.

2.8. George$_i$ avait fait fermer au public cette partie des toilettes. . . . Le Padre et le directeur$_j$, agenouillés de part et d'autre du cadavre, se taisaient. (38–39)

George$_i$ had closed off this part of the toilets to the public. . . . The Padre and the director$_j$, kneeling either side of the body, were silent.

In order to understand the reference to the *directeur*, the reader must make the link between this social function and the name *George*.

Grammatical Coherence: Pronominal Reference/Anaphora and Cataphora

The next tightest link is created by pronominalization:

2.9. Tiff$_i$ avait coutume de me lancer, du plus loin qu'elle$_i$ m'apercevait. (14)

Tiff$_i$ was in the habit of yelling as soon as she$_i$ caught sight of me.

The *elle* of the second clause must be understood to refer anaphorically to Tiff. If readers fail to make the link to the antecedent noun phrase, they will have no referent for *elle*. The pronoun may precede the noun phrase in what is known as a cataphoric link:

2.10. Je la$_i$ reconnus à l'eclat de ses paillettes et de ses strass. . . . Tiff$_i$ avait coutume de me lancer . . . un bonjour. (adapted from p. 15)

I recognized her$_i$ by the brightness of her spangles and paste jewelry. . . . Tiff$_i$ was in the habit of yelling hello.

Pronominal linking allows of more variation than ellipsis, but less than the preceding devices. It should be mentioned, however, that since the unmarked strategy is anaphor, cataphor can be ambiguous in the absence of intonational clues. Because of its marked status, requiring extra effort on the part of the reader to find the referential link, cataphor may be used to indicate that a particular character will be prominent in the discourse that follows. In a novel that opens with a cataphoric pronoun, like Nathalie Sarraute's *Vous les entendez?*, the reader is expected to understand that *il* is an important character and that the actions he performs are highly salient.

2.11. Soudain il s'interrompt, il lève la main, l'index dressé, il tend l'oreille.

Suddenly he interrupts himself, he raises his hand, forefinger pointing, he listens.

In fact, no proper name or other designator is ever provided for *il* in *Vous les entendez?* He remains the sum of the actions attributed to him.

Grammatical Coherence: Ellipsis

The tightest grammatically cohesive link is created by ellipsis:

2.12.   A*** n'imaginait plus systématiquement le pire, ne présidait plus de désastres. (94)

(A*** no longer systematically imagined the worst, no longer presided over disasters.

It is only by activating the link between the verbs *imaginait* and *présidait* (of which the subject has been elided) that we understand the subject of the second verb to be A***.

Repetition of the Proper Name

As we have seen, it is repetition of the proper name that creates the weakest sense of cohesion in a text, while pronominalization creates a much stronger link. The lack of pronominalization of A*** makes it seem as though this character is continually reintroduced, and the resulting text is loose and disconnected. In their work on episode markers, Teun van Dijk and Walter Kintsch (1983) list seven factors that identify the beginning of a new episode, of which "full noun phrase introduction of old participants" is the fifth. A***, despite being a central character and therefore an "old participant," is continually reintroduced, as though each time the narrator's beloved is mentioned a new episode begins. This, too, promotes a sense of discontinuity.

2.13.   A***$_i$ m'entretint longtemps de choses diverses; il y avait de la chaleur dans son ton. Nous étions ivres et A***$_i$ plus que moi. (111)

A***$_i$ talked to me for a long time about different things; there was warmth in his/her tone of voice. We were drunk and A***$_i$ more so than I.

2.14.   Je l$_i$'accusai en vrac d'indifférence et de narcissisme. . . . A***$_i$ me reprocha en retour. (147)

I accused him/her$_i$ of both indifference and narcissism. . . . A***$_i$ reproached me in turn.

2.15.   Cette affection que j'éprouvais pour A***$_i$ réclamait son incarnation, ce plaisir que je ressentais en sa compagnie exigeait sa plénitude. Je voulais A***$_i$. (81)

This affection I felt for A***$_i$ demanded its incarnation, this pleasure I felt in his/her company clamored for fulfillment. I wanted A***$_i$.

In 2.13 (repeated from 2.6) since A*** is considered to be a sufficiently active referent for the possessive *son* to be used anaphorically (*son ton*, his/her tone, stands for *le ton de A****, A***'s tone), it is unusual that the proper name A*** is reintroduced in the following sentence, where one would have expected *lui/elle plus que moi*. Similarly in 2.14, A*** is anaphorized in the direct object pronoun *l'*, thus one would have expected a subject pronoun *il* or *elle* instead of the repetition of A*** in the next sentence. The reasons for this repetition are clearly due to gender avoidance rather than to the activity status of the referent. Since in French the possessive pronoun agrees with the possessed, not with the possessing, noun, use of *son* in *son ton* does not reveal A***'s gender, whereas the disjunctive pronoun *lui* or *elle* would. Similarly, the direct object pronoun *le* or *la* takes the elided epicene form *l'* before a vowel, whereas the subject pronoun *il* or *elle* does not elide. *Je l'accusai* does not reveal A***'s gender identity, whereas *je le/la voulais* (I wanted him/her) would.

One could argue that the proper name is repeated in 2.15 to avoid ambiguity, since in *je le voulais* the masculine object pronoun might refer to *ce plaisir* (this pleasure), while in *je la voulais* the feminine object pronoun might refer to *sa plénitude* (its fulfillment). In French, as in many other languages, however, there is a hierarchy of animacy in which human beings are perceived as more salient than objects or abstract ideas. Readers will assume the pronoun *le* or *la* refers to an animate antecedent unless there is good cause not to. As Bernard Comrie's (1976) work on language universals demonstrates, morphological distinctions between nominative and accusative correlate with high animacy, thus functionally differentiated pronouns tend to be used only for human or other high-animate referents (cf. *she/her* versus *it*). In French, these formal distinctions are now limited to the pronominal system, as can be seen with the personal pronouns *je/me*, *tu/te*, *il/le*, *elle/la*, *ils/les*, and *elles/les*, in which the first of each pair is in the nominative, the second in the accusative. Furthermore, all pronominal reference is marked as higher in animacy than all non-pronominal reference. Although grammatically a subject pronoun may refer to an inanimate object and a full lexical noun phrase to a human being, in fact it is much more common to find the human being pronominalized and the inanimate object referred to with a definite descriptor. In example 2.16, because the nail is pronominalized, it is seen as more salient than the director.

2.16.   Ce clou m'a griffé; il a griffé le directeur aussi.

      This nail scratched me; it scratched the director too.

For this reason, referents lower down the animacy scale are much more seldom pronominalized than those higher up.

Closely associated with pronominalization are topicworthiness, individuation, and saliency (Comrie 1976, 190–93). A referent that is pronominalized is more likely to be singled out as a focus of attention (indi-

viduated) and to become the topic of the next or subsequent clause (demonstrating high topicworthiness). This fact may be illustrated by an example
involving Tiff, a minor character in *Sphinx* whose gender is given in the
usual way (as seen in examples 2.9 and 2.10). First the character is introduced in a full lexical noun phrase (i.e., by her proper name, Tiff), then
reference progresses to pronominal anaphorization.

2.17.   La voix de Tiff avait vrillé dans mon cerveau. (15)

         Tiff's voice had drilled into my brain.

2.18.   Elle me commanda, comme à elle-même, une fine et un café. (16)
         She ordered a brandy and a coffee for me, and one for herself.

In example 2.17, the grammatical subject is not Tiff, but her voice, yet it is
clear to the reader, when confronted with the pronoun *elle* in example 2.18,
that this refers to the woman herself. It should be noted, furthermore, that
there are nine lines of text between these two passages that provide details of
the narrator's confused psychic state, and that the latter marks the beginning
of a new paragraph. Given such a quantity of intervening matter, one might
have expected *Tiff* to become inactive, yet there is no processing difficulty.

   What is remarkable about this treatment of Tiff, a character who serves
only to introduce the narrator to A***, is the contrast it provides with the
treatment of the two main characters. *Sphinx* does not avoid mention of
gender for all protagonists. Thus Je and A*** are continually set apart from
less salient characters, such as George, the cabaret owner; Jeanne, the old
woman who runs Je's favorite restaurant; and Elvire, the "dame-pipi" who
keeps the cabaret toilets clean. The narrator and her/his beloved do not
occupy an ungendered world, and the reader is reminded constantly by the
traditional linguistic treatment of the other characters of the marked status
of Je and A***.

Synecdochic Lexical Substitution

The consequences of Garréta's use of lexical items instead of pronouns to
refer to A*** are similar to those of repetition of the proper name. As we
saw above, lexical substitution creates less-cohesive text than does anaphorization. A*** is continually referred to in terms of his/her body parts,
giving an impression of fragmentation rather than of a whole, complete
being. Although the lexical substitutes are pronominalized, this does not
increase reader empathy for A***.

2.19.   J'avais la sensation dans ma chair du contact de ses membres$_i$ alors qu'ils$_i$
         n'étaient plus là. (83)

         I had the sensation in my flesh of contact with her/his limbs$_i$ even though
         they$_i$ were no longer there.

In example 2.19, *ses membres* is used to represent A*** and is anaphorized at its second mention as *ils*. While this creates a grammatically cohesive sentence, it fails to arouse or maintain reader empathy, since the referent is presented not as an animate agent but as a collection of body parts. Examples 2.20 and 2.21 provide further examples of lexical substitution for A***: *un corps* (a body), *le modelé musculeux* (the muscular molding), and *le visage* (the face).

2.20. Je m'émerveillais des soins que requiert un corps pour paraître lisse, imberbe, souple. (25)

I was amazed by the care required to keep a body looking smooth, hairless [beardless] and supple.

2.21. Le modelé musculeux de ses hanches . . . ses cheveux rasés . . . le visage ainsi rendu à sa pure nudité. (27)

The muscular molding of her/his hips . . . her/his shaven hair . . . the face thus restored to its naked purity.

In example 2.22, where the narrator is describing the admiration he or she feels for A***, the qualities under consideration are all physical, but static and impersonal, as though the narrator were contemplating a statue (an analogy made more salient by the oblique reference to Michelangelo's David).

2.22. Qui ne se fût épris de cette charpente élancée, de cette musculature comme modelée par Michel-Ange, de ce satiné de peau? (10–11)

Who would not have been taken by that elegant frame, by that musculature as though modeled by Michelangelo, by that satinity of skin?

This fragmentation of A***'s identity into parts of the body—necessarily shared with every other human being, since to describe specifically male or female attributes would be to reveal gender information—presents yet another obstacle to reader empathy. There is no sense of A*** as a unique individual. The narrator's beloved is merely a sum of common parts.

Deverbal Nouns

Deverbal nouns are substantives formed from verbs. The move from verbal to substantive status has consequences on the temporal sequencing of events as well as on the agentive status of the character to whom these events are related. In the section on lexical substitution, we saw that in order to avoid revealing his/her gender, A*** was frequently represented by parts of his/her body. In this section, we will look at a related phenomenon: the translation of A***'s acts from verbal predicates to nouns describing those acts as completed states. Instead of moving from place to place, the subject of his/her own actions, A***'s life is seen as a series of states, the end points of movements rather than the movements themselves; thus, A*** is deprived of both agency and temporality.

2.23.   Après le baiser sur les lèvres (24)

After the kiss on the lips

2.24.   Je pris l'habitude de contempler . . . le lent office du maquillage et l'ajustement de la tenue de scène. (24)

I got into the habit of gazing at the slow make-up ritual and the adjustment of the stage outfit.

2.25.   Au plaisir de sa contemplation . . . s'ajouta celui de sa conversation. (73)

To the pleasure of his/her contemplation was added that of his/her conversation.

Verbal constructions such as *après qu'il/elle m'eût baisé/e sur les lèvres* (after he/she had kissed me on the lips) would, again, reveal or create the sex of the participants. Example 2.25, has the further ambiguity of mixing the objective genitive (*sa contemplation*—in which A*** is the object, i.e., someone else contemplating A***) and the subjective genitive (*sa conversation*—in which A*** is the subject, i.e., A*** conversing with someone else).

The effect of using nouns rather than verbs to describe A***'s and the narrator's actions and reactions to each other is to produce a series of atemporal states, seemingly without active participants. This device is used much more frequently with reference to A*** than to the narrator. Finite verbs in French obligatorily carry tense information, whereas nouns do not. Plot-advancing temporality, which establishes a temporal sequence among different events, is missing from many of the episodes involving A***.

2.26.   Sa présence et sa conversation m'étaient un agrément tout comme la contemplation de son corps ou de sa danse. (74)

Her/his presence and her/his contemplation were an attraction to me just like the contemplation of her/his body or her/his dance.

A*** is, we know, a dancer in a discotheque, which must involve vigorous body movement, yet her/his body is permanently caught in the static moment of the narrator's gaze. Stativity is enhanced by the use of the *imparfait* in both examples 2.26 and 2.27. The imparfait is used in French for durative actions described without reference to their beginnings or endings, in contrast to the passé composé, which describes actions at a particular moment, and places them along the timeline in relation to each other.

2.27.   Je ne savais . . . si je devais m'avancer à sa rencontre ou bien attendre sa venue auprès de moi. (109)

I didn't know whether I should go to his/her meeting or wait for his/her coming to me.

In example 2.27, although the narrator suggests the possibility of her/his own or A***'s movement toward the other, in fact only Je's thought processes are involved in this statement; Je is the only grammatical subject, the only one whose actions are invested with a sense of temporality. Both the finite verbs *savais* (knew) and *devais* (had to) are modals of mental state and are therefore very low on the scales of activity and transitivity themselves, a fact that contributes to the static impression of the scene. Even in the narration of the first time A*** approaches the narrator to make love, A***'s action is described in terms of the narrator's perception, as though it too were a possession of the narrator's.

2.28. J'eus la vision de son visage près du mien. (99)

   I had a vision of her/his face near mine.

A***'s movement toward Je is summed up in the phrase "J'eus la vision de son visage." A*** is depersonalized and represented synecdochically by a body part: the face.

   At one point, after this first night, Je states explicitly, "L'ordre temporel des évènements et jusqu'aux simples repères dans l'espace s'abolirent" (112) (temporal sequence and even simple spatial reference points were abolished). This is hardly surprising, since the scene has been described largely in terms of a series of bodily sensations rather than as intentional movement in space and time.

2.29. Le goût d'une peau, de la sueur sur cette peau. Contre mes mains l'impression tactile que me firent et cette peau et le modelé de cette chair. (112)

   [T]he taste of a skin, sweat on that skin. Against my hands the tactile impression that skin and the shape of that flesh had upon me.

This scene is introduced by the sentence "Je chancelai lorsque A*** s'approcha de moi pour m'embrasser" (my legs trembled when A*** came up to me to kiss me). A*** was clearly the one responsible for the narrator's experiencing these sensations, but we hear nothing of A***'s consequent actions; this would cause problems for the author, since, after the initial mention of the proper name, A*** would normally be pronominalized.

   When a definite determiner is used with a deverbal noun, as in examples 2.23, and 2.24 (repeated here as examples 2.30 and 2.31)—*le baiser, le lent office, l'ajustement du maquillage*—the impression created is that these are well-known, routine activities, since the definite determiner is normally used for referents that are already active in the discourse or for generics, as opposed to the indefinite, which introduces brand-new referents. In this context, this strategy is intended to obscure gender. Deverbal noun phrases are, anyway, much more common in French than in English.

2.30. Après le baiser sur les lèvres. (24)

       After the kiss on the lips.

2.31. Je pris l'habitude de contempler ... le lent office du maquillage et l'ajustement de la tenue de scène. (24)

       I got into the habit of gazing at the slow make-up ritual and the adjustment of the stage outfit.

The narrator's presentation of A***'s life is not only that of a series of states, but of a series of repeated, familiar states, the way one might describe the actions of machines in an assembly line: expected, unvarying, and automatic. This effect is increased by the racial difference between Je and A***. Since A*** is prevented from becoming a character whose point of view the reader can share, being described in terms of his/her body rather than his/her whole self, the racial distinction becomes more salient. A*** is represented as a set of black body parts, eroticized and exoticized but never familiar. Only A***'s dark skin is commented on. The white characters are not described in terms of their race.

Empathy

Earlier in this chapter, we looked at the inferences drawn by cooperative readers when faced by a novel in which the gender of the two protagonists is unknown. We saw that they needed to create a working hypothesis for themselves to explain why the usual gender markers were withheld in order to restore their sense of a coherent narrative at the macro level of the novel as a whole. We then examined in detail some of the linguistic devices available in French for creating textual cohesion at the micro level of the sentence or episode. We now combine the two approaches by looking at empathy, one of the effects created by these linguistic devices, and discuss how it influences the reader's view of the characters.

Empathy conveys the perspective from which events are related, indicating which character's point of view is shown. The reader will, in all likelihood, share this point of view. Susumu Kuno and Etsuko Kaburaki's (1977) scale of empathy in many ways parallels Halliday and Hasan's scale of grammatically cohesive devices. The lowest degree of empathy for a character is shown by repetition of the proper name, the highest by pronominalization and zero anaphora (ellipsis). The principal features of each scale, cohesion and empathy, are presented in table 2.3 so that their points of coincidence become clear. Empathy is shown by the use of ellipsis and by pronominalization, while repetition of the proper name indicates lack of empathy.

Table 2.3   Coherence and empathy

Grammatical coherence	Degree of empathy
Proper name repetition	Proper name repetition
Reference	—
Lexical substitution	—
Pronominal reference/anaphor	Pronominal reference
Ellipsis	Ellipsis

Just as a character whose name must be repeated makes the text less cohesive, so that character cannot become the focalizer of the narrative. It is difficult for a narrator to show empathy for a character who cannot be referred to by a pronoun. If the character never receives pronominal reference, it is difficult, if not impossible, for his or her own words, thoughts, or feelings to be assumed by the narrator, since the use of the proper name produces a certain distance between named and namer. It has the formality of a title (an unusual way for people to refer to themselves).

This impression is confirmed by Patricia Clancy's (1980) study of empathy in oral narrative. Clancy examined the English and Japanese renditions of the "pear stories," narratives told by viewers of a film constructed by Wallace Chafe in which various events take place concerning a farmer, his pear tree, the pears, and different groups of passersby, but that has no speech or voice-over. Respondents narrate the events according to their own interpretations, uninfluenced by any authoritative account in the film itself. Clancy's work involves an analysis of the types of reference used by speakers from the two different cultures. She concludes: "By using an explicit form of reference, such as a pronoun or ellipsis, the speaker . . . is telling the listener that he should be able to identify the referent in question without further information. . . . Use of inexplicit reference serves to make the reader identify most closely with, and to some extent, take the point of view of that character" (Clancy 1980, 178). In other words, repetition of the noun phrase tends to reduce reader/hearer empathy, whereas pronominalization may be an indication of "hero" status (i.e., that of someone whose point of view everyone should share).

The narrator usually takes the point of view of the character most often pronominalized, though in certain cases, particularly in literary contexts, this may not be the case. In Flaubert's *L'Education sentimentale*, for example, the woman whom the hero adores from a distance, Madame Arnoux, is almost always referred to as *elle*, suggesting a familiarity the hero would like to claim but cannot. The narrator may utilize the conventional meaning attached to pronominalization—familiarity or accessibility—to convey a character's desire for familiarity, rather than the actual state of affairs.

Clancy remarks that one way of working out where the narrator's focus of attention lies is by observing which referent she chooses to clarify and which to leave ambiguous in making subject switches; in other words, if a character is referred to by zero anaphora or by pronoun, despite the possibility of ambiguity, then that is the character who acts as the object of focalization for the narrator. In the film from which the various pear stories come, there is only one female character. Both Japanese and English speakers use a full noun phrase to refer to her even after she has been introduced and is an active referent. By doing this they indicate her peripheral status compared with that of the male characters. Without pronouns, or ellipsis in the case of Japanese, the sense of familiarity, as for an already established referent, is missing. The recurrence of the noun phrase creates a sense of distance instead.

Reviewer Response to Sphinx

An obvious question in response to this analysis is whether French readers actually notice, or are in any way disturbed by, these techniques in *Sphinx*.[5] Although they do not comment explicitly on the features examined here—it would be somewhat unusual for literary critics to pay particular attention to such linguistic phenomena as deverbal noun phrases or the use of cataphora versus synecdochic lexical substitution—all the reviewers in a sample of more than thirty reviews in major French magazines and newspapers remark upon the distinctive style of the novel and make some attempt to guess the "real" gender of the two protagonists, or at least the reasons for gender avoidance. Many also note the disparity between the depiction of the narrator and that of A***.

Gender assignment varies from reviewer to reviewer: *World Literature Today* (spring 1987), for example, describes "the studious theologian and his vulgar beloved" and how "the narrator becomes enamoured of her." With equal confidence at having found the answer to the riddle of the sphinx, *Paris-Match* (30 May 1986) describes A*** as "un danseur noir" (a black male dancer) and the narrator as "une jeune personne" (a young woman, although *une personne* may be either male or female, the phrase *une jeune personne* has strong connotations of femininity, while *jeunes gens* [young people] connotes the masculine). *Le Républicain lorrain* (7 March 1986) writes of the "étrange périple que celui du narrateur, un étudiant en théologie" (strange odyssey, that of the narrator, a male theology student) who "se prend de passion pour 'A,' un danseur d'origine noire" (is overtaken by passion for "A," a male dancer of black origin), while *Le Canard enchaîné* (March 1986) describes "une jeune théologiennne" (a young female theologian) and "une danseuse noire" (a black female dancer). All bases are covered; each of the four possible combinations is cited as the correct one: male narrator, female beloved; female narrator, male beloved; male narrator, male beloved; female narrator, female beloved.

Other reviewers produce complicated evidence for their claims. *Libération* (27 March 1986) identifies the narrator with the author, since a first novelist will not have the confidence to distance herself from the narrative voice and because, when pleading her cause from bar to bar, she does not simply slip her arm round her beloved as would a man. In a more nuanced explanation, the *French American Institute for International Studies* (29 November 1986) discusses the *pôle masculin* (masculine end of the spectrum) which, apparently, "domine chez 'je'" (dominates in 'I'), and *le pôle féminin* (feminine end of the spectrum) which "domine chez A***" (dominates in A***). In this version, no specific gender is assigned to either character; instead, there is a suggestion of a continuum of gender characteristics that may be displayed by either men or women.

Some critics offer sophisticated hypotheses as to the reason for the creation of a nongendered text. *Esprit* (May 1986) suggests linguistic motivation: "A partir du moment où dans la langue disparaît le genre, ce n'est plus le masculin qui commande les rapports d'assujetissement" (the moment gender disappears from language, it is no longer the masculine that rules relations of subjection). *Roman* (September 1986), on the other hand, explains the rationale in ideological terms, suggesting that the text aims at "la transcendance d'un sentiment qui peut ne dépendre ni du sexe ni de la race, ni de la culture ou des centres d'intérêt" (the transcendence of an emotion that may not depend on sex, race, culture, or a community of interests). Garréta has explained that she had both linguistic and ideological motives for the writing of *Sphinx;* indeed, her own account is not dissimilar to those suggested by *Esprit* and *Roman.*

Both *Libération* (27 March 1986) and *Le Figaro* (1 April 1986) imply that the very question as to the characters' gender comes from prurient interest. *Libération:* "n'est-ce pas grossier, avant de tomber amoureux, de demander aux gens ce qu'ils cachent sous leur string?" (isn't it vulgar to ask, before one falls in love, what people are hiding beneath their g-string?); *Le Figaro:* "c'est sans doute nous qui avons tort de nous poser ces sortes de questions" (doubtless it is we who are wrong to entertain this sort of question). The irony of these remarks is clear from the tone of each paper. That of *Libération* is exaggeratedly vulgar. In a society built largely around the differences between the sexes, where clothes, coiffure, color scheme, tone of voice, and language use (to mention only the most obvious features) all work together to produce clearly delineated gender projections, one hardly needs to look at a person's genitals to work out their sex. That of *Le Figaro* is exceptionally dry and matter-of-fact, but the "sans doute" (doubtless) rings false, a way of showing that the writer has guessed at Garréta's intentions and is politely mocking them.

Many critics describe not the freedom of androgyny vaunted by Garréta, but "une certaine pudeur des mots" (a certain prudishness of vocabulary— *Le Républicain lorrain*); "une préciosité académique" (academic preciosity— *La Suisse*, 29 May 1986); "(une) langue recherchée, voire précieuse" ([an] affected, even prissy linguistic style— *Culture et bibliothèque pour tous*, April 1986). It would seem that for these reviewers the absence of gender marking signifies not an end to sex-role stereotyping, but a return to the seventeenth-century rules of suitable behavior, or *bienséance*, according to which one draws a veil over markers of sexual difference, and indeed of sexuality. *La Presse étrangère* attributes the lack of gender markings to "un vieux fond de puritanisme" (an old leftover Puritanism) and remarks, "ce livre ne me semble pas . . . favoriser la levée de l'interdit qui pèse encore sur la bisexualité ou l'homosexualité" (this book does not seem to me to be in favor of a lifting of the ban that still weighs on bisexuality and homosexuality). Evidently, silence on matters of gender can be interpreted in two very different, even contradictory, ways: either gender is unimportant and need not be mentioned, or gender is of such importance and so powerful that it needs to be muted and left to the reader's imagination.

The varied comments on the distinctive style of *Sphinx* are instructive. While some reviewers see it as a return to classical purity, with its outmoded *passés simples* and sometimes archaic vocabulary, others, particularly the more literary, see its excesses as sophomoric. The *passé simple*, the usual tense for third person narration, is almost never seen in modern novels in the first or second person. In *Sphinx*, however, it is used frequently to describe the narrator's actions, especially where the use of the *passé composé*, with its accompanying agreement rules for verbs conjugated with *être* (to be), would reveal the narrator's gender. "Je me levai du canapé et m'apprêtai à sortir dans le couloir" (I got up from the sofa and prepared to go out into the corridor) (148); "Lorsque nous rentrâmes à l'hotel . . . nous nous couchâmes dans le lit" (when we returned to the hotel . . . we lay down in the bed) (127–28). There are even some imperfect subjunctives and pluperfect subjunctives, tenses that are extremely rare in modern French, even in literary texts: "J'eusse désiré [pluperfect subjunctive] qu'à cette heure la tragédie me livrât [imperfect subjunctive] au moins un confident" (I could have wished that the tragedy had given me at least a confidant by now) (166). A more modern rendering of this sentiment would probably have employed the past conditional with a present subjunctive: "j'aurais désiré que la tragédie me livre au moins un confident" (I would have liked to the tragedy to give me at least a confidante). These tenses would not have betrayed the narrator's gender any more than the archaic subjunctives do. One must conclude that they are employed to support the use of the *passé simple* and give an old-fashioned slant to the style.

La Presse étrangère (April 1986) admires the text, written in "le plus pur style XVIIe siècle" (the purest seventeenth-century style);[6] for *Esprit* it is "écrit dans une langue classique portée à la perfection" (written in a classical prose that reaches perfection); *Marie-Claire* (April 1986) describes the style as "d'une autorité et une élégance confondantes" (of extraordinary authority and elegance). *Le Quotidien de Paris* (6 May 1986), on the other hand, condemns "les monstruosités normaliennes" (sophomoric monstrosities typical of the *ecole normale supérieure*),[7] while *Le Monde* sighs lugubriously, "on aurait pu se passer de 'la désertitude de la ville'" (one could have done without "the desertitude of the town"). The creation of those "sophomoric monstrosities" is, to a large extent, due to the need to avoid gender markers by bringing into play the more arcane reserves of the French language. *Le Monde*'s disapproval of the word *désertitude* expresses an irritation with stylistic grandiloquence when simpler, more straightforward expressions are available. There is no reason for Garréta to employ the term *désertitude*, since the town could safely be described as *déserte* without giving away the gender of either A*** or the narrator; but seeking out unusual words has become a part of the author's rather contrived style, as we have seen with her use of the past tenses of the subjunctive. *Paris-Match* describes Garréta's style ironically as "le meilleur français académique dont le passé simple ad nauseam" (the best academic French including the *passé simple* ad nauseam). *Le Figaro* complains, "[C]e court récit est très écrit avec une volonté d'élégance, de préciosité, ce qui n'empêche ni les scories ni les extravagances" (this short tale is overwritten, aiming at elegance and preciosity, which prevent neither dross nor folly).

Reviewers also comment on the difference between the depiction of the narrator and that of A***. Jean-Claude Bologne notes in *Télérama* (March 1986), for example,

> Quant à son sphinx impénétrable, dont il faut à chaque instant traduire les paroles pour qu'elles soient intelligibles, elle est . . . beaucoup moins finement dessinée que le narrateur.

> As for his/her impenetrable sphinx, whose every word must be translated to make it intelligible, he/she is much less intricately designed than the narrator.

It is true that A*** is rarely allowed sentences of direct speech. Instead, his or her words are embedded in the speech of the narrator, as in the following, which encapsulates A***'s reply to the narrator's declaration of love: "Sa réponse fut claire. Elle se résumait en substance à cette sentence: 'Tu ne dois pas m'aimer'" (89) (his/her reply was clear. It could be summarized in essence as: 'You must not love me'). The narrator does not attempt to quote A***'s own words, but gives a brief précis that is not even colored by A***'s manner of speaking. If A*** were permitted passages of direct speech, a *verbum dicendi* (or verb of introduction to speech, such as *elle dit* [she said]) would become necessary, with accompanying pronominal subject. Hence Bologne's perception that A*** is a more nebulous character than Je, filtered always through the perceptions of the narrator.

Sphinx is an example of the extreme end of narrator control. Justifying the abrupt summary of A***'s reaction to the narrator's protestation of love, the narrator adds, "Je ne rapporte ni les termes exacts de sa plaidoirie ni le mouvement de sa logique personnelle. A*** ne formulait pas de rapport entre les sentences successives" (89). (I report neither the exact terms of her/his speech nor the process of her/his particular logic. A*** did not formulate any relation between successive sentences). The double meaning of this last sentence is telling. There is a lack of logical progression in A***'s thoughts: the different utterances do not relate to each other in a semantically satisfying way. More significantly, there is no formal or grammatical relation between one sentence and another, thus A***'s discourse lacks cohesion—exactly what we have found in the lack of pronominalization of A***'s name. A*** could serve either as use or as mention in the sentence "A*** ne formulait pas de rapport entre les sentences successives." There is no formal connection between one appearance of A*** the character and another, just as there is no formal connection between one appearance of "A***," the linguistic device for referring to that character, and another.

An even stronger statement is made by the critic from *Esprit* who observes: "L'image renvoyée par A*** est toujours la même, figée. Le sentiment suscité par le corps n'est en rien modifié à la vue de son cadavre" (May 1986) (the image projected by A*** is always the same, frozen. The feeling provoked by the body is in no way modified by the sight of its corpse). A body that is not in any way altered by becoming a corpse can hardly be said to have been alive. Supporting this impression, *World Literature Today* asks, "[I]s A [*sic*] any more than a symbol of the enigmatic other? As a person she is reduced to her movements on stage." One might be tempted to add that these "movements" consist of stylized, repetitive gestures executed by parts of A***'s body, since A*** cannot be described as a whole person without revealing gender. As we have seen, because descriptions of A*** so often take the form of deverbal nouns, which do not encode tense-aspect information, A***'s body seems as though frozen, a static, unmoving entity. There is thus no action to be placed on the time line and to participate in the sequence of events that make up a narrative, to play a part in the chain of cause and effect. Instead, the nominalizations present the reader with states rather than actions, entailing no urgency, incapable of having consequences—an encapsulation outside time.

It is evident that while neither narrator nor A*** is accorded grammatical gender, the effect on the reader is somewhat different in each case. The narrator has no proper name, always being referred to by the pronoun *je*, while A*** is restricted to an initial letter. As we have seen, pronouns create a sense of familiarity and empathy in the reader and serve to produce a strongly cohesive text. While the narrator may seem somewhat mysterious, readers are nevertheless able to empathize with him or her. In contrast, there is little empathy for A***, because the various means of reference indicate that A*** never becomes a "given" in the discourse but must be continually reintroduced. The net result of this avoidance of grammatical gender is that A*** has only a very attenuated self, since no cohesive element is present that can link all references to A***, showing that they are the actions, feelings, or body parts of the same person. A***'s existence is restricted to the letter "A" with its train of asterisks, showing a deleted persona.

A major achievement of *Sphinx*, therefore, is not so much that it is a novel without gender, but that it shows how crucial gender is, for the effectiveness of *Sphinx* goes beyond the stagnant, depersonalized relationship of the novel. Without gender, the very concept of selfhood is tenuous outside of the first and second persons, which, being deictic rather than anaphoric, gain their ability to refer from the context of discourse. The pronoun *je* anchors the person uttering this word to the *situation d'énonciation*, or the context of the speech event. The narrator has an identity, created by the use of that pronoun (which is not the case when narrative relies on so-called third person forms). The reader is able to recognize the narrator as an individual who remains the same under varying conditions, a being distinct from others. In contrast, there is no necessary—that is, grammatical—link between one appearance of A*** and another. The reader is obliged to forge the link from the scant details of A***'s life.

The French gender system has spread its tentacles, as it were, from morphology, morphosyntax (showing which qualifiers belong with which nouns), and morphosemantics (providing some indication as to the gender of a referent) to cross clausal and sentential boundaries and exert a strong binding effect at the discourse level. Its marks cannot be eradicated without doing serious damage to the text as a whole. The writing of *Sphinx* is undoubtedly an extraordinary achievement, but the trap set for the unwary reader may instead have caught the overhasty champion of androgyny. Employing a method of analysis similar to that used for *Sphinx*, in the next chapter I will examine a body of literary works in English that avoid mentioning the gender of their principal protagonists.

3

"Was I, perhaps, castrato/a?"

Nongendered Characters in English

In chapter 2, I examined the effects produced by the creation of non-gendered characters in the French novel *Sphinx*, noting that the devices used to avoid betraying the gender of the two protagonists caused certain disruptions to the text. A***, in particular, described in the third person, seems distant, fragmented, and static. In this chapter, I turn to an investigation of a corpus of novels written in English that feature characters whose gender identity is not given by the usual grammatical and lexical means. An analysis of the workings of these novels, particularly with regard to the features examined in *Sphinx*—repetition of the proper name, lexical substitution, and ellipsis—will tell us much about the construction of a gender identity in English and why the omission of formal gender markers is not sufficient to erase gender from a text. Although gender is not as widespread in the morphosyntactic structure of English as it is in French, being limited to the forms of the third person singular pronoun in the contrasting pairs *he/she* and *him/her* and the corresponding possessive adjectives *his/hers*, nevertheless, as we shall see, the absence of these morphemes and the strategies required to repair the lack have important consequences for the resulting discourse.

Genderless narrators are more common than genderless characters described in the third person. As we have seen with reference to *Sphinx*, it is less disruptive to the text to conceal the gender of someone who refers to himself or herself in the first person, since *I* and *je* are epicene, while third person reference, *he/she* and *il/elle*, reveals gender. All the novels I have found with at least one genderless character are written in the first person.

First person novels tend to feature a higher degree of narrator control of the narrative than third person novels. The non-omniscient first person narrator cannot, for example, enter the minds of other characters, to give alternative points of view. Thus empathy is stronger for the narrator than for other characters.

Although *Sphinx* was greeted as a unique achievement by French critics, many similar experiments with gender have been conducted in English, beginning with the publication in 1930 of Natalie Clifford Barney's *The One Who Is Legion, or A. D.'s After-Life*. Apart from this early work, most of these books were written in the last quarter of the twentieth century, especially during the 1970s and 1980s, inspired by the feminist concern with language discussed in chapter 1. Brigid Brophy's *In Transit* (1969); Maureen Duffy's *Love Child* (1971); Sarah Caudwell's three mysteries *Thus Was Adonis Murdered* (1981), *The Shortest Way to Hades* (1984), and *The Sirens Sang of Murder* (1989); and Jeanette Winterson's *Written on the Body* (1992) all involve at least one prominent character who is described without recourse to traditional gender markers. Nor is this phenomenon limited to English (or Anglo-Irish—Brophy is Irish) and French writers: Cristina Perez-Rossi, the author of *Solitario de amor* (1987), another novel featuring a genderless narrator and a genderless beloved, was born in Uruguay and now lives in exile in Spain. These fictional works represent three distinct genres: the lesbian love story (Duffy's, Perez-Rossi's, and Winterson's novels), the transsexual novel (Barney's *The One Who Is Legion* and Brophy's *In Transit*), and the detective story (Caudwell's three mysteries). What they have in common is the idea that gender categories are themselves problematic, especially when tied to grammatical gender.

It is the presence of nongendered characters described in the third person that most undermine the structures for creating textual cohesion. *The One Who Is Legion*, *In Transit*, and *Love Child* are all principally narrated in the first person, though both *The One Who Is Legion* and *In Transit* switch back and forth between first and third person. An added complication, in the case of *The One Who Is Legion*, is the switch between singular and plural reference. All three novels also involve a genderless character described in the third person. It is this character, in each text, whose identity is fragmented, by which I mean not simply their gender identity but, more fundamentally, their ability to be recognized at a second appearance. This is because the devices that can be used to avoid gender reference in English—repetition of the proper name; reference (i.e., use of a noun phrase description); lexical substitution; ellipsis; and free direct speech, which omits any introduction to speech that would tie an utterance to a specific character—all create a more fragmentary sense of self than does the use of an anaphoric pronoun (*he* or *she*). As we will see, the techniques used in English to avoid gender reference, and their effect on the text, are strikingly similar to those reported in French in my analysis of cohesion in *Sphinx*. In this chapter, I will concentrate on a discussion of *Love Child*, since of the three novels it is the most classically narrative in form, though an analysis of the other two works produces similar results. I conclude my examination of English novels featuring nongendered protagonists with a brief consideration of Caudwell's three mysteries and Winterson's *Written on the Body*. Discussion of these latter works will be much less detailed, concentrating mainly on reader hypotheses rather than in-depth linguistic analysis. This is because they feature only nongendered first person narrators and so pose fewer challenges to the gender system as a whole.

Nongendered Narrators

Plot Summary: Love Child

Love Child tells the story of the child narrator's obsessive jealousy toward his/her mother's lover. No clue is given to the gender of either the child, Kit, or the lover. The lover in question is referred to either as "Ajax" (a name Kit has invented) or as "my mother's lover." Employed as the father's secretary, Ajax becomes the mother's lover while the family is on holiday in Italy. Kit's jealousy increases as s/he spies on the couple, until one day s/he manipulates Ajax into believing the mother unfaithful, whereupon Ajax, under the influence of too much alcohol, crashes a car and dies.

The novel opens with the announcement, "It was I who christened my mother's lover." This striking claim presupposes that the mother has a lover and asserts that it was the narrator who gave this person a name. Since "my mother's lover" is one of the two designators used to refer to this person throughout the text, by stating "It was I who christened my mother's lover," Kit is in effect naming the person "my mother's lover." Two paragraphs further on, the reader is taken back to this person's first entry into Kit's house. Kit comes across his/her father asking his assistant what he/she wants to be called. Before he/she can answer, the father presents his assistant to his child, calling him/her "my secretary." This is the first and last time the term "secretary" is used to designate this person. Kit offers the name "Ajax" in answer to the father's question, and from then on everyone in the family will refer to the secretary as Ajax. Thus Kit has named Ajax not once but twice, first as "my mother's lover," a term Kit shares with the reader, and then as "Ajax," a name Kit shares with the family.

Neither *Kit* nor *Ajax* reveals the gender of the person referred to. *Kit* may be short for either "Katherine" or "Christopher," and *Ajax* is a nickname suggested by a child. One might assume that Ajax is a man, named after the ancient Greek hero, but nicknames for upper-class girls frequently have overtones of masculinity, for example, "Timmy" for Artemisia or, "Charlie" for Charlotte (and Kit's family is upper class). Lest readers assume from the description "secretary" that Ajax is a woman, Kit hastens to inform us that the father's personal secretaries have consisted of both "boys and girls" (4–5). No gendered lexical item is used in reference to Ajax. Although Kit is called "man" by some hippy beachbums (113), in the next line the bums call him/her "kid": If Kit can be referred to as both *man* and *kid*, then the age specificity of each term must be set aside. Hippies in the 1960s used the word *man* as a form of address encoding equality rather than sexual specificity.

Kit's parents have no proper names but are referred to as "my mother" and "my father". All terms revolve around Kit as the deictic center, since the parents are named only in relation to their child and the father's secretary loses his/her own name upon entering the house. The deictic center supplies a fixed referent point from which a set of shifters (like family terms) can be understood. In scenes involving all four of the major characters (father, mother, Kit, and Ajax), *he* is always Kit's father, while *she* is Kit's mother; from personal pronouns they appear to solidify into rigid designators.

Pronominalization: Anaphoric Linking

Father as *he*:

3.1. Why did he$_i$ fail so with Ajax$_j$? Is it the onset of age, the crumbling of him$_i$? (5)

Mother as *she*:

3.2. "There might be more air outside," said Ajax$_i$. My mother$_j$ fumbled with the door but got the window winder by mistake. . . . As my mother's lover$_i$ levered the handle, my mother$_j$ looked up. . . . She$_j$ got out. (71)

Repetition of Ajax

3.3. Ajax$_i$ sat beside him$_j$; my mother and I in back. Already my father$_j$ had abandoned any attempt to flirt with or subjugate Ajax$_i$. (39)

3.4. "Why does Ajax$_i$ want this job?" I asked my mother later.
      "To travel. . . . Why do you ask?"
      "Ajax$_i$ is different." (6)

As may be seen from these examples, the name *Ajax* is often repeated in the verb phrase following a previous mention where a pronoun would be expected, implying that a second Ajax has appeared. In example 3.1, the father is consistently referred to pronominally, telling the reader to treat the referent of *he* and *him* as accessible and to examine the context for the most likely candidate. Since Ajax is referred to by name twice in the space of three sentences, involving only four verbal predicates, the message to the reader is that, in contrast to the father, Ajax is not accessible, not familiar, either in terms of the immediate textual discourse or in terms of the narrator's worldview.

In the first sentence in example 3.2, Ajax suggests that they get out of the car; in the second, "my mother" attempts to open the door. In the next sentence the mother, now considered an active referent, is designated by the pronoun *her*, anaphorically creating a tight cohesive link between the two mentions of the referent. In contrast, the proper name *Ajax* is repeated, suggesting that Ajax, unlike the mother, can never become inferentially accessible. The reader has by now no difficulty accessing the referent for Ajax, since Ajax is not only an important protagonist but has been mentioned in the immediately preceding clause. The author is using the device of proper name repetition to denote coreference, in obvious contrast to that of anaphorization, in order to show, by the contrasting presuppositional status of the two devices, that the narrator refuses to presuppose the presence of Ajax.

What is at issue is the *presupposition* of Ajax's presence in Kit's family. At the level of assertion, the narrator has told the reader plainly from the beginning that Ajax had come to Italy on the family holiday as the father's secretary. Repetition of the proper name not only presupposes the lowest level of familiarity (in fact, none), as has been seen in chapter 2, it also creates the weakest cohesive tie (following Halliday and Hasan 1976). The second mention of Ajax does not require the reader to make a referential link between this proper name and another linguistic item further back in the text, in the way that *my mother* and *she* must be successfully linked to each other. Each mention of Ajax stands alone. Where the name *Ajax* alternates with the descriptor *my mother's lover*, rather than enhancing Ajax's identity by providing further information, it suggests that a second person has appeared.

In example 3.3, we see again the repetition of Ajax's name in contrast to the pronominalization of *my father*. The members of Kit's tightly knit family appear to have occupied all the singular personal pronoun positions save the second person *you*, for Kit, as deictic center, holds onto the first person *I* (rarely giving it up to the other characters), while the father occupies the masculine singular *he* and the mother the feminine singular *she*. Since the reader is given the position of addressee, interpolated by Kit at the very beginning of the novel—"You notice that I say 'I'" (3)—all spaces in the singular pronominal paradigm are conveniently filled. Ajax is left with no pronominal possibility in Kit's megalomaniac world, condemned instead to be the outsider. Needless to say, there are no fourth person pronouns. This underlines Ajax's position in Kit's mind as a gate-crashing fourth party. As in *Sphinx*, narrator control of the text is paramount.

In example 3.4, it is the child, Kit, who repeats Ajax's name on the second mention. The mother, whose lover we are told Ajax is, considers the referent so active that she uses the expression "to travel," an infinitive from which the finite verb "he/she wants this job" has been elided in surface structure. For the mother, Ajax's name does not need repeating; for the resistant child, it should never be assumed.

Reference and Ellipsis

3.5.   Ajax_i spieled _[1], pattered _[2] manipulated _[3] unseen puppets, drew _[4] scenes and characters with a charlatan's fluency. Then my mother's lover_i began to question deftly. (50)

Example 3.5 is particularly informative in that it combines two different kinds of referential device. The link between *Ajax* and *my mother's lover* is often termed reference proper: a noun phrase description of Ajax that presupposes that the referent is unfamiliar and needs to be explicitly singled out by having more information provided about him or her than is available solely from the proper name. The string of verbs without a preceding noun phrase, on the other hand—*pattered, manipulated,* and *drew*—are examples of ellipsis, in which all referring items are omitted. Unlike reference, ellipsis presupposes the familiarity or accessibility of the referent. In order to understand who the subject of the predicate *pattered* is, the reader must link this verb with the preceding verb *spieled*. The contrast between the two devices, reference and ellipsis, in two contiguous sentences is striking. In the first sentence, with its string of elided subjects, Ajax has become so familiar that even when all subsequent reference is omitted, the reader will still make the connection between the verbs and their subject. In the phrase immediately following, however, a new descriptor is used: *my mother's lover.* The abruptness of the change in empathy causes Ajax to appear doubly strange. Elliptical linking is used only when the referent is termed *Ajax,* as can be seen in examples 3.2 and 3.5. The actions of "my mother's lover" are always of a singular nature, emphasizing the singularity of the appellation and of the narrative situation. Mothers are not meant to have lovers; if they do, their children are not mean to know of it; and if the children do know, they are not meant to make this knowledge public.

A similar effect is produced in example 3.6, though instead of a new designator, the proper name is repeated.

3.6.   I pictured Ajax_i climbing up_[1] the hill at night and slapping down_[2] in the morning feet smacking up little puffs of dust, . . . lying_[3] in bed, . . . drawing_[4] on a cigarette. Did Ajax_i smoke? (43)

The four present participles *climbing up, slapping down, lying,* and *drawing,* all recounting imagined actions of Ajax, express a high degree of narrator empathy for this character. Clearly, Kit empathizes strongly with Ajax in this brief reverie but cuts this intimate insight off abruptly by the repetition of Ajax's name and an expression of his/her own ignorance of Ajax's habits: Kit does not know whether Ajax smokes. The evocative mental picture of Ajax's bare feet in the dust is nullified by this shrug of ignorance.

This scene reveals an important aspect of empathy, which should not be confused with sympathy, fellow feeling, or any such good-hearted sentiments. Empathy refers only to the angle from which events are related. The narrator may often share the feelings of the character from whose perspective a scene is envisaged, but there is no necessary connection. In Kuno and Kaburaki's classic examples, "John hit Mary," "John hit his wife," and "Mary's husband hit her" (1977, 627), in which the first is empathically objective, the second reveals John's perspective, and the third Mary's, one assumes that the speaker has a different emotional reaction in each. This need not be so, however. Empathy is like understanding. As decent human beings, we like to imagine a necessary connection between understanding and compassion. If we understood each other, we would feel for each other. If we saw the world from the same point of view, we would sympathize. A brief look at the lines of sympathy and empathy at any murder trial will prove us wrong. The jury must concentrate on the actions and motives of the defendant, not on the pain of the victim, yet they are not expected (at least by the prosecution) to sympathize with the murderer but to put him to death. In the same way, an antiterrorist squad strives to understand the motives of the terrorists they seek, but not to share them.

These examples, though significant, admittedly demonstrate the marked rather than the unmarked case. In general, empathy and sympathy tend to collocate. What the examples show is that the connection between empathy and sympathy may be canceled by the context. Kit's bitter enmity toward Ajax, whom he/she considers to have usurped his/her mother's love, allows him/her to enter into Ajax's world at times in order to understand the workings of his/her rival's mind and place Ajax as the focalizer of the narrative (for brief passages). Kit is, however, extremely careful to cut off any welling of reader sympathy toward Ajax.

A switch in descriptor may also indicate a change or loss of empathy. The change in designator from *Ajax* to *my mother's lover*, or the other way round, sometimes takes place within the same sentence.

3.7.   Ajax$_i$ and my mother didn't speak to each other but my mother's lover$_i$ talked briskly to amuse my father. (75)

In example 3.7, it sounds very much as though there were two couples in the room: Ajax and the mother sulking, and the mother's lover and the father chatting away. Ajax seems to be split in two by the two designators, reflecting his/her duplicitous position in the family as the father's secretary and the mother's sexual partner.

In the last scenes of the novel, in which Ajax commits suicide, the two designators, *Ajax* and *my mother's lover*, break apart for good, no longer indicating coreference.

3.8.   My mother's lover has killed Ajax. (214)

In example 3.8, the two designators appear not only in the same sentence, but as arguments of the same verb. It is a highly transitive verb, and one designator refers to the agent, the other to the patient. The jealousy of the lover, so easily kindled by Kit's clumsy plotting, overcomes the good sense of the secretary, but in killing Ajax, the lover also kills himself/herself. In the penultimate sentence of the novel, a new referent for the designator *my mother's lover* appears:

3.9. I am my mother's lover now. (215)

Kit has taken over the role of lover. The connection between *Ajax* and *my mother's lover*, which throughout the narration Kit has been trying to suggest is peculiar and unnatural, is now sundered.

Lexical Substitution

Another tactic the author uses to avoid pronominal reference that would reveal gender information is that of synecdochic lexical substitution, where parts of the body stand for the whole person. As we have seen in reference to *Sphinx*, this strategy is an important weapon in Garréta's antigender arsenal; in *Love Child*, in contrast, it is of less importance. The structure of the language of each novel easily accounts for the difference. In French, Garréta can divide A*** into a series of body parts and write of *sa taille* (his/her waist), *son crâne nu* (his/her bare skull), and *ses hanches étroites* (his/her narrow hips) without giving away's A***'s sexual identity. In English, on the other hand, only *their*, the third person plural possessive, is epicene. In the singular, *his* and *her* are clearly gendered. Since, in English, the possessive agrees with the number (and, in the singular, the gender) of the possessor, a plural possessor is required for the use of epicene *their*, as seen in example 3.10 below.

3.10. Ajax' eyes$_i$ were cool, they$_i$ smiled. Whatever lay behind them$_i$ was not to be drawn up easily. (34)

Here Ajax's eyes are pronominalized, not Ajax. Parts of Ajax's body may become familiar enough, accessible enough, to be referred to by pronoun, but the reader must never be allowed to identify with Ajax as a whole person.

3.11. I pictured my mother's lover$_i$

"Hurld headlong flaming from th' Ethereal Skye,"

the yellow hair streaming back from *the face* as if in waves . . . Icarus-Phaeton-Lucifer$_j$ . . . smiling as wings sprouted. . . . I was a little surprised not to see them$_j$ arcing above Ajax' head. (38)

In example 3.11, the mythological figures of Icarus, Phaeton, and Lucifer are anaphorized as *they* despite possible confusion with the antecedent plural nouns *wings* and *waves*, either of which might well "arc" over Ajax's head. It is only the hierarchy of animacy that tells the reader that Icarus-Phaeton-Lucifer is the referent for *them*, since animate subjects will take precedence over inanimate ones. The name *Ajax* is reintroduced after minimal intervening material, although it is unlikely that the reader has forgotten to whom the head belongs. Whereas in example 3.10 parts of Ajax's body may be pronominalized without revealing gender, in the singular this is impossible; thus, in example 3.11, instead of *his yellow hair*, or *her face*, we read *the yellow hair*, or *the face*, suggesting yet again disconnected body parts, separate items in a disjointed collage rather than elements integral to a human being.

This disjointed effect is even more remarkable in example 3.12.

3.12.   *Abstract:* Ajax had been drinking. 1 {The near empty bottle of scotch stood on the floor. One hand gripped the glass, the other was splayed over the face . . .} 2 {Ajax moaned and the free hand beat with the heel of the palm against the broad forehead.} 3 {The glass was emptied and set down.} 4 {My mother's lover got up wildly, hands clawing at the face.} (201) (The division of this passage into an abstract and four frames is my addition.)

In this passage, Kit is spying on Ajax through the vent from the bathroom; Ajax is framed by the square of light visible to the child. The scene appears as a series of stills (enclosed in braces in the examples), or sketches of the human body, in which the person portrayed is no more than a model. Each of the various body parts—hand, forehead, and face—is introduced by the definite determiner, suggesting that they are generic, rather than personal. There are four freeze-frames, introduced by an abstract of the sequence we are about to read: Ajax had been drinking. The first frame is of a nearly empty whiskey bottle and a human figure with one hand on the glass, the other on his/her face. The second focuses on the figure, the palm of the hand against the forehead. The third focuses on the now empty whiskey glass. The fourth shows the figure on its feet, both hands held up to the face. Despite the use of highly emotive terms such as *gripped*, *misery*, *moaned*, *wildly*, and *clawing*, this picture of human wretchedness remains strangely distant; our attention is concentrated on the hand gripping the glass, the tear-drenched face, but only as objects in a framed landscape. Nothing is told from Ajax's point of view; the focalizer—the one who sees—is safely outside the frame (hiding in a bathroom vent). No empathy is created for Ajax. Kit hardly needs to announce that he/she observed each detail with cold precision (201); the coldness of the description is manifest in the absence of personal pronouns and possessives. The last, frantic action, which might have been the culmination of a scene full of pathos as Ajax springs to his/her feet and claws his/her own face, is attributed to "my mother's lover," the switch in designator cutting off any empathy that might have developed. The figure does not even claw its own face, but the face assigned to it, geographically proximate but without physical connection.

Free Direct Speech

Two of the strategies I have discussed so far that avoid pronominal reference and thereby gender information—proper name repetition and synecdochic lexical substitution, serve to lessen empathy for Ajax. The third strategy, ellipsis, however, heightens empathy. When we turn to an investigation of the different techniques used to indicate represented speech in *Love Child*, we see that free direct speech (FDS), which uses no introduction to speech but quotes what was said without assigning the utterance to any one character, works in a similar way to ellipsis. Passages in which Ajax's name is elided are ended by the reintroduction of the proper name or the designation *my mother's lover*. The same is true of passages of FDS, which produce a similar effect of drawing in and then brusquely throwing back.

One might assume that FDS would be used frequently to report Ajax's speech, since this device avoids the necessity for a *verbum dicendi* with its accompanying noun or, more likely, pronoun (*he said, she commented*) and thus avoids revealing the gender of the speaker. However, FDS has two distinct, even opposite functions. During a conversation recorded in FDS, either each of the participants is considered to be so active in the reader's mind that it is not *necessary* to distinguish them explicitly, or the ideas and opinions expressed are thought to be so similar that it is not *possible* to distinguish them. Thus there may be either a permanent divergence or a complete convergence in the views recorded. In either case, the views of the characters are assumed to be so recognizable that it is not necessary to state formally who says what. Neglecting to provide a formal tie between Ajax and the words s/he speaks causes the reader to assume narrator empathy for Ajax. FDS, which is so convenient in excising gender markers, brings with it a level of empathy that is at odds with the narrator's purpose. Consequently, while it is used frequently to record the conversational turns of the other members of the household, it is used very sparingly with Ajax. Considerations of empathy rank higher than simple gender avoidance.

The narrator of *Love Child* continually emphasizes the family unit, as we have seen when considering the names and descriptors of family members. A multiparty FDS (involving conversations among father, mother, and Kit) is commonly used to show that the individual voices can merge without incoherence. The opposite strategy is employed with Ajax, however, whom the narrator will not allow to merge with anyone. Multiparty FDS is broken up by speech explicitly attributed to Ajax by *verba dicendi* (set in boldface).

3.13. "Which of the dead are we honouring?" asked my mother.
"Philosophy, that ancient Sibyl. . . ."
"I've always imagined her like Michelangelo's Sistine Sibyl . . . ," **Ajax said**.
"That's it exactly. . . . ."
"And her death is a matter of falling apart into the constituent elements . . . ?"
"Exactly so. . . . ."
"She was a Titaness in fact," **Ajax offered**. (61) (My bolding.)

The conversational turns in example 3.13 are not formally assigned to any of the characters save Ajax (and the mother upon her first entry into the conversation). There is no substantial difference between Ajax's contributions and those of the rest of the family. Ajax's first speech offers an elaboration on the image of Sibyl introduced in the previous turn, while the second speech sums up the different elements listed in the preceding line. Yet Ajax's name is reintroduced with each contribution, unlike those of the other participants, whose names occur only when they speak for the first time. Since Ajax's speech is unexceptionable, the constant repetition of the proper name, especially in circumstances where the names of the other characters are withheld, serves to make Ajax's participation itself seem strange. Ajax has no natural right to speak at the family table.

An exception to this pattern is a dialogue between Kit and Ajax that takes place in Ajax's room. During this dialogue, Kit pretends to be relaxed and friendly in order to "case the joint" for signs of the mother's presence. This state of mind is neatly ironized by the author in the descriptor *consciously relaxed*. An extract from this interchange is given in example 3.14. The name *Ajax* appears immediately before and immediately after, but not during, the conversation. This is despite the fact that the dialogue continues for eleven turns and the reader could easily lose sight of who is saying what. Instead of adding to a common theme, as in example 3.13, the conversation rambles over several topics—polite formulas, national identity, swimming—and it is only by following the order of the turns (and assuming neither character misses a turn) that the reader can keep track of the speakers.

3.14. $Ajax_i$ smiled.
         "You should say: 'you're welcome.'"
         "The English don't have a polite equivalent. Is that because we don't mean it?"
         . . .
         "Have you got an American passport?"
         "At the moment. . . . Do you swim?"
         . . .
         "Perhaps I could join you sometime?"
         "You do that." I was back on the bed, consciously relaxed, smiling across the gap as $Ajax_i$ raised the glass. (86)

Clearly, the reason the proper name *Ajax* is reintroduced at the end is not to avoid ambiguity, since it has not been used throughout the dialogue. *I* contrasts with every other person by virtue of its deictically central position, and no other characters besides Kit and Ajax are present. The name is used to avoid the introduction of a pronoun, which would reveal gender information. The effect produced by its reintroduction is abruptly to cancel any intimacy that has built up between Kit and Ajax during the conversation.

We have seen the effect produced by repetition of the proper name in many of the examples above. What is unusual about example 3.14 is that throughout the conversation itself, Ajax's name is omitted, suggesting a high level of empathy from the narrator. As we have explained earlier, empathy may be double-edged, and in this example it is clearly so. It would appear that Kit is gradually warming toward Ajax, since empathy may suggest sympathy. This impression turns out to be part of a deliberate tactic on the part of the narrator to throw the reader off the scent, as it were, so that Kit's homicidal intent comes as a surprise.

From this discussion of the textual strategies used in *Love Child*, it is evident that there are substantial similarities, both in the strategies themselves and in their effect upon the narrative, between this novel and *Sphinx*. Kit's antipathy toward Ajax and Ajax's peripheral status in the family go some way to explaining why the secretary appears distant and fragmentary, providing contextual motivation for effects produced by the avoidance of gender. Where the potential exists for a clash between empathy and gender avoidance in the use of any particular device, that device will be avoided in favor of one that does not produce such a clash, as has been seen with regard to FDS and proper name repetition.

Parody

When we turn to parody, we see how these devices, which have become conventionalized, may be used to comic effect.

Plot summary: In Transit

In Transit tells the story of a sexually ambiguous figure who finds himself/herself in an airport lounge having forgotten what gender s/he is. It relates the various contortions and social misadventures that befall this figure in quest of its true sex. Before reaching the gender grail, however, Pat/Patricia falls to his/her death on the airport runway. Alternative endings are given for the masculine and the feminine character.

Brigid Brophy's transsexual fantasy *In Transit* (1969) spells out the dilemma faced by the creator of a genderless character.

3.15. I . . . could hardly . . . commit myself to a main character at whose every appearance in my narrative I would be obliged to write he/she, his/her etc.
   For which reason
      I have,
         dear Sir/Madam,
            to remain
               your
                  I (69)

Brophy uses the first person pronoun in order to avoid the clumsy neologism *he/she*, a stance that might well be shared by the authors of *Love Child* and *Sphinx*. Elsewhere, however, she has made clear her opposition to such neologisms on stylistic and aesthetic grounds. In a review of Casey Miller and Kate Swift's *Handbook of Nonsexist Writing*, ironically entitled "He/She/Hesh," Brophy asserts that a writer's "duty is to the language, and to its elasticity and metaphorical power" (1987, 67). She recommends that authors brush off feminist nagging about nonsexist language with the exclamation "Co, E, tey, and hesh," each of which has been suggested as a nonsexist pronoun to replace the generic masculine. In *In Transit*, she parodies feminist concern with language, particulary the controversy over the generic masculine, seen in other works examined here. Although her intention is to point out the ludicrous side of the endeavor, her novel stands as something of a tribute to feminist experiments, since they provide the conventions by which her parody may be recognized.

Anticipating the writing of *Sphinx* by some fifteen years, Brophy remarks upon the necessities and possibilities provided by the French system of grammatical gender.

3.16.   They're sly, though, these romance languages, in this matter of sex. Sly rather than shy, I shurmise; for they sometimes do, sometimes won't, the girlish things. Sometimes the adjectives don't change. Vous êtes triste? Tick:—masc. [ ] fem. [ ]. Strik(e) out whichever does not apsly. J'en suis content(e). (1969, 41)

In saying "they sometimes do, sometimes won't," the narrator is referring to gender concord in French, which may or may not be made, depending on complex rules of grammar and phonology. S/he proceeds to supply two examples, one of an invariable adjective, *triste*, for which no gender concord is made, and one of an adjective that does change form according to the gender of the antecedent noun: *content/e*. Since the theme of the novel is the narrator's amnesia concerning his/her gender, the latter adjective is written with a slash to show that either a masculine or a feminine reading is possible. As we have seen, Garréta makes great use of invariable adjectives in *Sphinx*, calling them "marvelously convenient" for her purposes.

The quotation that serves as the title of this chapter, "Was I, perhaps, castrato/a?" comes from *In Transit* and is doubly significant. The termination *-o/a* (taken from the Italian gender system) indicates that the referent may be either masculine or feminine. But since castration means the removal of the testicles, essentially masculine organs, the *-a* ending would indicate a castrated male, rather than a female; thus, *castrato* and *castrata* denote exactly the same thing (though the connotations are, of course, different in each case).[1] Brophy's parodic intent is evident in the spurious slash in *castrato/a*, a reference to feminist forms that place the masculine and the feminine on equal footing, instead of recording only the masculine: *candidat/e*, *professeur/e*. The spelling "strik(e)" above, in which the *-e* is wilfully interpreted as a feminine ending, although the word is a verb and in English to boot, underlines the fact that Brophy is mocking feminist and linguistic conventions.

Patrick/Patricia O'Rooley, hero/ine of *In Transit*, has forgotten what sex s/he is and is therefore obliged to undergo a series of contortions, linguistic and otherwise, in search of the missing information. This search makes plain some of the pitfalls of the gender system, as well as its sometimes contradictory assumptions. Not being able to work out from the clothes s/he is wearing what sex s/he must be, O'Rooley is relieved to bump into someone who knows him/her and who will be able to reveal his/her gender. Unfortunately, gender is so basic that one's acquaintances do not habitually remind one of it. The conversation therefore proves frustrating, and it is some time before Patrick/Patricia gains any infomation that will help him/her in his/her search.

The acquaintance greets Pat with a jovial exclamation of his/her full name, "Hilary Evelyn O'Rooley" (106), for which "Pat" turns out to be a nickname. Since all three first names are epicene, they advance O'Rooley's quest not a whit. By piling on these common gender names, Brophy is taunting the reader, for all three have become something of a cliché of the gender-neutral genre. (Witness Pat, the gender-indeterminate and somewhat unsavory character on the American television show Saturday Night Live). Having at last been told that Betty Bouncer considered him/her to have been her first date, O'Rooley, assuming the heterosexual prerogative, believes *himself* to be a man and strides off to the men's toilets (an act that the narrators of both *Sphinx* and *Written on the Body* will later emulate; the men's toilet seems to be one of the most sacrosanct domains of masculinity).

3.17. O'Rooley$_i$ approached the lavatory, unzipped his$_i$ trousers and reached his$_i$ hand inside. There was nothing there. . . . Patricia$_i$ staggered against the wall and dully heard that she$_i$ had knocked her$_i$ briefcase . . . to the floor. (114)

The mark of masculinity, the penis, is discomfortingly absent, preventing O'Rooley from taking his manly part in the signifying net. After the discovery of this absence, the surname, a traditionally masculine designation, is dropped in favor of first name reference; hence, *O'Rooley* becomes *Patricia*, and the pronoun changes from its masculine form, *he/his*, to its feminine form, *she/her*. Usually a change in the gender of a pronoun would be the signal of a change of referent. In Brophy's parody of traditional gender roles, this is not the case.

Our hero/ine's quest is, however, not at an end, for Pat reflects that he/she may simply not have reached far enough into his/her pants for conclusive evidence to be found. O'Rooley turns from anatomical to linguistic evidence and concludes that what is needed to clarify his/her gender is a third person reference to him/herself. He/she therefore seeks a discourse situation in which s/he will be present to hear how s/he is designated, but in which s/he will not be considered a discourse participant, for that would entail second person address (the gender-neutral *you*). Since it is considered rude to refer to people in the third person—Emile Benveniste's (1966a) *non-personne*—while they are in hearing distance, such a situation is, pragmatically, extremely marked. O'Rooley finds his/her answer in the radio talk show presentation, where the host speaks to the (absent) audience about the (present) guests. The host exclaims, "[W]e come to our mystery panelist who, when invited onto the panel, wouldn't even tell us his name" (132). It takes a moment or two for O'Rooley to realize that the talk show host's use of the masculine pronoun does not solve the gender dilemma, for this is a generic masculine, leaving O'Rooley no better off. Indeed, O'Rooley states the problem explicitly:

3.18.   I am . . . a he/ a she a "he," a "she." The clue to it all . . . resides in disentangling that enigmatic inverted-comma'd He. (141)

O'Rooley must discover whether this "he" is masculine or feminine.

After the débâcle of the radio show, Pat embarks upon a series of adventures that show the need to add orientation to the sexual paradigm, for, as s/he discovers, gay men and lesbians may be referred to, and refer to themselves, by gender markers traditionally limited to the opposite sex. Accordingly, Pat writes out what s/he calls "the paradigm of the possible truth of my own situation":

3.19.   I am a man
        I am a woman
        I am a homosexual man
        I am a homosexual woman (89)

Pat's gender paradigm posits heterosexuality as an integral part of "being a man" and "being a woman." Homosexual masculinity and femininity need their own separate mentions. If Pat is a gay man, then feminine pronouns will sometimes be applied to him; conversely, if Pat is a lesbian, she may be referred to in the masculine. Pat's paradigm is intended as lighthearted criticism of the assumption that investigations of gender and sexual orientation give the same results since women are sexually oriented toward men, while men are sexually oriented toward women. In this Brophy anticipates by twenty years Eve Sedgwick's now famous Axiom Two: "The study of sexuality is not coextensive with the study of gender; correspondingly, antihomophobic enquiry is not coextensive with feminist enquiry, but we cannot know in advance how they may be different" (1990; 27).

Believing *himself* to be a male homosexual, Patrick plans, when asked *his* name, to "look demurely down and confess his name was Pat or 'to my intimate friends, Patricia'" (150). The narrator continues with the feminine version of the name in quotation marks: "'Patricia' titupped along, every moment expecting the exploratory touch of a prospective purchaser

on 'her' buttocks" (150). Further on, s/he discovers that another character, whom s/he believed to be a woman and a lesbian, is in fact a man who
had found "some stress living up to the rather flamboyant standard of
manliness so constantly and drivingly expected" among the lesbians (195).
Thus, in discovering his/her own sexual identity, O'Rooley must be aware
not only of cultural and linguistic signs that indicate the gender of the referent, but also of indications that these signs are in fact being used to convey sexual orientation. Stereotypical masculinity may be a mark of lesbian
behavior, while feminine pronouns and mannerisms may signal homosexual
masculinity.

    After a crash between two heavily laden airplanes, whose occupants will
be harvested for spare body parts, O'Rooley's missing member is discovered.
Brophy offers alternate endings to the story, one in the feminine for Patricia,
the other in the masculine for Patrick. The two versions are laid out on the
page in two columns in the original (of which an abbreviated version is given
below). The reader is told to make the choice of Pat's true sex:

	Patricia	Patrick
3.20.	Neatly Patricia swung her legs over the side of the girder.	Convinced by his interlocutors (he was always a rational being), Patrick decided to come out of his perilous predicament.
	Holding on by her fingertips, she lowered herself till her body hung free. Someone screamed below. Patricia swung. She let go.	With a slowness that caught the crowd's breath . . . he slid his left knee backwards along the girder and began cautiously to back out the way he had come.
	Her body, spread-eagled, was flattened by the fall, like an animated-cartoon hero who's been run over.	After a few paces . . . his right knee slipped over the edge.
		. . . He slipped wholesale, and plummetted when neither he nor anyone else was expecting him to. (229–30)

Though Patricia and Patrick start off in the same position, stranded on a
girder high above the runway, and their fates are ultimately the same—both
fall to the ground and are killed—the two descriptions of the events leading up to the fall are very different. Without clear motive, Patricia jumps;
her jump is described in a series of short phrases narrating bodily movements: "Patricia swung. She let go." Her corpse resembles a cartoon char-

acter. There is no explanation for her actions, she is simply a figure moving through space. Patrick, on the other hand, is described as "rational," determined to do what is necessary to save his life. His movements are slow and deliberate; his death is unexpected, accidental. In this last scene, Brophy is parodying the literary (and cultural) convention of the rational, decisive, logical man and the inconsequential, inarticulate woman. When she finally restores gendered pronouns and a stable gender identity to her characters, it is to show that conceptions of gender run far deeper than their morphosyntactic representations.

The Plural Narrator

So far we have considered only texts concerning characters whose gender is concealed. When we turn to an examination of Natalie Barney's *The One Who Is Legion*, we encounter a character who is plural in nature and both male and female.

Plot Summary: The One Who Is Legion, or A. D.'s After-Life

The One Who Is Legion tells the story of a strange, shadowlike figure who emerges from the grave of his/her master/mistress and goes on to reconstruct the life of his/her employer. What follows is a journey through the Paris of the belle époque, complete with drives in the country, seaside visits, and mountainous hikes.

Natalie Clifford Barney's symbolist novel *The One Who Is Legion* is separated from *Love Child* and *In Transit*, both written forty years later, by period, genre, and sensibility. Symbolism was an aesthetic made popular by the nineteenth-century painters Gustave Moreau and Odilon Redon; as a literary genre, it is perhaps best exemplified by the poems and short stories of Gérard de Nerval such as *Les Filles du Feu*. Barney's emulation of this aesthetic was already, in 1930, old-fashioned and antimodernist. The symbolist style is characterized by a gothic sensibility and a fascination with death, transmigration, and the afterlife. In Barney's meditation on the essential androgyny of the soul, she uses these symbolist concerns and images to present the asexual nature of the spirit. She presents this androgynous, dual being to demonstrate the expanded consciousness of the homosexual who must know both how his/her own gender functions and how the lover of this sex should behave. The subject matter of her novel is in keeping with that of her stylistic models. Moreau and Redon's paintings also frequently feature androgynous figures.

The reader is introduced to the first person narrator in a graveyard:

3.21. I, the most faithful of dead shadows, have hovered about this spot since my master-mistress' burial. (11)

The "master-mistress" in question is the physical body who has died and whose shadow the narrator used to be. We are never told whether this person was anatomically a hermaphrodite, a particularly masculine woman, or a remarkably feminine man, although there are many references to bisexuality, hermaphroditism, and transsexuality in the text. The novel begins with a quotation from the preface to *Paradise Lost:* "For Spirits, when they please / Can either sex assume or both." Later the narrator reminds us, "Angels are hermaphrodites" (38), elaborating further on the theme of a third sex with mention of the sphinx, the centaur, the siren, and other mythical, dual-natured creatures (100). The narrator remarks that its master-mistress was "a couple so united that I never could cut out one from the other in separate silhouettes" (14), suggesting that they are in fact two people, a Platonic duo whom not even death can sunder.

In the sentence immediately following the shadow's introduction, a further blurring of boundaries is presented (emphasis added):

3.22.   This is *our* tomb-stone—the double of the urn in which *their* ashes are mingled and sealed together. (11)

Not only the usually rigid gender binary but the singular/plural distinction as well is swept aside. The narrator is both masculine and feminine, singular and plural. The narrator refers to the master-mistress in the plural, since it contains both masculine and feminine elements, alternating between third and first person reference depending on whether only the physical body is under discussion or the whole entity. Thus the narrator speaks of "my master-mistress" when considering only the relationship between this person and itself, but "our tomb-stone," since the urn belongs to all aspects of the being, and "their ashes" because only the physical body has been burned.

Upon returning to consciousness after suicide, the being asks not the classic "where am I?" but "where are we?" (22). The whole entity is subsequently referred to as "the One," in the third person singular, hence the title of the novel, *The One Who Is Legion*. This form of reference alternates with the first person plural. Although there is a separate possessive form of the pronoun *we*, namely *our*, none such exists for One, and the definite determiner is used when referring to parts of the One's body. Thus we read (emphasis added):

3.23.   *The* seraphic head charged with new life. *The* electrical eyes seemed fed from a near battery. . . . A cloudiness settled down upon *the* spirit. (24)

3.24.   *The* rhododendrons' reflection made a stained glass of *the* transparent flushed cheeks and *the* translucid eyes. The thin enamel of *the* teeth let the under-light through. (39)

The effect of this device is similar to that noted above in *Love Child* and *Sphinx*: like A*** and Ajax, there is no sense of a united self behind each mention of the One.

The effect of this systematic plural and third person reference is to distance the reader from the actions being performed and the agents who perform them, as we have seen before with both *Sphinx* and *Love Child*. In *Sphinx*, because this fragmentation affects the beloved and not the narrator, A*** seems like a collection of desirable body parts, resembling the montage figures of perfume or toothpaste commercials. Since A*** is black and Je white, this fragmentation increases the exoticization of A***'s body. In *Love Child*, we understand the distancing of Ajax and the interruption of empathy as effects willed and caused by the jealous Kit. In *The One Who Is Legion*, we sense a different motivation on the part of the narrator. In the last chapter, entitled "The One Takes Leave of the Legion," the One asserts for the first time, "I am I," finally distinguishing itself from the hordes of forces that have inhabited it up until now: the Sensualist, the Poet, the Philosopher, Health, Desire, and so on. As these figures depart, the shadow begins to fade, dissolving its awkward connection with the One.

3.25.   A shadow threw itself before the One . . . an imploring shape upon the floor, and swayed there in fear at no longer being in attendance. . . . Our shadow became but the shadow of a shadow. (155)

Since so many of the small details of the story come from the life Barney shared with Renée Vivien, including the manner of Vivien's death and the location of her grave, I would argue that Barney uses the clumsy, emotionally distancing device of the third person singular pronoun "One" to mask her feelings after her lover's death. The "shadow of the shadow" is arguably Barney after Vivien's demise. The description of "our" hands—"we looked at our hands, through our hands, our bloodless, shadowless hands, relieved from form and motion, folded within each other" (157)—seems to confirm this reading. The work was published in 1930 but describes the Paris of thirty years before, the time of Barney's relationship with Vivien. In its move to the first person plural, it confirms Barney and Vivien as a couple, united, leaving the question of how many hands are intertwined deliberately ambiguous. It might be either Vivien's hands clasped together in a semblance of prayer as she lies dead in her coffin (an image Barney has described in her poetry) or the two lovers' four hands intertwined.

The Mystery Genre

With the mystery, we move on to a genre in which concealment and the carefully controlled provision of information to the reader has become conventionalized. Ambiguity is a textual strategy the mystery reader expects and welcomes.

The least complex of the English texts featuring nongendered protagonists are Caudwell's three mysteries and Winterson's *Written on the Body*, all four of which are told by a genderless narrator but whose third person characters are described with the usual gender markers. Accordingly, we will examine them only cursorily, retracing the reader's search for gender information. Caudwell's novels are each little gems in the classic tradition of British detective fiction, which saw its heyday in the 1930s with Dorothy L. Sayers's Lord Peter Wimsey books. Most literary theorists name Edgar Allen Poe as the father of detective fiction and his character C. Auguste Dupin, created in 1841, as the first sleuth (Klein 1995, 6; Paul 1991, 1). However, Poe's repertoire of locked rooms, improbable criminals, macabre crimes, misdirections, and seemingly supernatural plots have their origins in the gothic horrors of the eighteenth century, such as Anne Radcliffe's *The Italian* and *The Mysteries of Udolpho*.

The detective genre relies for its effect on building suspense around one central question: who is the murderer? The British or "cozy" tradition often involves aristocratic detectives who combine mental and physical agility with arcane knowledge to solve the puzzle. The American or "hard-boiled" tradition, typical of Raymond Chandler and Dashiell Hammett, pits aggressive, hypermasculine lower- or middle-class detectives against organized crime. This latter tradition began in the 1920s and reached its greatest popularity in the 1940s and 1950s (Priestman 1990, 169–93). The British tradition tends to be socially conservative, the phrase "the butler did it" indicating a threat to the old order by which social inferiors and outsiders attempt to improve their class position. Caudwell's novels are situated easily in the British tradition, too easily perhaps, for at times they sound almost like a parody of it. All three of her books are narrated by Professor Hilary Tamar, an Oxford don, who solves the crime by astonishing feats of deduction. Tamar is almost a pastiche of the gentleman detective who works not for money but to satisfy a burning intellectual curiosity. The masking of Tamar's gender cloaks the don in the same aura of mystery with which the asexual monks of the castle of Udolpho are shrouded.

Because of Tamar's position in the text as omnipresent narrator, he/she is never referred to in the third person, except, jokingly, by himself/herself. Even in these rare and playfully self-laudatory passages, the narrator retains an epicene designator. The don imagines reviewers praising his/her latest article but does not go beyond the opening phrase, thereby avoiding the necessity for anaphoric pronouns: "Professor Tamar's masterly exposition," "Professor Tamar's revolutionary analysis" (1981, 8). Indeed, the professor's mock-serious tone seems to indicate a game of tag with the reader and the reader's persistent desire to know Tamar's sexual identity. The professor writes, for example, of "the penetrating scrutiny of the trained scholar, that is to say my own" (1981, 7) when the student is "inspired by the reverence which ought to be felt for his former tutor, that is to say myself" (8). In these examples, the deictic indicators *my own* and *myself*, introduced by the explanatory phrase "that is to say," are supposedly intended to add to the reader's knowledge of a specific, already designated referent: *the scholar, his former tutor*. The indexing of these epicene nouns to the narrator himself/herself should have the effect of revealing the referent's gender, yet the link remains uninformative since the reader does not know the gender of the narrator. Thus the referential system becomes a closed circuit, pointing only to other signifiers.

In the opening paragraph of the novel, the narrator parodies the usual working of gender reference:

3.26.   Scholarship asks . . . no recompense but Truth. It is not for the sake of material reward that she (Scholarship) pursues her (Truth) through the undergrowth. (Caudwell 1981, 7)

The nouns in parentheses (an integral part of the original text, and not my addition) appear to clarify the referents of the subject and object pronouns *she* and *her*, but since the same order has been observed as that of the previous sentence in which the nouns themselves appear, this clarification is unnecessary. The reader has no difficulty in understanding that since Scholarship's reward is Truth, it must be Scholarship who pursues Truth through the undergrowth. The first noun is assumed to be the subject, the second the object, following the canonical (unmarked) English word order of subject-verb-object (SVO). Instead, the device serves to mock the reader's curiosity about gender, imputing femininity to the abstract nouns, as though in scholarly recognition of their Greek and Latin counterparts, while the gender of the narrator, a sentient being, remains obscure. This subverts the hierarchy of animacy, discussed in chapter 2, according to which animate referents are more salient than inanimate referents.

Professor Hilary Tamar plays two roles in the text, sleuth and storyteller. His/her behavior is decorously unisex throughout. Tamar's reaction to a speech by one of the women characters is the strongest clue that the professor is a man, since *he* seems to be placing *himself* as an outsider, in need of information only a woman may have.

3.27.   My dear Selena, you quite persuade me that no woman of breeding and refinement could be expected to know the surname of any young man whom she was trying to seduce. (1981, 106–7)

Yet this detail is merely an indication, leaving the reader in search of corroboration. Tamar uses the logical deductive processes acquired during his/her Oxford law school training to discover the murderer, rather than any feats of athleticism that, given prevailing notions of gender roles, might cause *him* to be identified as male. The immediate discourse context, then, provides no conclusive evidence as to the narrator's gender, and the reader is obliged to seek this information elsewhere.

Although the first name *Hilary* is epicene, its attribution is nevertheless age related. There is a common progression in English names by which those that have served as last, or family, names in one generation are often given to sons in the next and may be given to daughters in succeeding generations when they are no longer popular for boys. *Hilary* is such a name.

(*Shirley, Sidney, Brooke,* and *Dale* are other examples.) If one cross-references this piece of information with Tamar's profession, one might reason that although there are both male and female dons, the overwhelming majority of dons are male and tend to belong to the older generation. Thus it would seem that this Hilary must be male. Tamar is also a detective, a métier that mostly falls to men. In the absence of signs to the contrary at the contextual, intertextual, and paratextual levels, readers will assume Professor Tamar is male, the masculine being the unmarked term.

The reader might be tempted to believe Tamar androgynous were this hypothesis not inadmissible in the realist genre of detective fiction. This turning toward the intertext and its conventions—here, the genre, which classifies the narrative—demonstrates the next step in the reader's search for the narrator's true sex. Denied information at the micro level of the morpheme (no comforting *he* or *she* comes to assuage the reader's desire to know), as well as at the contextual or cultural level (unisex intellectual prowess takes the role usually played by superior strength or gunmanship) the reader turns to the intertext, to the genre itself. Science fiction abounds in androgynous beings, as we will see in chapter 6, but mysteries require their protagonists to be either male or female.

Since we are dealing with a detective story, we should also pay attention to a method of interpretation that appears to be an important clue, that of the *lectio difficilior* (the most difficult reading), which comes, we are told by Tamar, from "the science of textual criticism." This principle is revealed as all important in the solving of the murder and may aid us in our own search for gender information. Since in fields such as romance philology or medieval legal history, one rarely has the original text to study, one is often obliged to rely on a copy, or a copy of a copy, penned by a hasty and inattentive scribe. According to the principle of *lectio difficilior*, the most difficult reading is to be preferred since the scribe has almost certainly mistaken a less common word for a more common one, rather than the other way round. What is of interest to us, in dealing with gender in the absence of the traditional markers, is the contrast this principle poses to the idea of markedness. Indeed, it suggests a strategy diametrically opposed to that which usually orders our assumptions about unknown quantities The most difficult, that is, the most marked, is to be preferred in order to rectify previous mistakes. According to this logic, Tamar's erased gender must be reinstated in the feminine.

The reader's hypotheses as to the gender of the first person narrator in *Written on the Body* (Winterson 1992) take a rather different trajectory. Winterson's novel is a love story, and since her other novels are on lesbian themes, most readers will assume it is a lesbian love story. Of course this assumption immediately solves the puzzle as to the narrator's gender, but it poses a different question: how is our understanding of the narrator affected by the lack of grammatical reinforcement? Lesbian love stories do not form a genre of their own; they cannot be categorized in the same neat fashion as mysteries or science fiction, with their more formulaic plots and worldviews. Nevertheless, Winterson is not the first to tell a tale of homosexual love in which gender markers have been obscured, as we have seen with Garréta's *Sphinx*. This strategy has been more common in poetry than in fiction, from sixteenth-century poets such as Louise Labbé and William Shakespeare to their twentieth-century colleague Marguerite Yourcenar. The recent literary movement to "queer the canon," or discover the hidden lesbian and gay themes running through apparently heterosexual fiction, demonstrates that novels considered classics of heterosexual sensibility may also be read as homosexual texts. Eve Sedgwick's *Epistemology of the Closet* (1990), with its rereadings of mainstream authors such as Henry James and Herman Melville, is probably the best known of these. Marion Zimmer Bradley's *The Mists of Avalon* and Willa Cather's *My Ántonia* have also been given homosexual interpretations (Bradley in Farwell 1990, Cather in Fetterley 1990 and Butler 1993). Reading *Written on the Body* in the light of this new trend in textual criticism provides an answer to the question posed by the narrator's apparent lack of gender. It also endows it with a literary history, instead of compelling it to stand alone, an idisosyncratic curiosity.

Winterson's narrator has no name, and no gendered lexical items are used to refer to him/her. The reader knows only that the narrator is in love with a married woman called Louise. Louise reports that she has told her husband she is sleeping with the narrator, and the reader waits to see what terms she will use to describe the relationship.

3.28. "I told him what you are to me. I told him we'd been to bed together."
       (82)

Here she seems to name, and yet fails to name, for her description is self-referential, relying on information that she and the narrator share but the reader does not. This self-referentiality teases the reader in the same way as Hilary Tamar's clarification that "the scholar" is none other than himself/herself.

Whereas Hilary Tamar's behavior is studiously androgynous, appropriate for either sex, the narrator of *Written on the Body* seems more hermaphroditic, alternating between the sexes. In this, Winterson's project seems to echo Garréta's, promoting gender fluidity as social progress. Like Garréta's Je, Winterson's narrator displays an in-depth knowledge of the insides of men's toilets. "Men's toilets are fairly liberal places. . . . Why do men like doing everything together?" (22); "[l]ike men in johns, cows and sheep do things in unison. I've always found it disturbing" (186). Dare the reader assume from this that the narrator is a man? The evidence is at best circumstantial, and the lightly mocking tone might suggest a woman disturbed by the masculine herd instinct.

We must turn to the intertextual level for more commanding proof. The litany of body parts the narrator addresses to his/her lover Louise is strongly reminiscent of passages from Monique Wittig's *Le Corps lesbien*

(The Lesbian Body), a parellelism underlined by the similarity in the titles of the two works. Wittig's novel is punctuated with a list of body parts and products, written in block capitals so that they stand out, filling a double page every thirty pages or so. Wittig's list begins:

3.29. LE CORPS LESBIEN LA CYPRINE LA BAVE LA SALIVE LA MORVE LA SUEUR (22)

THE LESBIAN BODY THE CYPRINE THE SLOBBER THE SALIVA THE SNOT THE SWEAT

Readers familiar with this text will see in the list of Louise's facial bones in *Written on the Body* an obvious intertextual reference to Wittig, especially since in each case the narrative is temporarily interrupted by this anatomical inventory.

3.30. Frontal bones, palatine bones, nasal bones, lacrimal bones, cheek bones, maxilla, vomer, inferior conchae, mandible. (132)

Although Winterson never states that the relationship between Louise and the narrator is lesbian, this is powerfully suggested by the parallels between *Written on the Body* and *The Lesbian Body*. Eclectic readers may remember James Mitchell's poem "Gay Epiphany," which celebrates a young man's "external urethral orifice" with similar anatomical humor. The opening lines of this poem are as follows:

3.31. o sperm, testes, paradidymus! o scrotum, septum, and rectum! o penis! o prepuce, urethra (Coote 1983, 330–31).

Spurred by these intertextual clues, the reader examines the paratextual level for similarities between Wittig and Winterson (and Mitchell, if it occurs to them). Both Wittig and Winterson are known to be lesbians, a fact that seems to close the possible readings of *Written on the Body*. In the absence of any signs to the contrary on the contextual level, Louise's lover is assumed to be female, her sexuality paralleling that of the author.

The reader's hypotheses regarding both Caudwell's and Winterson's novels concern not only the sex of the narrator, but also the writer's reasons for obfuscating it. Given Caudwell's championing of the power of the mind, an obvious conjecture is that she has concealed Tamar's gender in order to make a feminist case for the prioritizing of mental faculties, which are shared by the sexes and which therefore put women on an equal footing with men. Such a hypothesis requires the reader to recognize the contrast Caudwell is making between Hilary Tamar and Chandleresque detectives such as the hard-boiled, heavy-fisted Philip Marlowe, for example. With *Written on the Body*, the intertext reinforces a hypothesis made plausible by the paratext of Winterson's lesbianism. There is a common tendency to identify the narrator of a first person narrative with the author, if the two are of the same sex.

While questions may hover over the gender identity of Hilary Tamar and Louise's lover, the two narrators are nevertheless recognizable as whole and discrete beings upon each appearance, like Garréta's Je and unlike A***, or Duffy's Ajax, Brophy's Patrick/Patricia, and Barney's the One. Brophy's parody makes explicit what may be felt only unconsciously in the other works examined here. Since the masculine is the unmarked term, as well as the generic, readers faced with ungendered characters will tend, all things being equal, to assume these characters are masculine, in the manner of the driver who sees another car flagged down by a traffic cop and shrugs, "Glad it was him and not me."

In her introduction to *Love Child*, the British literary critic Alison Hennegan asserts that "discussions of this novel constantly assume that Kit is female" (Duffy [1971] 1994, xv). Though Hennegan declares that the uncertainty about Kit's and Ajax's gender "focuses attention purely on the emotions themselves" (16), the one thing these novels do not do is make gender irrelevant. In fact, they focus the reader's attention on it as never before. An ungendered text is a marked text, and with the marked element of any opposition, one can never lose sight of the mark. However, far from being constrained by the linguistic gender system in English, the individual authors use the possibilities offered by the language to create a variety of effects, from the elimination of reader sympathy for Ajax to the sense of passionate but contained grief in the One. As we saw in our earlier analysis of *Sphinx*, describing a third person character without using pronouns creates a sense of fragmentation in both English and French, but the meaning of this fragmentation may vary widely from text to text. The novels I have discussed so far employ the existing resources of the language to avoid gender. In the next chapter I will move on to a discussion of linguistic innovation and its effects on the text.

4

"La sphyngesse, la taure, et les agnelles nouvelles-nées"

Experiments with Lexical Gender in French

A cause de tous les déplacements de sens, glissements de sens, pertes de sens que les mots ont tendance à subir, il arrive un moment où ils n'agissent plus sur la ou les réalités. Il faut alors les réactiver.

Monique Wittig and Sande Zeig, MOT,
Brouillon pour un dictionnaire des amantes

Because of all the displacements of meaning, shifts of meaning, losses of meaning, that words tend to undergo, there comes a moment when they no longer act on reality, or realities. Then they must be reactivated.

WORD, *Sketch for a Dictionary of Female Lovers*

Lexical Innovation

In chapters 2 and 3 I looked at novels in French and English in which at least one prominent character is described without the usual gender markers. I now turn to an examination of lexical innovation, literary experiments that create new words to highlight the feminine, rather than decribing characters without recourse to gender. In this chapter, I evaluate the lexical neologisms introduced by Monique Wittig in her fiction. In the next, I move on to a consideration of Wittig's pronominal experiments, principally her use of the nongendered *on* as the main pronominal vehicle for her first novel, *L'Opoponax*.

My discussion of Wittig's novels is divided into two chapters reflecting two different features of her work: lexical innovation and pronominal experimentation. To the literary theorist, such a division may seem at first awkward, and indeed, it would be more orthodox to consider Wittig's work in a single chapter. However, the difference between experimenting with lexical items and experimenting with syntax (here, the pronominal system) is in linguistic terms vast. Lexical items are part of an open class, in which items may be added or subtracted as required. In quickly evolving fields, such as the Internet, new terms are created almost daily to provide names for previously nonexistent referents, or new meanings are given to existing but little used terms. "Wysiwyg," an acronym for "what you see is what you get," is an example of the former. "Brain dump," the act of filling someone in quickly on necessary information, is an example of the latter. In contrast, pronouns are a closed class, containing a limited number of items. Although this set may be modified, supplemented, or depleted, these changes take place over an extended period of time, often as long as one or several centuries, and are not perceptible synchronically. Several new second person plurals may be competing with each other for acceptance into the personal pronoun paradigm in English: "yous," used in Australia; "you all," used in the southern states of America; and "you both" (a dual rather than a plural pronoun) used in informal speech. We cannot tell at this stage of the language whether any one of these will be successful in its bid to be accepted as standard usage. Although Wittig's experiments with lexical neologisms and the feminization of the lexicon are challenging and innovative, they do not have the same radical consequences for the text itself as her experiments on the pronominal level, as we will see.

Monique Wittig was a prominent lesbian activist in the French women's liberation movement and a radical lesbian. She is famous for the declaration that lesbians are not women (1992a), meaning that *lesbian* is the only signifier that goes beyond the male/female binary to offer a third term, a position not defined by the heterosexual imperative.[1] Her work has had an enormous impact on both French and English feminism, especially in its advocacy of lesbian separatism. Her opposition to what she saw as the psychoanalytic essentialism of the Psych et Po (*psychanalyse et politique*) strand of French feminism (see note 6) made her a pioneer in the feminist struggle against heterosexism, or the assumption that a defining characteristic of women is their sexual interest in and availability to men. Taking a materialist rather than a psychological perspective on the origin of inequality between the sexes, Wittig turned her considerable intellectual energies toward language.

In the epigraph to this chapter, Monique Wittig and Sande Zeig point to the fact that language—at the level of the lexicon—is constantly in flux, evolving in new directions due to both internal and external forces: "les déplacements de sens, glissements de sens, pertes de sens" (displacements of meaning, shifts in meaning, loss of meaning). When the meaning of a word is altered, either because the relations between items in a given semantic field have changed ("glissement de sens") or because the referent itself has changed ("déplacement de sens"), the word must, as Wittig and Sande state, be reactivated if it is to remain in use. In her literary works, Wittig has been concerned with reactivating and creating feminist meanings.

What is true of the lexicon of a language is applicable to the morphosyntactic and phonological levels, albeit over a much longer time frame.

All linguistic features are subject to displacement, slippage, and erosion, though these processes are easier to discern at the lexical level, since individual vocabulary items have a much quicker turnover than grammaticalized features such as tense or word order. Once a feature has been eroded to an appreciable extent, it may be reactivated, redeployed, (retained but with a new function), or dropped. In chapter 1, I introduced the term "reanalysis" to refer to the retention of an already existing feature that manifests a new function. In this chapter, one of the questions I will be asking is whether the renaissance of linguistic gender in Wittig's work constitutes reanalysis or an ephemeral and momentary resuscitation.

Feminization of the Lexicon

Damourette and Pichon observed that throughout the centuries writers have reintroduced individual archaic feminine forms into their work (1911–27, §273–77). Wittig does this systematically, however, and on a wide scale. Other authors use feminine terms to point out the incongruity or poignancy of a female in a traditionally masculine role. A good example of this is Lucie Delarue-Mardrus's use of the feminized term *la majore* in the ironic exclamation "La majore de son ambulance, naturellement!" (The adjutant$_f$ of her ambulance, naturally!) (from *Le pain blanc* 4:60; quoted in Damourette and Pichon, 1911–27, §255), referring to women driving ambulances during the First World War. Here the use of the feminized form *la majore* highlights the social turmoil caused by war, since women were driving ambulances to replace the men called up to fight. *La majore* is a term that Delarue-Mardrus implies should not exist and that has only come to exist in the exceptional and difficult circumstances of the First World War. Wittig, in contrast, employs archaic feminines and creates neologistic forms where no feminine existed in order to present the feminine as the universal or unmarked term. One neologistic feminine would stand out, showing the exceptional nature of the referent or her situation, but a systematic feminizing of all generic and masculine terms creates a universe in which the feminine is the default option. Wittig's tactic provides a marked contrast to those, like the more traditional Delarue-Mardrus, who use the feminine to emphasize an unusual situation.

Since it is particularly in *Le Corps lesbien* that Wittig uses the feminine forms of terms more commonly found in the masculine, I will concentrate on that text in this discussion. It should be noted that both *Les Guérillères* and *Brouillon* feature the same technique and use many of the forms that appear in *Le Corps lesbien*. This cross-referencing provides a rich intertext and ensures that the technique of genericizing feminine forms is reinforced from work to work. The text of *Le Corps lesbien* is laced with the feminized names of famous men, of peoples made famous by the battles of classical antiquity or myth, of animals, and of occupations. One even finds a feminine adjectival form of the noun *soleil* (sun) in *Ishtar à la tête/soleille* (Ishtar of the sun$_f$-head) (1973, 73).[2]

Whereas any one of these items encountered individually would strike
the eye as significant and unusual, the systematic feminization of proper
names and other substantives with animate referents causes the reader to
expect feminine forms. *Achillea* (30), *Patroclea* (30), *Ganymedea* (39),
Ulyssea (16), and *Archimedea* (181) all appear in the text, not merely feminine versions of male names, but heroines taking the place of heroes, and
macho heroes at that. When Wittig begins her canto 8 with "Heureuse si
comme Ulyssea j/e pouvais revenir d'un long voyage" (Happy if like Ulyssea
I could return from a long voyage) (16), she is not only turning the Greek
hero Ulysses into a woman, but parodying, a little bitterly perhaps, the *felix
qui* (happy the one who) motif of poetry both Latin and French. Ulysses'
epic return home after the war is a common figure in the literary trope
popular in the Renaissance known as *patriae desiderium* or "longing for
the fatherland," perhaps the most famous example of which (for French
readers at least) is to be seen in Joachim du Bellay's *Les Regrets*, poem 31:
"Heureux qui, comme Ulysse, a fait un beau voyage" (Happy the man who,
like Ulysses, has accomplished a fine voyage).[3] Notice that in the original,
the proposition is constative, whereas Wittig's variation, "Heureuse si
comme Ulyssea," is hypothetical.

Not only are the names of legendary heroes given new feminine endings, and thereby a feminine perspective, but the originator of Christianity
himself appears in feminine form as *Christa la très crucifiée* (Christa the
very crucified) (30), as well as a voice crying "mère, mère, pourquoi m'as
tu abandonnée" (sic) (mother, mother why have you abandoned$_f$ me) (139),
as Christ is reputed to have done on the cross, though his lament is traditionally understood to have been addressed to a male rather than a female
parent. The Egyptian god Osiris, too, undergoes a sex change, to be addressed as *m/a très belle* (my very beautiful$_f$ one) (87). The first effect of
these changes is a sense of surprise and shock, a realization that the feminine forms refer not to the wife of Achilles, Archimedes, and the others—
as *Madame la Présidente* refers to the wife of the president—but to a woman
fulfilling the same role as the man himself. The second effect is to provoke
one to ask how we know the heroes of antiquity actually were men and
whether *men* should be taken in its specific or its generic sense. We are
reminded, once more, that "un homme sur deux est une femme" (one man
in two is a woman).[4]

Two of the races Gulliver encounters on his travels are transformed
in a way perhaps even Jonathan Swift would not have anticipated, for
Wittig writes of *les hargneuses Lilliputiennes* (the cantankerous$_{fpl}$ Lillipu-
tians$_{fpl}$) and *un peuple de géantes* (a race of giants$_{fpl}$). *Les Lyciennes, les
Lydiennes, les Macédoniennes, les Libyennes*, and *les Tracéennes* all parade
through the text, reversing the common tendency to consider a people
only from the point of view of its menfolk. One of the most striking examples of this tendency is to be found, ironically perhaps, in Lévi-Strauss's
Les Bororo, (1936):

Le village entier partit le lendemain dans une trentaine de pirogues, nous laissant seuls avec les femmes et les enfants dans les maisons abandonnées. (Quoted as an epigraph in Michard-Marchal and Ribéry 1982)

The whole village left next day in about thirty canoes, leaving us alone with the women and children in abandoned houses.

In this account, although the whole village is said to leave, the women and children stay put. The European anthropologists are then described as alone, despite the presence of a village full of people. Finally, the houses are abandoned, although manifestly occupied by women and children. Thus, three times in one sentence Lévi-Strauss makes it clear that he does not consider women or children fully human.

The range of female animals that appear in *Le Corps lesbien* is wide and exotic, from the *sphyngesse* (female sphinx) (45) to the *giraffe* (180) and the *guenon* (long-tailed monkey) (32). They include animal names of which the feminine is the generic form, even in the most orthodox of French grammars, such as *tourterelles* (turtledoves) (32);[5] the female forms of domestic and farm animals, more commonly used in the context of animal husbandry: *agnelles nouvelles-nées* (new$_{fpl}$-born$_{fpl}$ ewe lambs) (8), *taure* (heifer) (117), *génisse* (heifer) (117), *agnelle de lait* (suckling ewe-lamb) (99, 117), and *chiennes* (bitches) (47); and *serpentes* (female snakes) (126) and the exclusively feminine *jument* (mare) (109). Many of these feminine forms of animal names are also used to refer, derogatively, to women. *Guenon*, for example, denotes both the long-tailed monkey and female monkeys in general and has the colloquial meaning of "ugly old woman," while the phrase "c'est une pauvre chienne-chienne" (lit., she's a poor bitch-bitch—fig, she licks the boss's boots) is said of a woman who cajoles her way into the boss's good books. The only form Wittig has created is *sphyngesse*. The feminine form *sphynge* already exists, but, lacking the hyperfeminine morpheme *-esse*, it is not as clearly feminine as Wittig's neologism. In *Brouillon*, written three years later, one finds similar feminized forms for animal names—*animales* (animals$_f$) (18, 21), *ourse blanche* (white$_f$ bear$_f$) (18), *caméléonne* (chameleon$_f$) (47), and *serpentes* (snakes$_f$) (216)—a tactic that no longer seems like a tactic but has become the status quo in Wittig's work.

Names for occupations and activities for which Wittig gives the feminine forms include those that may refer either to men, or to women, or to both, but that are more commonly found in the masculine: *vivantes* (living women) (89), *une nouvelle arrivante* (a newly arrived woman) (116), and *occupantes* (women occupants) (107), each of which is formed by adding the morpheme *-e* to the past participle; and *porteuses* (women bearers) (182), *nageuses* (women swimmers) (20), *promeneuses* (women strollers) (25), *pêcheuses* (fisherwomen) (107, 179), *cueilleuses de lavande* (women lavender gatherers) (132), and *bateleuses* (women jugglers) (187), each of which is regularly formed from the masculine by changing the *r* to an *s* and adding *e*. As well as these largely unmarked occupations, the list of feminized

forms includes some unusual jobs for a woman: *ravisseuse* (female rav-
isher) (85), *voyeuse* (female voyeur) (152), and *bourreleuse* (female tor-
turer, executioner; the term feminine *bourrelle* already exists and is cited
in Damourette and Pichon) (8). Since these last four are formed the same
way as the more gender-neutral occupations listed above, they become less
startling once one has become accustomed to seeing feminized forms. The
same forms also permeate the earlier novel, *Les Guérillères*, which features
dormeuses (sleepers$_f$), *parleuses* (speakers$_f$), *joueuses* (players$_f$), and both
chasseuse (hunter$_f$) and *chasseresse* (hunter$_f$—the form traditionally used to
refer to Diana the hunter), as well as two others formed from the present
participle; *combattantes* (fighters$_f$) and *manifestantes* (demonstrators$_f$). In
the *Brouillon*, one finds *les chevalières du Graal* (the knights$_f$ of the Grail)
(112) and *les donastères* or *maison communautaires des amantes* (commu-
nal houses of the women lovers) (79). Readers inculcated into Wittig's style
expect the feminine to prevail.

That this tactic works may be seen from the fact that in certain places
the feminine plural *elles* anaphorizes both grammatically feminine and grammatically masculine referents without causing any pronoun angst in the
reader. Thus we find "la terre les arbres les eaux les fleuves les rivières les
mers les étoiles du ciel ne tremblent-elles pas" (the earth$_f$ the trees$_m$ the
waters$_f$ the rivers$_m$ the streams$_f$ the seas$_f$ the stars$_f$ in the sky do they$_f$ not
tremble) (102), in which there are two grammatically masculine items (*les
arbres* and *les fleuves*) while the other five are feminine. Traditional grammar would require that a mixture of masculine and feminine items be
anaphorized by the masculine pronoun, yet this set of nouns is anaphorized
by the feminine *elles:* "ne tremblent-elles pas?"

Critical Opinion

Many critics have claimed that there are no masculine referents in *Le Corps
lesbien*, at least no animate ones. Hélène Wenzel writes, for example:
"Personne, en fait aucun être vivant, y compris les animaux, n'est du genre
masculin . . . donc la différence de genre n'est pas la question" (no one,
that is no living being, is masculine in gender, so gender difference does
not enter the picture) (1985, 44).

Echoing Wenzel, Erika Ostrovsky writes, "All nouns in the text (relating to living beings, human or animal) are either feminine or feminized"
(1991, 95). For her part, Marthe Rosenfeld declares:

> Renversant les lois que construisent grammaire et société pour défendre la
> hiérarchie des genres, ce langage révolutionnaire nous transporte au-delà des
> catégories de sexe. (1984, 60–61)

> Overturning the laws constructed by grammar and society to defend the hi-
> erarchy of the genders, this revolutionary language transports us beyond the
> categories of sex.

This feat is accomplished, according to Ostrovsky, by abolishing "les dualismes . . . du 'féminin' et du 'masculin'" (the dualisms of "feminine" and "masculine") (1991, 61). It is striking that all three critics agree about the absence of animate masculine referents in *Le Corps lesbien* and that all interpret this purported fact as indicating an eradication of gender dualism and its concomitant hierarchy and antagonism. If there is no grammatical distinction to reinforce the difference between the sexes, then the gender hierarchy seen in the social and political arena will be overturned. This reasoning is in keeping with Wittig's own stated aim "to make the categories of sex obsolete in language" (1986, 70).

Ignoring the received wisdom of critics and author and investigating the text itself, one does indeed find an array of animate masculine referents in *Le Corps lesbien*, ranging from the animalian *petit rat* (little rat) (155), *papillons* (butterflies), *requins* (sharks) (119–20, 148), and *deux cygnes noirs* (two black swans) (32) to the elemental *le feu* (fire) (184) and *le vent* (wind) (88) and parts of the human body such as *les deux yeux* (the two eyes) (152), *tes regards* (your looks) (154), and *les globules des noyaux cellulaires* (the globules of the cell nuclei) (173). These last items may initially seem surprising in a list of animate referents, for while eyes and cell nuclei may be organic, they seldom figure high enough up the animacy scale to be possessed of independent thought and automotive faculties. However, the pathetic fallacy that runs through Wittig's work attributes thought, movement, and feelings to a multitude of animals, organs, and elements usually considered, if not inanimate, at least brute, unreasoning entities propelled either by instinct or by outside force.

The verbs associated with the referents in this list are highly active, including many verbs of movement. Thus, the butterflies, for example, "reviennent d'un long voyage, obscurcissent le soleil; se reposent sur tes doigts" (return from a long voyage—like Ulysses, block out the sun, come to rest on your fingers) and "s'abattent sur les épaules" (collapse on the shoulders) (155), while the sharks "obscurcissent la mer; dévorent (mes membres)" (119–20), "mettent en danger de chavirer (la barque); arrivent de plus en plus nombreux; se heurtent dans leur effort pour fuir; s'écartent; reviennent" (148) (darken the sea, devour (my limbs), put the boat in danger of capsizing, arrive in greater and greater numbers, bump into each other in their effort to flee, swim away, come back) and "croisent sans relâche" (148) (cruise incessantly). Not only are the verbs themselves active, but many of them subclassify for highly animate agents. The wind, which combs, brushes, and shines the two women's hair, seems possessed of unusual intentionality, as does the fire, which smolders, devastates, is fanned, and finally attacks.

From this list of the movements and actions of these animals, elements, and body parts, all endowed with considerable animation and all grammatically masculine in Wittig's text, it is clear first of all that animate masculine referents do indeed occur in the text and, in the case of the butterflies and the sharks, are prominent agents whose activities continue over many lines. Must one conclude that since the first premise of the critic's argument is shown to be false—that is, there are animate masculine referents—then their conclusion that the text serves to reverse the usual gender hierarchy must be false too? No, indeed. The fact that three critics and the author herself all believe that there are no animate masculine referents is significant in itself. It indicates that Wittig's strategy of feminizing nouns has been so successful that even in cases where nouns remain in their traditional masculine form, anaphorized by masculine pronouns and qualified by masculine adjectives and past participles, readers assume they are looking at feminine forms. This shows that the feminine has become the generic, the unmarked, the form one expects to see and believes one does see even when it is not there. Wittig's "reactivation" of lexical gender is not merely a resuscitation of a system on the wane, but a reanalysis, an inventive exploration and redeployment of gender in furtherance of feminist aims.

Elsewhere Wittig herself has stated explicitly that "gender must be destroyed" (1986, 67), suggesting that in her own work the gender system is eradicated, not reinforced. Indeed, Wittig believes this so strongly that the idea provides a leitmotif for her theoretical works, continually recurring in different forms but always with the same passionate feminist sensibility. In "The Mark of Gender," Wittig condemns gender as "a primitive ontological concept that enforces in language a division of beings into sexes" (1986, 63). She restates this idea several times: "gender is the linguistic index of the political opposition between the sexes and of the domination of women" (1986, 64) (this phrase is repeated word for word in "The Point of View," 1992c, 60); "gender is the enforcement of sex in language" (1986, 65); and "gender, by enforcing upon women a particular category, represents a measure of domination" (1986, 66). In "The category of sex" (first published in 1976), she states, "[T]he category of sex is a totalitarian one. . . . It grips our minds in such a way that we cannot think outside of it. This is why we must destroy it and start thinking beyond it if we are to start thinking at all" (1992a, 8). In "The Straight Mind" (first published in 1980), she declares, "[T]here cannot any longer be women and men . . . as classes and categories of thought or language they have to disappear" (1992b, 29). In her 1980 essay "The Point of View: Universal or Particular?" she remarks, "Djuna Barnes cancels out the genders by making them obsolete, I find it necessary to suppress them" (1992c, 61). Throughout these essays, whether the topic is politics, literature, or philosophy, Wittig adamantly proclaims her opposition to the linguistic gender system.

Reading these declarations, one might expect Wittig to avoid all marks of grammatical gender, as Garréta does for A*** and the narrator in *Sphinx*. Yet Wittig relies on the lesser-used facets of the gender system, rather than eradicating it from her work. The key to this paradox lies in the chameleon-like properties of the system itself, for the gender to which Wittig voices such outspoken objection is the obligatory classification of human beings into two biological sexes, not the assignment of inanimates to two distinct noun classes. Wittig elucidates her intentions by explaining that "to destroy the categories of sex in politics and in philosophy, to destroy gender in language (at least to modify its use) is part of my work in writing" (1986, 67). It is the material in parentheses that is most informative, for the empassioned indictments of gender turn out to be invested with metaphoric rather than literal intent. Wittig proposes to modify the use of the gender system and adds, "[W]hat is really in question here is a structural change in language, in its nerves, its framing." The term "structural change" is not used lightly or innocently, for Wittig's concept of the functioning of language comes directly from the work of the French structuralists and their insistence on the tenet that language is a system in which everything works together. By championing the more neglected elements of the gender paradigm, Wittig hopes to sabotage it from within, rather than simply turn her back on it, which is Garréta's tactic. To this extent, Wittig's strategy is more subtle, for it is not apparently revolutionary but uses the possibilities of the system to change the pattern of relationships within it. Language is continually in flux, as the epigraph to this chapter claims; Wittig's strategy has been to intervene in the direction of its flow.

The idea of language as being in constant flux may be traced back to Edward Sapir. Using the metaphor of flux in its original sense of the flow of a liquid, from the Latin *fluxus* (m), Sapir makes clear the relationship between individual innovation and societal takeup.

> Language exists only in so far as it is actually used—spoken and heard, written and read. What significant changes take place in it must exist, to begin with, as individual variations. . . . Yet they themselves are random phenomena, like the waves of the sea, moving backward and forward in purposeless flux. The linguistic drift has direction. Only those individual variations embody or carry it which move in a certain direction, just as only certain wave movements in the bay outline the tide. (Sapir 1978, 155)

According to Sapir, linguistic changes must relate to cultural changes taking place at the same time, or they will not become an organic part of the language. Wittig's writings attempt to influence linguistic drift in a particular direction. As we will see, many of her assumptions about the nature of language can be traced back to Sapir, coming, if not from direct exposure to his writings, at least via the intermediary of French anthropologists and language philosophers such as the structuralist Claude Lévi-Strauss and the post-structuralist Michel Foucault. The title of Wittig's polemical condemnation of the organizing principles of heterosexism, *La Pensée straight* (The Straight Mind) (1992, 21–32), is an avowed calque on Lévi-Strauss's famous anthropological work, *La Pensée sauvage* (The Savage Mind) (1962). In *La Pensée straight*, Wittig criticizes such noteworthy theorists as Lévi-Strauss, Jacques Lacan, and Roland Barthes for not bringing a materialist analysis to bear on the exciting new (at the time) science of semiology.

Parody of Lévi-Strauss

There are frequent references to the structural anthropology of Lévi-Strauss in Wittig's *Les Guérillères*.

4.1.   N'a-t-il pas écrit, le pouvoir et la possession des femmes, le loisir et la jouissance des femmes? Il écrit que tu es monnaie d'échange, que tu es signe d'échange. Il écrit, troc, troc, possession acquisition des femmes et des marchandises. (1969, 166–167)

Has he not written, power and the possession of women, leisure and the enjoyment of women? He writes that you are a token of exchange, that you are a sign of exchange. He writes swap, swap, possession acquisition of women and merchandise.

This is a parody of Lévi-Strauss's well-known theory that women and the exchange of women provide not only the elementary structures of kinship, but also the symbolic basis of language itself, providing a fixed point in the endless play of signifier over signified—the phallogocentrism discussed in the introduction. Although no referent is given for *il* to tell us who writes, readers familiar with Wittig's work will make this connection for themselves.[6]

Il en est donc des femmes comme de la monnaie d'échange dont elles portent souvent le nom, et qui, selon l'admirable mot indigène, "figure le jeu d'une aiguille à coudre les toitures, et qui tantôt dehors, tantôt dedans, mène et ramène toujours la même liane qui fixe la paille." (Lévi-Strauss 1967, 549)

The same is true of women as is true of the tokens of exchange whose names they often bear, and which, according to the admirable native saying, "functions like the play of a sewing needle which, now outside, now inside, pulls the same liana back and forth to hold the straw in place."

Women, like the monetary system, like the liana woven through the thatch, keep the structure in place and are central to the social, economic, and material fabric. By not specifically attributing these statements to Lévi-Strauss, Wittig tacitly condemns all who espouse his credo. In her essay "On the Social Contract," Wittig spells out her criticism of the notion that women are reducible to the signs of a language (1992e, 43).

Elsewhere, Wittig refers to the theories of structuralism themselves:

4.2.   Elles disent qu'un raisonnement mécaniste . . . met en jeu une série de termes qui sont systématiquement mis en rapport avec des termes opposés. (1969, 112)

They$_f$ say that a mechanistic reasoning process . . . puts into motion a series of terms that are systematically related to opposite terms.

In the next passage, proponents of structuralism more generally are taken to task for promoting the belief that language is based on binary oppositions, one of the most salient being that between the masculine and the feminine, a hierarchical opposition that takes the masculine as the universal, or unmarked term.

4.3. Elles disent, esclave tu l'es vraiment si jamais il en fut. Ils ont fait de ce qui les différencie de toi le signe de la domination et de la possession. (Wittig 1969, 153)

They$_f$ say, slave you truly are if ever there was one. They$_m$ have made of what distinguishes them from you the sign of domination and possession.

The association of *ce qui les différencie de toi* with the pronoun *ils*, designates "them" as masculine, while *tu* (you) is clearly feminine. In other words, you are a slave (i.e., a woman) because they (masculine) have made the penis (which distinguishes you from them) into a symbol of domination. This serves as an oblique reference to phallogocentrism and hence to the writings of Jacques Derrida and Julia Kristeva. What distinguishes *elles* most saliently from *ils* is the lack of a penis, the sign that has been made the symbol of phallocratic power, organized around the centrality of the word or *logos*, the power to speak and to name.

Each of the paragraphs in *Les Guérillères* in which these dicta are found is prefaced by the phrase *elles disent*, showing that the *guérillères* are evaluating them to expose their masculine bias. The statements are not permitted to stand by themselves but appear only in the reported speech of the women. The universalizing pronoun *elles* rewrites reality from the perspective of the *guérillères*. In what reads like a reworking of the Sapir-Whorf hypothesis, the *guérillères* warn,

4.4. Il n'y a pas de réalité avant que les mots les règles les règlements lui aient donné forme. . . . Elles disent qu'en premier lieu le vocabulaire de toutes les langues est à examiner, à modifier, à bouleverser de fond en comble, que chaque mot doit être passé au crible. (192)

There is no reality before words rules regulations have given it form. . . . They$_f$ say that, in the first place, the vocabulary of every language must be examined, modified, completely overturned, that each word must be screened.

It is, in fact, by appeal to the Sapir-Whorf hypothesis of linguistic relativity that the *guérillères* escape from the rigid binary of the structuralist system. For where Lévi-Strauss posits women as the unit of exchange, the unit that underpins the linguistic system and provides a fixed point for the play of the signifier over *signifié*, the signified, Sapir-Whorf veers away from the minefield of language universals, asserting that different languages segment reality in different ways. There is a covert didacticism, a deliberate polemic, built into the Sapir-Whorf hypothesis, whether or not this was intended by its original designers as they encouraged linguists working with

Native American languages not to import Western bias into their analysis. Other languages should be seen as other, different, and separate from the Indo-European tongues that had formed the basis of Western linguistics, not as the Other within the Western system. An awareness that words shape reality allows the *guérillères* to test the lexicon of the language they inherited for gender bias and propose new terms and new relations among them.

Wittig's conception of the role of language in influencing and creating perception may well originate in her reading of Foucault. In *L'Archéologie du savoir* (1969; published in English as *The Archaeology of Knowledge* in 1972), Foucault argues that discourses should be considered not simply as groups of signs or signifying elements that refer to specific content, but "as practices that systematically form the objects of which they speak" (1972, 49). This is a restatement, or perhaps a development, of the Sapir-Whorf hypothesis of linguistic determinism, transferred to the level of discourse rather than of language in the abstract. For Foucault it is the discourse, or the linguistic presentation of a social phenomenon, that organizes and mobilizes knowledge about that phenomenon, but this knowledge cannot precede the manner of its description. The terms of the debate thus create the debate.

In fact, Foucault echoes the Sapir-Whorf hypothesis at many points in his writings, but without crediting its American originators. In *Les Mots et les choses* (1966; published in English as *The Order of Things*, 1970), for example, in a subsection on structure, one finds "la structure, en limitant et en filtrant le visible, lui permet de se transcrire dans le langage" (structure, by limiting and filtering the visible, allows it to transcribe itself in language) (1966, 147), suggesting that it is the preexistence of the structure that provides a grid by which the visible may be articulated. In a paragraph discussing the importance of linguistics, Foucault notes:

> Elle permet—elle s'efforce en tout cas de rendre possible—la structuration des contenus eux-mêmes; elle n'est donc pas une reprise théorique des connaissances acquises par ailleurs, interprétation d'une lecture déjà faite des phénomènes; elle ne propose pas une version linguistique des faits observés dans les sciences humaines, elle est le principe d'un déchiffrement premier . . . les choses n'accèdent à l'existence que dans la mesure où elles peuvent former les éléments d'un système signifiant. (1966, 393)

> It allows—or rather it endeavors to make possible—the structuring of the contents themselves; it is not, therefore, a theoretical recapitulation of knowledge acquired elsewhere, an interpretation of a reading that has already been made of the phenomena; it does not propose a linguistic version of facts observed by the humanities, it is the origin of interpretation. . . . Things do not come into existence except insofar as they can form elements in a signifying system.

The last phrase of this passage is patterned on the Sapir-Whorf hypothesis, with its insistence that things only exist inside a system that can explain them and give them structure, relating them to other like, or unlike,

phenomena. Foucault's emphasis on the importance of language to interpretation gives language a central place in perception and comprehension.

The verb *agir sur*, in the epigraph to this chapter on the ability of words
to "act on" reality, is interesting in its echo of Foucault's thoughts on the
role of linguistics (and every other discipline in the humanities) in constructing its field of study. This emphasis on the power of language to construct
reality suggests that the world-to-word fit of the classic directive speech
act, in Elizabeth Anscombe and John Searle's terminology (see Searle 1979,
1–29), takes precedence as a function of language over the word-to-world
fit of the classic assertive speech act. To understand the concepts of word-
to-world and world-to-word fit more clearly, a visual example may help.
We can think of the assertion as a sketch of a building after it has been
constructed. In this case, the words (or sketch) are being fitted to the world
(or building), for it is the world that has changed (a new building has appeared); the words merely keep up with this change. For the directive, we
may think instead of a blueprint of the same building: this is a command to
the builders to erect the edifice in this fashion. In this case, the world (or
building) is being made to fit the architect's words (or blueprint) (John
Searle's examples from lectures on the philosophy of language, University
of California, Berkeley, spring 1992).

Wittig often describes words as a blueprint for social change, rather
than simply a record of it. As we have seen with regard to her reworkings
of the tenets of structural anthropology, she is particularly concerned with
language's role in the creation of sociocultural categories and their influence on perceptions of reality. Thus, when she writes of reactivating words
that have lost their meaning, it should be borne in mind that she is referring to their ability to frame and reframe reality, in the active sense of causing people to see the world in a particular way, to make their perceptions
fit the language used, rather than to the more passive conception of words
as simply referring expressions.

Judith Butler comments on Wittig's strategy of renaming in *The Lesbian Body:* "The name confers morphological distinctness, and names which
expliclitly disavow the patronymic lineage become the occasions for the
disintegration of the (paternal) version of bodily integrity as well as the
reintegration and reformation of other versions of bodily coherence" (1993,
259–60, n. 17). Wittig's dismemberment of the lesbian body, her lists of
the organs that compose it, her rewriting of the names of Greek male heroes in the feminine, are, according to Butler, occasions, or opportunities,
for the body to be reconceptualized in a less paternalist frame. The normal
process of signifying has been disrupted, and from this disruption more
liberatory versions can come. As we noted in chapter 1, Butler is at times
determinist in her view of the power of language. She often presents a very
narrow view of human agency, limiting it to a tiny wriggle-hole in which
repeating patterns may be (temporarily) disrupted: "'agency' . . . is to be
located within the possibility of a variation on . . . repetition" (1990, 145).
Butler also describes the speaking subject as merely an effect created by

speech, not the actor behind the speech event: "the subject is a consequence of certain rule-governed discourses" (145). I would argue, with all the stolid insistence of the antigun lobby, that people kill, weapons shoot, and, likewise, people signify, words refer. Wittig's texts create a challenge to the reader whose job it is to re-member the body in his or her search for textual coherence. It is not the text itself that produces this effect. As we have seen in our discussion of cohesion, ellipsis produces the tightest textual link because it requires the reader to activate the relationship between the elided material and its antecedent. The reader may fail to do this, in which case the text fails to cohere. Similarly, in Wittig's apparently incoherent use of lists of body members and feminized heroes, this is no more (and no less) than an invitation to the reader to imagine the world differently.

Although Wittig's reworkings of structuralist (and indeed Whorfian) tenets are most apparent in *Les Guérillères*, all her works show an intense interest in the nature of language. In *Brouillon pour un dictionnaire des amantes* (1976), a retelling of the history of lesbians that takes the form of notes for dictionary entries, we see the same belief that language not only structures perception but creates it. In the entry under "langue" (language), we read, "La légende dit que la vieille langue était capable de créer la vie ou au contraire de 'frapper' à mort" (The legend says that the old language was capable of creating life or of "striking" death) (translation by Wittig and Zeig 1979). If the old language had power of life and death, it could clearly create reality. Yet its syntax and construction (morphology?) were less "rigid, rigorous, repressive" than those of the modern language. Here we see again Wittig's concern that the structure of a language may itself be oppressive. The epigraph to this chapter comes from the *Brouillon*, from the entry on "mot" (word); the project of reactivating the meanings of words is that of the *Brouillon* itself.

Feminist complaints that traditional dictionaries present the world from a masculist perspective, and the recognition that dictionaries have a powerful normative effect on those who consult them, have been the motivation for a number of feminist dictionaries, more or less poetic in nature, of which Wittig and Zeig's 1976 *Brouillon* was the first. Cheris Kramarae and Paula Treichler's *Feminist Dictionary* (1985) and Mary Daly and Jane Caputi's *Webster's First Intergalactic Wickedary of the English Language* (1987), both witty subversions of traditional lexicography, owe an important debt to Wittig and Zeig.

In what might have been a conscious reference to the film *Alphaville*, Jean-Luc Godard's 1965 science fiction classic, Wittig and Zeig note under the entry "dictionnaire":

4.5.   La disposition du dictionnaire permet de faire disparaître les éléments qui ont distordu notre histoire. . . . Elle permet également d'utiliser les lacunes à la façon d'une litote dans une phrase où il s'agit de dire le moins pour dire le plus. (Wittig and Zeig 1976, 77)

> The arrangement of the dictionary allows us to eliminate those elements
> that have distorted our history. . . . It also allows us to use the gaps in the
> manner of a litotes in a sentence in which one says the most by saying the
> least. [My own translation: Wittig and Zeig's, while more poetic, is not a
> literal one.]

Here Wittig appears to support the strong version of the Sapir-Whorf hypothesis: omitting words from the dictionary that refer to women in a disparaging way, or that suggest women are inferior to men, will prevent speakers from perceiving women as inferior, since they will have no words with
which to articulate their perceptions. Of course, this assumes that a dictionary is not merely a reference work for those interested in normative spelling and canonical meanings, but, like George Orwell's "Thought Police"
(and Orwell's *1984* is another novel steeped in Whorfian determinism),
legislates which words are to be used and what they may mean, exercising
an omnipotent ideological control over speakers' minds.

The emphasis on the dictionary as an ideological tool places enormous
importance on the ability of individual lexical items to classify reality, as
though the whole of language could be contained in its lexicon. This view
of the role of dictionaries is similar to that found in *Alphaville*, where
Natasha von Braun explains to Lemmy Caution, the outsider:

4.6.   Presque tous les jours il y a des mots qui disparaissent parce qu'ils sont
       maudits, alors à la place on met de nouveaux mots qui correspondent à
       d'idées nouvelles.

       Almost every day words disappear because they are damned, then new
       words are put in their place, corresponding to new ideas.

As the words are lost, so too are the concepts to which they refer. In every
room in the city's hotels can be found a Bible. When Caution introduces
Natasha to words like "love" and "conscience," she turns to the Bible for
an explanation. Caution examines this Bible and, Magritte-like, declares,
"Ceci n'est pas une Bible. C'est un dictionnaire" (This is not a Bible. It's a
dictionary). In Alphaville, the citizens are, to repeat Edward Sapir's often-
quoted words, "very much at the mercy of the . . . language which has
become the medium of expression of their society" (1929; quoted in
Mühlhäusler and Harré 1990, 3), so much so that their ability to form a
mental concept of a referent is dependent on the appearance of a term for
that referent in the Bible/dictionary.[7]

The degree of success that may be attributed to conscious attempts to
alter or reactivate elements in a language is always difficult to calculate. In
Sapir's concept of linguistic change, it is clear that drift has purpose, as
opposed to flux, which is random. Sapir sees language as an organic, dynamic device, a tool that both reflects and constructs the culture of its users.
It is resistant to ideological constraints and dictates imposed from without

or by an unrepresentative group from within. The question of whether language can be changed by design is discussed in two overviews of work on language and gender, *Gender Voices*, by David Graddol and Joan Swann (1989), and *Les Mots et les femmes*, by Marina Yaguello (1978). What Graddol and Swann term "linguistic intervention," suggesting the influence of an outside force that does not quite belong, Yaguello calls "l'action volontariste sur la langue" (voluntarist action upon language). She subtitles her concluding chapter "Peut-on infléchir l'évolution naturelle des langues?" (Can one divert the natural evolution of language?). The phrasing of Yaguello's question and the use of the term *volontariste*, which emphasizes the role of the will in social change, suggest that there is something unnnatural or unrealistic in trying to change language, that its evolution is in some way separate from the evolution of the people who use and create it. Graddol and Swann conclude that while conscious intervention on its own has little effect, most interventionist strategies are accompanied by social change, and the two forces tend to work together (195). Yaguello's conclusion, reached after an overview of the attempts of different revolutionary governments to change the speech of their citizens, is remarkably similar to that of Graddol and Swann:

> Il est certain que l'action volontariste dans ce domaine ne peut rien en dehors d'une évolution parallèle des structures mentales et sociales, ce qui suppose avant tout: prise de conscience, explicitation idéologique, analyse critique. (185)

> It is certain that volontarist action can achieve nothing in this domain unless there is a parallel evolution in mental and social structures, which presupposes above all: consciousness of the problem, ideological explanation, critical analysis.

It would seem from the number, range, and longevity of projects to change language for ideological or political reasons that this desire must itself be considered a natural part of language use, as Deborah Cameron (1995) argues. Indeed, Cameron has coined the expression "verbal hygiene" for what she sees as the ingrained desire to "clean up" language and sanitize it.[8] She states, "[M]aking value judgements on language is an integral part of using it" (3). Strategies that do not "enhance communication by rendering the writer's meaning transparent," but instead distract attention from the content to the form of a message, are useful in causing people to stop and consider the cultural baggage attached to a particular phrasing (156–57). The surprise and perplexity caused in the reader by many of Wittig's neologisms such as *sphyngesse*, *bourreleuse*, or *Ishtar à la tête/soleille*, interrupt the smooth flow of the text in a way that is entirely intentional.

It is difficult to imagine a context in which linguistic intervention would be divorced from a desire for social change of some kind. The absolute solipsism of Humpty Dumpty's "when I use a word it means just what I choose it to mean, neither more nor less" is intentionally anomalous, even

in Alice's looking-glass world. Advertising companies, which have no political agenda beyond the marketing of a new product and the making of
another megabuck, nevertheless spend millions of dollars simulating social
change and new social contexts in which their products will be consumed,
and as much again doing market research to find a name that will be well
received and perceived as culturally innovative. Thus the Japanese company
launching "Sweat," a soft drink that, like the American Gatorade, is intended
to replenish the body's vital minerals after a hard workout, had two tasks
to accomplish. First, it needed to find a name that was new and unusual to
Japanese consumers but had connotations of fast-paced American living.
Second, it needed to portray the drink in nontraditional, high-tech gyms
to promote the kind of lifestyle that would support the buying of the product. Even in the ultimately unreal world of product promotion, linguistic
change (the name "Sweat") and social change (the high-tech gym) must
be seen to go hand in hand.

For social theorists, the success of any attempt to reactivate, alter, or
abandon a particular linguistic feature must be judged by the degree to
which the modified feature is taken up by the society at large. The success
or failure of a literary work is not, however, an easy matter to judge, as I
elaborate in chapter 6. Some literary experiments may be contained within
the binding of their own covers, their linguistic pecularities never adopted
by any native speaker, yet they may still have a profound and observable
effect on the linguistic community. People do not have to speak like the
characters in George Orwell's *1984* (1948) or Jean-Luc Godard's *Alphaville*
(1965) for these works to be effective and for their message about language
and language use to be widely disseminated.

Wittig's reanalysis of linguistic gender as culturally motivated has not
caused any disruption to the language practices of native speakers. It has,
however, been extensively commented on by gender theorists like Judith
Butler. The shock value of phrases like "Les agnelles nouvelles nées" (the
newly born she-lambs) causes readers to reassess the cultural values trans-
mitted by French grammar.

5

"On est quatre dans le même tas"

French Epicene on

"Personal pronouns engineer gender through language, and personal pronouns are . . . the subject matter of each one of my books," Wittig asserts when asked about her intentions in writing (1986, 67). In *L'Opoponax*, *Les Guérillères*, and *Le Corps lesbien*, Wittig either uses a pronoun that has low frequency in literary works or invents a new pronominal form to express one of the essential messages of the text. In *L'Opoponax*, *on* is used as the principal pronominal vehicle; in *Les Guérillères*, the story is told through the third person feminine plural, *elles*, while *Le Corps lesbien* features the first person singular neologism *j/e*. In this chapter, we will mainly be concerned with an examination of the epicene *on* of *L'Opoponax*, Wittig's first novel, which has far-reaching effects on almost every aspect of the text.

Observing that the masculine is the abstract, the general, and the universal, Wittig explains that in her first novel she was concerned with the problem of subjectivity. "I wanted to restore an undivided 'I,' to universalize the point of view of a group condemned to being particular"(1986, 68). She therefore looked for a "strong device" that would be "beyond sexes" and came upon the "munificent" pronoun *on*, which "locates characters outside of the social divisions by sexes." And so *on* became the pronominal hero/ine of *L'Opoponax*, representing the voice of the narrator, as well as that of the other characters, in an undifferentiated third person singular form, for *on* can be used to refer to first, second, or third persons in either the singular or the plural. Although the context will usually serve to clarify which person is intended, reference may remain intentionally vague."'On' est 'un négatif,' utilisé pour supprimer devant le verbe toute référence à la personne, ou plutôt pour recouvrir, pour accumuler toutes ces références," writes Jacques Cellard in *Le Monde* (*on* is a negative, used to suppress all reference to persons in the verb phrase, or rather to recover, to accumulate all possible references) (Mühlhäusler and Harré 1990, 182). Gender divisions, too, are obfuscated by *on*, though the agreement of adjectives or past participles may provide gender information: *on est assis* (we are seated$_{ms}$) and *on est assises* (we are seated$_{fpl}$) are both grammatically correct forms of the past participle (*assis:* seated) describing a feminine plural antecedent. The utility of this pronoun for a writer concerned with the "tyranny of gender" is clear.

Functions of on

Before turning to a systematic analysis of the functioning of *on* in *L'Opoponax*, it will be useful to see that Wittig is not unique in her use of *on* to replace other persons in the pronominal paradigm. The following examples (taken from Mühlhäusler and Harré 1990, 180–91) will show that in contemporary, colloquial speech and its literary representations, *on* is frequently pressed into service throughout the pronominal system.

First person singular: *On arrive* (one is/ I am coming), spoken by Mado Petits-Pieds, the barmaid in Queneau's *Zazie dans le métro*, called back to work by her employer (1959, 72).

First person plural: *On y va?* (shall we go?), *On se déplace* (we're off), spoken by one person as a suggestion to the group. *Qu'est-ce qu'on pourrait dire de cette mer?* (what can we say about this sea?), spoken by a teacher to the class. In informal speech *on* has replaced *nous* as the most common pronoun for expressing the first person plural. (Cellard, 1978)

Second person singular: *Alors mon enfant, on a un gros chagrin?*, spoken by a would-be child molester to Zazie (so, child, you have a great sorrow *or* you're very upset about something?) (Queneau, *Zazie dans le métro*, 1959, 41).

Second person plural: *Et vous, qu'on se retire* (and you, you may withdraw), spoken by Nero to his guards (Racine, *Britanicus*, 1669, 2: i).

Third person singular: *On a souvent besoin d'un plus petit que soi* (one often needs someone smaller than oneself), maxim of La Fontaine. Here *on* has the meaning of people in general, everyone.

——*On est venu te voir.*——*Qui?*——*Quelqu'un* (someone has come to see you.——Who? ——a person.) Here *on* is indefinite. (Wagner and Pinchon, 1962: p. 198, ex. 213)

Third person plural: *On balaie les rues chaque matin à quatre heures* (one/they sweep the streets every morning at four) (my invented example).

What is noticeable about these sentences is that, apart from those that express the first person plural (a use now so common it has become unmarked) or the third person indefinite, each conveys a sense of discretion. This type of oblique reference does not formally state the connection between the person implicated in the action and the action itself. *On* is often used in the second person as a hedge on a direct question, statement, or imperative that might be interpreted as rude or invasive. In the first person singular, it is intended to express a degree of humility, although if overused or used ironically, it may indicate the reverse. It will be useful to remember, in the analysis to come, that *on* implies indirectness or indefiniteness, obliging the hearer or reader to examine the context in order to identify the correct referent, thus implicating the reader in the supposition made. (See M. Harris 1978, 122–23, and M. Harris 1988, 231–35, for discussion of the increasing frequency of *on* in popular speech, especially in the first person plural. See Maingueneau 1986, 8–9, for discussion of the plasticity of *on*.)

By eliminating, or rather neutralizing, personal reference, the systematic, sustained use of *on* forces the reader to invest a significant amount of processing time in identifying the referent (since nominal antecedents are either obscured or nonexistent). During this process, which requires the reader to pay closer attention than usual to such textual features as cohesion, focalization, and reported speech and thought, the reader must pick out the lens, the central processing unit (CPU), and the mouthpiece to answer three questions: who sees this? who thinks this? and who says this? The questions themselves demonstrate that these three functions (seeing, thinking, and speaking) may be filled from three different centers of consciousness.

Plot Summary: L'Opoponax

L'Opoponax (1964), Monique Wittig's first novel, tells the story of a group of children growing up in a small village in rural France. Focusing on one child, Catherine Legrand, it follows her through her first day in kindergarten to preadolescence and her first feelings of love for another girl. All events, major and minor, are seen through the eyes of a child in an uninterrupted flow.

In *L'Opoponax*, *on* is associated with a large number of different proper names. As Marguerite Duras puts it, "Il s'agit de dix, cent petites filles et garçons qui portent les noms qu'on leur a donné mais qui pourraient aussi bien les échanger contre des sous neufs" (it's about ten, a hundred little girls and boys who carry the names they have been given but who could as well exchange them for new pennies) (1964, 284). Whether the actions of one little girl, two girls, a large mixed group of children, or a group of anonymous adults are being recounted, *on* remains the grammatical subject. Claude Simon writes of Catherine Legrand, the narrator and focalizer, "I see, I breathe, I chew, I feel through her eyes, her mouth, her hands her skin. I become childhood" (*L'Express* 1964; quoted in Wittig 1986, 69).

It might seem from the preceding discussion that *on* is the only pronoun used in the novel to anaphorize animate antecedents and that, as in Garréta's *Sphinx*, there are no formal indications of gender. It should be noted, therefore, that the children's names, apart from a couple of Dominiques and a Laurence (both gender neutral in French), are all sex specific: Catherine Legrand, Véronique Legrand, Valerie Borge, Robert Payen, Alain Trévise, Vincent Parme, and so on. As will be seen, in many places the pronouns *elle* and *il* are used to describe the activities of one of the children or the nuns; this referent is thereby set apart from the rest of the group, for whom the nonspecific *on* is reserved. Catherine Legrand herself is referred to at times as *elle*, especially when the situation is presented as counterfactual (in this case the shift from *on* to *elle* is often accompanied by a shift in tense from the present to the future; more will be said on this point further on.) Furthermore, the gendered lexical items *les hommes* (the men), *les femmes* (the women), *la mère* (the mother), *le père* (the father), *le petit garçon* (the little boy), and *la petite fille* (the little girl), and even terms for sexual organs such as *la quéquette* (the peepee or penis), all appear in the text, making the sex of the referent perfectly clear. *On* is used in contradistinction to the sex-marked terms, making them seem overly specific.

If Wittig's technique works, then the point of view of one little girl as she matures from a four-year-old to a thirteen-year-old becomes that of every reader. In a sense, this is precisely what happens with any successful literary work; indeed the term *focalizer* indicates that, like the eye of a camera, the character through whose eyes the action is observed will orient readers' understanding of events. Wittig aimed at more than orientation through a child's eyes and sympathetic understanding: she wanted readers to accept this perspective as unmarked in terms of age or gender so that it would appear universal. From the responses of the French critics Simon and Duras, quoted earlier, it seems that Wittig was successful.

Wittig's success cannot, however, be explained merely by the fact that the predominant pronoun in the text is ungendered. This is an important point, since so many critics have noted the effect of her innovative style and imputed it to the choice of an epicene pronoun. Hélène Wenzel states, for example:

> Tout sens stricte de genre et de nombre est ainsi éliminé, créant une zone libre quasi utopique où ces jeunes enfants peuvent grandir en-dehors des limites . . . de la différence sexuelle. (1985, 44)

> All clear sense of gender and number is thus eliminated, creating an almost utopic free zone in which these young children can grow up outside the limits of sexual difference.

I will argue instead that it is by the almost complete eradication of personal deictics (terms like first person pronouns whose referent is determined by the immediate speech situation) and the consequent lack of a fixed reference point for perceptual and psychological deictics (perceptual and psychological deictics relate to the cognitive processes or state of mind of the speaker, like modal expressions and conditionals) that Wittig achieves her effect. To demonstrate this, it will be necessary to consider many different aspects of the text—deictics, tense, episode boundaries, focalization, and the use of direct speech—since each of these elements is in some way marked in this novel, and each contributes to the text's overall effectiveness.

Critical Opinion

Many reviewers, sensing Catherine's growing sense of autonomy and an independent self, have related this purely to the use of different pronouns. These critics assert confidently but incorrectly that *je* appears for the first time in the last line of the novel, where it takes over from *on* to refer to Catherine in a quotation of the first line of Maurice Scève's poem "Délie." Jean Duffy writes, for example, of "the *je* which displaces the impersonal *on* at the end of the *Opoponax*" (1987, 399), while Wenzel writes:

> L'auteur/Catherine Legrand s'approprie le "je" pour la première fois, empreignant sur le texte le sujet parlant qui a émergé, sans genre: "On dit, tant je l'aimais qu'en elle encore je vis." (1985, 50)

> The author/Catherine Legrand appropriates the "I" for the first time, stamping on the text the speaking subject who has emerged, genderless: "One says, so much did I love her that in her I live on."

Erica Ostrovsky writes that, "the impersonal *on* gives way to the personal *je*, thus imprinting on the text the speaking subject who has emerged finally and for the first time" (1991, 23). Like the other critics mentioned here, Jan Hokenson asserts, "The first-person pronoun 'I' is withheld until almost the end of the text." She then quotes the first line of Scève's poem (1988, 66). Finally, Y. Went-Daoust declares, "'Je' n'apparaît que dans cette phrase ultime pour marquer la fin de l'enfance et le début d'un nouveau discours" ("je" appears only in this last sentence to mark the end of childhood and the beginning of a new discourse) (1991, 365). It begins to sound as though these critics are quoting each other rather than reading the text. Monique Wittig herself has made the same claim: "the only appearance of the narrator comes with a *je*, 'I,' located at the end of the book in a small sentence . . ., a verse from Maurice Scève, in *La Délie*" (1986, 72).

That five literary critics and the author should make the same mistake is significant. One might be tempted to assume poor reading and a too-credulous adherence to the author's statements about her work, were it not for the fact that two at least of these critical essays (Duffy's and Wenzel's) precede Wittig's own discussion and, more important, that the mistake indicates the impact the text has on the reader. What we are witnessing is an effect similar to that discussed in the previous chapter, where critics assumed there were no masculine entities in *Les Guérillères* because the feminine had become the unmarked element. Despite the appearance of a first person reference on the first page of *L'Opoponax* (*ma quéquette* [my peepee]) and its frequent occurrences throughout the text ("j'aime ma mère, oui j'aime ma mère" "(I love my mother, yes I love my mother)" [23]; "je suis l'opoponax" (I am the opoponax) [230, 240, 242]), these critics believe the first person emerges only at the end, providing a concrete, formally encoded deictic centre that becomes the reference point for the novel as a whole. Since even this last occurrence of *je* is framed in a quotation, formally introduced by the *verbum dicendi on dit*, it cannot be said to provide a deictic center any more than previous citations have done.

Ostrovsky and Went-Daoust claim further that all verbs in *L'Opoponax* are in the present tense (Ostrovsky 1991, 23, 26; Went-Daoust 1991, 358) save two *passés composés* (composed past) on the first page and the use of the *imparfait* (imperfect) in the last line of the book ("tant je l'**aimais** qu'en elle encore je vis"). Furthermore, Ostrovsky is under the impression that *on* most frequently appears in the phrase *on dit* (1991, 24), while Wenzel expresses the belief that *on dit* is used to relate the actions of the latter half of the book (1985, 50).

Put together, these erroneous claims are instructive because they describe an effect that is actually achieved by the very carefully restricted focalization of the novel. As we will see, personal deictics do indeed occur before the last page. *On* is used in an enormous variety of ways, only one of which is in the introduction to speech *on dit*. Although the present is certainly the main vehicle of the text, the *passé composé* is used throughout to establish the effect of prior actions (an aspectual rather than a temporal distinction), and the *futur* is used particularly to describe events considered counterfactual by the narrator-focalizer. The events of the novel seem to take place in a seamless, boundless present (an effect heightened by the blurring of episode boundaries), while the polyphonic nature of much of the narration might well suggest that the phrase *on dit* lurks behind each sentence. Focalization, though not a deictic device in itself, nevertheless serves to tie the events narrated to the point of view of the person watching at the time, Catherine Legrand. Since narrator and focalizer occupy the same ground, it could well seem as though the *je* of *tant je l'aimais* is finally coming forward and giving up the protection of third person reference.

Focalization through on

I have used the term "focalizer" in chapter 3 in my discussion of *Love Child* and Kit's description of Ajax. Since focalization is particularly important in the *L'Opoponax*, it will be useful to look more closely at this term here. The scene in *Love Child* in which Kit describes Ajax's despair is focalized (visualized) entirely by Kit, who is hiding in the bathroom vent. The boundaries of the vent circumscribe what Kit is able to see, and, more important, Kit's jealousy over Ajax's close relationship with Kit's mother color the entire account given to the reader. Kit is, then, both narrator (the one who tells the tale) and focalizer (the one who perceives the events told). *Love Child* is narrated and focalized entirely by Kit; the reader is never allowed to see events from any other character's perspective. We remain throughout inside Kit's limited, childish field of vision, for which the constricted bathroom vent is an excellent metaphor. Furthermore, Kit is so bound up in himself/herself that the tale is told entirely from Kit's internal consciousness.

Other types of focalization are also possible. Shlomith Rimmon-Kenan gives the example of James Joyce's *Portrait of the Artist as a Young Man*, which she describes as "a third person centre of consciousness" novel (1983, 72–73). In this novel, verbal communication and nonverbal visualization remain separate, although both are performed by Stephen, the protagonist.

> Once upon a time and a very good time it was there was a moocow coming down along the road and this moocow that was coming down along the road met a nicens little boy named baby tuckoo . . .
> His father told him that story: his father looked at him through a glass: he had a hairy face. (quoted in Rimmon-Kenan 1983, 72)

Focalization is through Stephen as a small child who still wets the bed; narration is by an adult capable of formulating complete sentences. The consciousness that sees the father's face through a glass is Stephen's; the voice that reports these events is that of the narrator.

In other types of novel, the separation between the roles of focalizer and narrator is even clearer. Where there exists an obvious class, race, gender or age difference between narrator and character, it is much easier to distinguish character focalization from narration. In Charles Dickens's *Great Expectations*, for example, Pip narrates what happened to himself as a child. During his first visit to Estella, Pip gazes at his "coarse hands" and his "common boots." "My opinion of those accessories was not favourable. They had never troubled me before, but they troubled me now, as vulgar appendages" (quoted in Rimmon-Kenan 1983, 73). As Rimmon-Kenan observes, words like "accessories" and "appendages" are those of an adult, while the center of consciousness is that of a child.

What is unusual about *L'Opoponax* is not so much that it is a novel narrated mainly through the indefinite *on*, but that this device, in conjunction with the other salient aspects of the text listed above, causes an almost perfect coincidence between narrator and focalizer. In other texts, such coincidence has created a narrator-focalizer who sees and relates events in an external narration, with a kind of bird's-eye view over the whole; in *L'Opoponax*, in contrast, we are dealing with a narrator-focalizer and an internal narration, more like that of Kit in the bathroom vent.[1] With infrequent exceptions, in which the child narrator tells of events focalized by an adult (usually a schoolteacher or a nun), Catherine Legrand narrates entirely from her own point of view.

The mother superior of Catherine Legrand's school warns the girls that private correspondence is grounds for dismissal (232). This warning could be taken as the key to the lack of correspondences in the novel, for the French term *renvoi* is polysemic, meaning both dismissal and reference. Too formal a correspondence between the thoughts, observations, and actions described in the novel and the person thinking, observing, and acting would give a clear and unambiguous reference point to which to tie the events. The novel would then be a traditional account of a French childhood told through the eyes of a little girl. Although the novel opens with Robert Payen's late arrival at school, within a few pages it becomes clear that *on* has a preferential referent in Catherine Legrand. Except in contexts where the actions must be ascribed to someone else, *on* refers to Catherine Legrand, either alone or as part of a group. Since the different uses of *on*, as well as the reference points it creates, are central to the creation of an internal focalizer-narrator, we will turn to an analysis of these uses. We should bear in mind also that this link must be made by the reader, who understands from contextual clues rather than formal cues that the story is told from the little girl's perspective and that this child is also the mouthpiece of the story.

Although the narrative is focalized through the eyes of one little girl, Catherine Legrand, whose actions and thoughts become more individualized as she grows older, the pronouns do not change correspondingly. *On* remains firmly in place, a feat made possible by its monomorphous diversity (to coin a phrase).

Indefinite, Generic on (*similar to* one *or* you)

5.1.   On voit sa maison de la porte de l'école. (7)

One/you can see his house from the door of the school.

The focal element of this sentence is Robert Payen's house and its topographical relation to the school; human agency is minimized by the generic pronoun.

Nonspecific (*similar to passive*)

5.2.   On fait dormir les enfants l'après-midi mais c'est pour rire. (8)

The children are put to sleep in the afternoon but it's not serious.

Plural, Inclusive Reference (*similar to inclusive* we)

1. Each person performs the same action.

5.3.   Quand on va dans le pré on fait très attention de ne pas parler fort. (15)

When we go into the meadow we are very careful not to talk loudly.

2. Either several people perform the same action or one person performs the action but represents the whole group (similar to inclusive *we* or indefinite *someone*).

5.4.   On demande à Mademoiselle ce que c'est qu'un fantôme. (90)

We/someone ask/s Mademoiselle what a ghost is.

Singular on, *Referring to Catherine Legrand* (*similar to generic* you, *although in English it sounds very awkward to have the third person* Catherine Legrand *coreferential with* you)

5.5.   Brigitte . . . prend Catherine Legrand par le cou. On$_1$ lui sourit. . . . Catherine Legrand tombe à plat ventre . . . Brigitte s'approche de nouveau, on$_2$ ne lui sourit pas, on$_3$ s'y attend cette fois. . . . elle tire elle est forte on$_4$ est tout de suite à plat ventre. (10)

Brigitte . . . takes Catherine Legrand by the neck. She smiles/you smile at her. . . . Catherine Legrand falls flat on her stomach. . . . Brigitte comes up to her again, she does/you do not smile at her, you are expecting it this time. . . . she pulls she is strong you are immediately flat on your stomach.

Rimmon-Kenan notes that a test for establishing whether a narrative has internal or external focalization is to try and rewrite it in the first person. If this exercise can be achieved, the narrative is internally focalized; if it cannot, focalization is external (1983, 75). It is the repetition of the proper name "Catherine Legrand" in example 5.5 that renders a first person translation in English impossible. The second person *you* sounds clumsy, but it does convey the sense of the child talking to herself. A proper name is usually used to introduce a new or textually inaccessible (animate) referent. Anaphorization—in the form of *elle* for an animate female antecedent—would be the usual form of reference for known, active subjects. The use of *on* suggests instead a switch reference, possibly Catherine Legrand and Brigitte's classmates watching the skirmish. It is only by following the pattern of the verbal predicates that the reader is able to link the four mentions of *on* in example 5.5 to Catherine Legrand. First "on$_1$ lui sourit," then "Catherine Legrand tombe à plat ventre." The juxtaposition of the two actions suggests a relation of cause and effect. Next time, "on$_2$ ne lui sourit pas, on$_3$ s'y attend cette fois." The person most likely to be expecting an attack is the child who has already been pushed to the floor, that is, Catherine Legrand. Once again, after an approach from Brigitte, "on$_4$ est tout de suite à plat ventre." Successful identification of the referent may only be achieved by observing the lexical linking of the predicates, creating tight cohesion despite the neutralizing effect of *on*.

Although Catherine Legrand functions as the focalizer for the text, she sees herself from the outside. The question of designation is very important in assessing focalization, and the consistent third person reference to Catherine Legrand would strongly suggest external focalization, yet spatial, temporal, psychological, ideological, and emotive clues all point directly to the little girl as the center of consciousness. Each scene is observed through her eyes, from her angle of vision, and with her understanding and attitudes. In example 5.5, I have translated *on* by the second person generic *you* rather than by a third person pronoun. In its generic sense, as an indefinite (like "one") rather than a true second person pronoun, *you* may serve to neutralize the boundaries between self and other, parallelling Wittig's use of *on*.

Plural, Exclusive on (*similar to* they)

In the system established by Wittig, an exclusive use of *on* will primarily exclude Catherine Legrand. In the uses of *on* I have examined so far, there is coincidence among lens, CPU, and mouthpiece: it is Catherine Legrand who sees, conceptualizes, and tells the story. In the following examples, however, the *on* who sees inside the story world is separate from the character Catherine Legrand who is seen. The child has begun to watch herself being seen and spoken to by others, although there is still no internal focalization. (Catherine is still not ready to say *je* (I).)

5.6. Catherine Legrand se penche . . . on la voit entre la chaise et le plancher. (12)

Catherine Legrand bends over. . . . They see her between the chair and the floor.

In example 5.6, Catherine Legrand narrates the words or actions of others as they relate to herself, though narration remains in the third person. It will be useful to look at the whole passage from which example 5.6 comes, for it provides examples of a more complex use of *on:* switch reference.

On Used with Switch Reference (*similar to* alternation between we, you, *and* they)

5.7. On [1] est à table. On [2] parle de l'attaque de grand-père il ne peut plus bouger le côté droit. . . . Le père et la mère regardent Catherine Legrand. On [3] ne peut pas parler. Le côté droit glisse sur la chaise . . . Catherine Legrand se penche . . . on [4] la voit entre la chaise et le plancher. . . . Catherine Legrand est attaquée. La chose a monté le long de la chaise pendant qu'on [5] a mangé sans qu'on [6] la voie. On[7] la regarde sans bouger. On [8] ne peut pas l'aider. (12–13)

We[1] are at table. We[2] are talking about Grandfather's attack he can no longer move his right-hand side . . . The father and mother watch Catherine Legrand. You[3] cannot speak. The right side slips down the chair. . . . Catherine Legrand bends over. . . . They[4] see her between the chair and the floor. . . . Catherine Legrand is attacked. The thing has climbed along the chair while we[5] were eating without anyone [6] seeing it. They[7] watch her without moving. They[8] cannot help her.

In example 5.7, the first and second occurrences of *on* refer to the whole family, setting the scene for the conversation at dinner, during a discussion of the grandfather's health. They would be most felicitously translated into English using the first person plural. The intervening sentence "le père et la mère regardent Catherine Legrand" specifies the different components of *on* in occurrences 1 and 2 ("On est à table. On parle de l'attaque de grand-père") and assigns them new roles. The father and mother become agents, while Catherine is the patient. The third instance of *on*—"On ne peut pas parler"—refers to Catherine alone. Exhibiting the same stroke symptoms as her grandfather, she professes herself unable to talk. This sentence acts cohesively with the previous one and explains why her parents are looking at her. The third *on* would be translated by the second person singular in its indefinite, generic sense.

The whole scene is focalized through Catherine's eyes as may be seen by the fact that the girl's father and mother are designated by the definite article (*le père, la mère*) rather than by possessive adjective (*son père, sa mère*). Catherine Legrand's use of the definite article to refer to her own family members, while possessive adjectives are used to refer to the family members of others is idiosyncratic but it parallels the custom in French of using the definite article to refer to one's own body parts while possessive adjectives refer to the bodies of others. This usage is exemplified in the next sentence of the text, "Le côté droit glisse sur la chaise," in which *le* replaces *mon* or *son* as a determiner for *côté* (side).

The fourth instance of *on*, "on la voit entre la chaise et le plancher," returns to the third person, a reprise of the earlier sentence, "Le père et la mère regardent Catherine Legrand," in which the noun phrases have been replaced by pronouns: *on* (the father and mother) *la* (Catherine) *voit*. The use of the object pronoun *la* to refer to the girl makes it plain that Catherine is not included in *on* here. Occurrences 5 and 6, "pendant qu'on a mangé sans qu'on la voie," are particularly complex in that they switch reference within the same sentence. The former governs a temporal clause, the latter a complement of manner. They describe the time (while we were eating) and manner (without being observed) in which the thing attacked Catherine. The two clauses are syntactically parallel: both are introduced by the complementizer *que* and have the same structure: conjunction + complementizer + pronoun + verb. Yet occurrence 5 is inclusive of the whole family and could be translated by *we*, whereas occurrence 6 returns to the third person and excludes Catherine. Since the reader has already been informed twice that the parents are looking at Catherine, we assume that it is the parents who should have spotted the creature but failed to. Finally, in occurrences 7 and 8, "On la regarde sans bouger. On ne peut pas l'aider," third person plural use is continued and excludes Catherine, who is referred to by the direct object pronoun *la* or *l'*.

It is evident from the foregoing analysis of the changing referents for *on* not only that this pronoun is itself remarkably protean, but also that

because of its protean performance the reader must pay scrupulous attention to other textual clues, in particular focalization, to disambiguate the
referents. I should reiterate at this point, perhaps, that Wittig's use of the
varied functions of *on* is not unique. She is merely utilizing the possibilities
available in the system. As has already been elaborated, *on* may stand for
any person in the pronominal paradigm. Even the switch reference discussed
above has antecedents in both literature and spoken conversation. In his
article on the use of *on* quoted earlier, the *Le Monde* critic, Jacques Cellard,
calls attention to his own use of switch reference by putting the two occurrences of *on* in quotation marks:

> "On" ne peut (dans ce cadre modeste) démasquer tout à fait cet agent gram-
> matical double et triple, et "l'on" me pardonnera de ne faire qu'effleurer le
> sujet. (Mühlhäusler and Harré 1990, 179)
>
> One/**I** cannot (in this modest framework) unmask this double and triple
> grammatical agent, and one/**you** will excuse me for only scratching the sur-
> face of the subject.

The first occurrence refers to the author, the second to the reader; no native French speaker would have any difficulty processing this. Similarly, in
the following quotation from Sartre's novel *La Mort dans l'âme*, there is a
clear change in referent:

> Vous en faites pas, dit Lubéron: on sera bien reçus quand on va rentrer: on va
> nous voter des félicitations. (Sartre 1949, 69)
>
> Don't you worry about that, said Lubéron: one/**we** will be well received when
> one returns/**we** return: one/**they** will call for congratulations.

The first two occurrences of *on* have first person plural meaning, whereas
the third is third person plural. It is not hard to find further examples of
this switch reference, both in literary texts and in conversation, although
its use is condemned by traditional grammarians. What is unusual in Wittig's
championing of *on* is the frequency and insistence of its occurrence, coupled
with a restricted use of other pronouns that might have served to clarify
number, gender, and person.

What these different uses of *on* show is, first of all, that the reader must
pay particular attention to the context in order to make the correct anaphoric
links. In many, even most, cases, however, there are no such links, strictly
speaking. If *on* commonly has an indefinite use, an inclusive singular or plural
use (i.e., for actions that include Catherine Legrand), an exclusive singular
or plural use (for actions that do not include the girl), a mixture of indefinite and inclusive in the same sentence, and a variety of ambiguous uses,
then it is clear that the reader must rely on other cues to understand who
does what. The fact that one can read the text and follow even the most
perplexing switches in reference shows not only that we are cooperative

readers (in the Gricean sense) but that Wittig is a cooperative writer, providing the clues we need in the context—and particularly in the techniques she uses to signal focalization—when the syntax is unclear.

Although chosen for its epicene nature, the pronoun *on* has many more properties than that of avoiding gender marking, properties that contribute to the creation of a universal from the particular. As we have seen, *on* avoids distinctions of number and person as well as gender. While it may show no concord but retain the form of the masculine singular when *on* is used with a verb in the *passé composé* conjugated with *être* (to be), it usually has feminine concord if it clearly refers to a feminine antecedent (Grévisse 1970, 782, n 4). This allows the French writer a rare moment of grammatical choice. It is notable, therefore, that Monique Wittig chooses to leave past participles governed by *on* in the unmarked or masculine form.

> 5.8. C'est la forêt de Catherine Legrand et de Véronique Legrand. . . . On s'arrache la peau. . . . On est arrêté. (82)
>
> It's Catherine Legrand and Véronique Legrand's forest. . . . One tears/they/we tear one's/their/our skin. . . . One is/they/we are stopped$_m$.

In the context described above, it is clear that *on* anaphorizes feminine antecedents—Catherine and her sister—but the lack of grammatical gender marking in the past participle *arrêté* makes this link less tight.

In contrast to the other commonly used third person singular pronouns, *il* and *elle*, *on* is marked for high animacy, or even humanity—that is, its referent generally must be a human being or a group of humans. Thus the reader does not have to consider rocks, trees, and abstract ideas when deciding the correct referent for *on*. This switch from traditional gendered pronouns that are neutral as regards animacy to a pronoun that is gender neutral but marked for animacy (and high animacy at that; *on* presupposes a referent capable of speech) shows a reversal of priorities whereby the essential, grammaticalized distinction is not that between masculine and feminine, but that between human and nonhuman.[2]

Catherine Legrand as Center of Consciousness

The scene in which Robert Payen makes his abrupt entry into the school is the opening scene of the novel, the point at which the reader is trying to identify narrator and focalizer (though in most texts these roles will vary throughout the story.) Since it is Robert Payen's late arrival in class and his offer to show the others his *quéquette* (peepee/penis) that starts the novel, one might expect him to be the focalizer, but it quickly becomes clear that this position is occupied by another character, one who watches Robert's arrival. The first use of *on* in the book, "on voit sa maison de la porte de l'école" (see above example 5.1) must be considered indefinite, in the manner of a street direction, since anyone standing at the school door would see the house, but it nevertheless contains indications that help pinpoint the center of consciousness. We are told shortly afterward that the mother of Robert Payen (the little boy who lives in the house opposite the school) sometimes calls him during school break.

5.9.   Elle est à la dernière fenêtre, on l'aperçoit par-dessus les arbres. (7)

She is at the last window, one sees her through the trees.

This use of *on* must be definite, for it refers to a specific witness of a re-peated series of events. Furthermore, the observer of these events must be inside the school. When Robert does not reply,

5.10.   On continue d'entendre la voix qui appelle. (7)

One continues to hear the voice calling.

Now both the eyes and the ears of the focalizer are clearly placed in the school building, focused outward.

Two indications link this center of perception to the name *Catherine Legrand*. Robert's eruption into the classroom is described as one casual event among many others to take place, whereas the events of Catherine Legrand's first day at school are announced as part of a series, as though recapitulating the reasons for her being in the classroom and her knowl-edge of what happens there.

5.11.   La première fois que Catherine Legrand est venue à l'école, elle a vu de la route la cour de récréation l'herbe et les lilas au bord du grillage. (7)

The first time Catherine Legrand came to school, she saw the playground from the road the grass and the lilacs on the edge of the latticework.

This is the reverse perspective from that of the schoolchild who regards the world from the schoolroom: it shows the little girl as the outsider looking in. This is underlined by the use of the pronoun *elle*, instead of *on*, which, as we will see, is frequently used to present one of the children as different in some important way from the others. While the collective *on* describes the undifferentiated acts of the children, the gendered pronouns *il* and *elle* single one or another of them out, expressing a unique position, though only Catherine acts as focalizer. This sentence introduces the *passé composé* (*elle a vu de la route*) for the first time: only Catherine Legrand's past is ever presented, and that at a minimal time distance with a direct bearing on the present, in the manner of an aspectual distinction of anteriority. This point will be discussed in greater detail further on. All other characters exist only in the present.

Not only does Catherine Legrand emerge as the perceptual center of the text, she is also the psychological center, and this too is established within the first couple of pages. On her first day it is reported that there are a lot of children playing in the courtyard but no *grandes personnes* (grown-ups).

5.12.   Seulement la mère de Catherine Legrand et il vaudrait mieux qu'elle ne
        rentre pas dans l'école c'est seulement les enfants, il faut lui dire, est-ce
        qu'il faut lui dire. (8)

        Only the mother of Catherine Legrand and it would be better that she did
        not go into the school, it is necessary to tell her, is it necessary to tell her.

Faced with the sudden string of modalized expressions—the conditional *il
vaudrait*, the epistemic *il faut lui dire*, and the interrogative *est-ce qu'il faut
lui dire*—the reader has to ask, who is the source of these doubts and di-
rectives? There are no formal marks to show whether this is a passage of
direct discourse: no quotation marks, paragraph indentation or *verbum
dicendi* ("she said," etc.). The comment reads more like a section of reported thought, except that there is no clear distinction between the narrator and the child to indicate who is reporting. The conditional *il vaudrait
mieux* and the interrogative *est-ce qu'il faut lui dire* act as evidentials, giving the narrator's attitude toward the events as they unfold. These modalized
expressions convey the anxieties, resolutions, and confusion of the little girl
faced with her first day at school. This passage proves to be a brief section
of internal monologue, an occasion on which focalization turns inward,
which, although not exactly rare in the text, is much less common than
externally focused narration.

     I should perhaps clarify that while the focalizer occupies a position
internal to the narrated events, her gaze is mostly turned outward upon
events external to herself, rather than toward the inner workings of her
psyche. In Rimmon-Kenan's terms, she is an internal focalizer with an external perspective. Immediately after this internal interlude, the narration
switches to a series of existential statements and presentatives as focalization is turned firmly back outward toward the world. We are told, for example, that the school is very big, that there are a lot of desks and that there
is a large stove (8). The school is described in terms of its physical dimen-
sions and the objects in it, but it is evident nonetheless that the center of
evaluation of the room is the little girl's, since an adult would hardly describe a one-room village school as big.

     The vocabulary of the text is colored by the use of children's terms
such as *grandes personnes, grande petite fille* (big little girl), *faire pipi*
(to pee), *quéquette* (peepee or penis). This demonstrates a close link between the focalizer, whose vision of the world is that of a small child, and
the narrator, who expresses herself like a child. There are, however, occasionally lapses into a more adult vocabulary, as when the narrator is describing a children's game and uses the more medical terminology *anus*
instead of *cul* (ass) and *vulve* (vulva) for *sexe* (55). These moments are
rare, for usually when a new concept or new vocabulary item is introduced
into the narrative, it is clear that the children have learned it from an adult,
and it functions almost as a citation—vocabulary half-digested for referents imperfectly understood.

For example, a group of children discovers totems in a picture book; the narrator explains that these are "yellow red blue beasts" which have been put together both end to end and one on top of another to make a whole (14). This is evidently a description Catherine Legrand has only half heard and half understood of Native American totem poles. Though she is trying to make the word *totem* her own; it is not entirely hers yet. The description of the different parts as "yellow red blue" suggests an impressionistic mixture of colors, while the structure of the totem pole, composed of beasts stuck both end to end and at the same time one on top of the other, implies an imperfect understanding of how the different pieces fit together. On another occasion, the children crawl on their stomachs under a barbed wire fence, mindful of the fact that this is dangerous since you can catch a fine (*un procès verbal*) (15). Whether they realize that a fine is not a new and irritating insect but a financial punishment is unclear, and one hears the voice of their parents or teachers behind the warning. The children will, in any case, not be called upon to pay the fine; this duty will inevitably fall to their parents. Also left intentionally vague is the question of whether the children are able to transform the indefinite *on* of their parents' probable injunction, which the reader reconstructs as something like "faut pas pénétrer les barbelés, les enfants, on peut attraper un procès-verbal" (it's wrong to go through the barbed wire fence, children, one can get a fine/ they fine people for that), to an *on* with a specific referent, that is, themselves. As has been noted, no personal deictics are used in the novel except in citation, so the whole question of indexicality and the children's comprehension of it is designed as a gray area.

The names used to designate the different characters are also "colored" (to use Rimmon-Kenan's term) by the perspective of a small child. Both the first name and the surname of each child are given systematically at each appearance of the referent, even when that referent may be assumed to be firmly anchored in the reader's mind. Thus the children are referred to throughout as *Robert Payen, Catherine Legrand, Valerie Borge, Vincent Parme*, and so on, as though the narrator were quoting the class register. It seems, again, as though the names are used in citation, quoting the nun who reads them out each morning in class. The names are often preceded by a descriptor, such as *le petit garçon qui s'appelle* . . . (the little boy named . . .), or *la grosse pettie fille qui s'appelle* . . . (the fat little girl named . . .), as though the connection between the names and the referents could not be taken for granted, but must be asserted at each mention. The adults are either referred to in terms of their relationship to one of the children (*la mère de Robert Payen* [Robert Payen's mother], *le père d'Alain Trévise* [Alain Trévise's father], or as they would be addressed as teachers in school (*Mademoiselle, ma soeur* [Sister], *ma mère de l'Enfant Jésus* [Mother of the Infant Jesus]).

Ma soeur refers to the nun in charge of Catherine Legrand's class, the possessive adjective *ma* being not a deictic reference, but part of her name;

the children have been taught to call the nun *ma soeur*, so *ma soeur* she is, regardless of whether she is addressed in the second person or referred to in the third. In similar fashion, *ma mère de . . . saint Jean-Baptiste, saint François d'Assise, saint Thomas d'Aquin . . .* , and so on, refer to the older, hierarchically superior nuns; the possessive *ma* is not deictic but a form of address that has become third person referent. In contrast, the narrator refers to Catherine Legrand's own sister not as *sa soeur* or *ma soeur*, as one might expect, but as *Véronique Legrand*, as we saw in example 5.8. This usage is systematic, occurring not just at the first or second mention of Catherine's sister, but throughout the novel. In a similar manner, when she first arrives at school, Catherine Legrand is described as holding "la main de la mère" (the mother by the hand) (7). The use of the definite article here, instead of the expected possessive adjective, is similar to its use in expressions such as "elle lève la main" (she raises the/her hand) and "elle ferme les yeux" (she closes the/her eyes). Catherine's uncle and aunt are always referred to as *mon oncle* and *ma tante*, a reference that is not deictic but citational since, like all French children, Catherine will have been taught to address her relatives in this way. One can hear Catherine's mother instructing her, "dis 'bonjour ma tante'" ("say 'hello aunty'"); thus, *ma tante* becomes a fixed designator.

The use of *on* is important not only in itself, but also for the dynamic it sets up between narration involving different kinds of pronouns. The clearest extended example of this movement may be seen in the scene introducing the new pupil, Suzanne Mériel. This scene is set with the usual series of existentials and external description: there is a new girl, she is very big, her hair is blonde, she has purplish-blue cheeks (49). This last descriptor is distinctly unkind, and Suzanne Mériel's fate is sealed in the following line, which establishes the relationship between the class as a group and the newcomer. She is described as the girl with hair like a mophead: *la fille à la tignasse*. This marks Suzanne as formally different from the others; she is not included in the undifferentiated *on*, but singled out as *elle*. The divide widens, and the situation turns into a free-for-all with Suzanne as the victim. She is seated on a bench apart; scabs are observed on her head; she is searched for lice; she is attacked with rulers; she is hit on the back. All these actions are narrated using the neutral *on*. Suzanne's reactions are then narrated using the third person feminine, *elle*, as she hunches her back and pulls her head down defensively between her shoulders; she makes no other move to defend herself. The contrast between the individual victim and the faceless attackers is rendered all the more poignant for this pronominal binary. The beating continues for another ten lines, gathering strength and becoming ritualistic, as can be seen from the description of its culmination: "On frappe en mesure, tout le monde à la fois, on crie" (one hits/we hit in time, everyone at once, one shouts/we shout) (50). All sense of individual responsibility is avoided by the use of *on*, which cannot be linked definitively to any one referent since the actions are synchronized and executed so that they form one act: the beating. *Elle* is not one of *on*, and so she is beaten.

If we look closely, we can see that in fact it was the teacher "Mademoiselle" who first established the distance between Suzanne and the others, for the *on* of "on la met toute seule à un banc" (she is put all alone on a bench) must be a person in authority. The children cannot decide for themselves where a classmate will sit. In this sentence, unlike the stream of first person plural uses which will follow it, *on* acts as a third person singular. The use of switch reference here is particularly interesting because it allows Mademoiselle to be assumed into the mass of bullying schoolchildren, without precisely stating that this has happened. Although we do not imagine that Mademoiselle participates in the beating, it is implied that she condones it, for there is no formal distinction between the *on* who sets Suzanne physically apart from the other children and the *on* who hit her with rulers. Nor can we tell the precise moments when Mademoiselle is acting alone, when she acts in unison with the children, and when the children act alone. Mademoiselle sets the unfortunate Suzanne apart on a bench, an act for which she alone is responsible. In the following sentence, describing how scabs are seen on Suzanne's head, both children and teacher are probably involved. By the next sentence, which narrates how the wretched little girl is searched for lice, Mademoiselle has probaby been eclipsed and is no longer included in *on*—although it was the practice of schoolteachers in the first part of the twentieth century to take liberties with their charges' bodies that we in an educational climate less tolerant of physical punishment would condemn.

At first sight, it might seem that the beating of Suzanne Meriel, recounted by the neutralizing pronoun "on," could either be focalized internally by Catherine or externally by an outside observer. Rimmon-Kenan (1983) has set out a series of criteria that may be used to show whether a narrative is focalized from within or from without, and whether we are dealing with a narrator-focalizer or with a narrator and a focalizer as two distinct entities. The traditional distinction between who speaks and who sees, or between the narrating self and the experiencing self, may collapse where there is minimal time and psychological distance between narrator and focalizer. According to Rimmon-Kenan, this typically happens with external focalization, that is, when the locus of perception is situated outside the represented events. Narrator and focalizer coincide as they experience and narrate events from either a retrospective or a panchronic vantage point. Their knowledge of events is unrestricted, their emotional attitude objective, and their ideological platform authoritative. Yet the two functions may also coincide at the other end of the scale, that is, where internal focalization results in imperfect knowledge of the events to unfold, a subjective attitude toward what is narrated, and a worldview clearly at odds with majority opinion. These three features (ignorance, subjectivity, and idiosyncrasy) may each be seen in the sewer episode discussed next.

The reason for Catherine Legand's fear of sewers is recorded by the narrator as self-evident truth: that is where they put dead people, and if you fall into one, you die.

5.13.   Tout le long de la route il faut se méfier des trous d'égout. On réfléchit
        qu'on ne veut pas passer tout près parce qu'on sait maintenant que c'est là
        qu'on met les gens qui sont morts et peut-être les enfants aussi. . . . On
        peut mourir avant c'est un fait et de toute façon c'est là qu'on va. (20)

        All along the road one has/you have to beware of the openings of the
        sewers. One reflects that one does not want to go too near because one
        knows now that that is where one puts/they put people who are dead and
        perhaps children too. . . . One/you can die before, that's a fact, and any-
        way that's where one goes/you go.

The superfactive verb *savoir* (to know) in "on sait maintenant" (one knows
now) presupposes the truth of the proposition it introduces; thus, the
gravelike nature of the sewer is presented as common knowledge of which
the narrator has only just become aware. This knowledge is, however, limited, since the narrator is unsure whether children are disposed of in the
same way. The modal expressions *il faut* (it is necessary) and *on ne veut
pas*, (one does not want to), the lexical modal *peut-être* (perhaps), and the
internally directed *on réfléchit* (one reflects) indicate the narrator's psychic
state: anxiety, doubt, and perplexity, despite the apparent confidence expressed in the use of *on sait* (one knows) and *c'est un fait* (it's a fact). The
clash between these elements conveys the narrator's mental state while
presenting the evil properties of sewers as well-known facts. The inherent
childishness in these fears marks the narrator as nonauthoritative, since her
worldview is clearly at odds with accepted wisdom.

   The questioning of beliefs first presented as uncontestable truth and
the modalization of propositions introduced as simple fact are common
features of interior monologue, where a character may muse on details recounted by the narrator. This technique usually sets up a clear distinction
between the two centers of consciousness, that of the character and that of
the narrator. Yet in *L'Opoponax*, because of the almost complete overlap
between the narrator, the character Catherine Legrand, and the focalizer,
it appears to be the narrator herself who is musing on the facts she has just
related, or indeed quoting facts told her by others, then considering their
validity for herself.

Speech, Deixis, Episode, and Tense

The overlap between these three usually separate entities (narrator, character, and focalizer) is created not only by the prioritizing of the epicene
pronoun *on*, but also from four other marked features of the text that combine to blur the traditional distinctions created by reported speech, deictic
reference, episode boundaries, and tense switching. Since each of these features will be discussed further in the following paragraphs, I will merely
outline them here. *L'Opoponax* is a novel of 281 pages, divided into seven
sections of approximately fifty pages each. Although each new section starts
on a new page, with the text set five lines from the top in a fairly traditional

page format, there are no paragraph indentations or other episode markers of any kind internal to each section. The text runs continually for fifty pages, one sentence separated from another by a full stop only, with scant use of commas.

Personal deictics such as *je*, *tu*, *mon*, and *ta* (I, you, my$_m$ and your$_f$) appear only in passages of reported speech. Although the forms themselves do appear quite frequently outside of speech, they are not deictic in this environment, as has been seen above in reference to the use of *ma soeur*, *ma mère*, and *ma tante*. Since no formal indicators, such as indentation or quotation marks (either the guillemets [<< >>] or the *tiret* (———]), are employed to mark off reported speech from the rest of the text, in the absence of *verba dicendi* one must rely on contextual clues to distinguish speech, interior monologue, reported speech, and thought from narration. (The guillemets traditionally mark off text as reported speech when situated within a passage of description or narration. The tiret is used to indicate that everything that follows is reported speech.)

´ The main tense of the novel is the present, with some use of the *passé composé* to relate events that immediately precede the main action and express anterior aspect and of the *futur*, *futur immédiat*, and *conditionnel* to relate imagined, anticipated, and contrary-to-fact events. These other tenses are used so rarely, however, that two critics have stated confidently that the whole novel is narrated in the present tense (Ostrovsky 1991, 23–26; Went-Daoust 1991, 358)—a fact I will comment on at greater length. The present, being unmarked, may have a minus interpretation, a plus intepretation, or indeed a zero interpretation with regard to past time. It can refer to the present ("j'**entends** un rossignol" [I **hear** a nightingale]), the past ("**hier** j'**étais** dans mon bureau et tout d'un coup un gars me **demande** une clope" [**yesterday** I **was** in my office when suddenly this guy **asks** for a cigarette]), the future ("j'y **vais** demain" [I'**m going** there tomorrow]), an unspecified moment or habit ("elle **va** à une crèche" [she **goes** to kindergarten]), or gnomic (eternal) truths ("les kangarous **sont** des mammifères" [kangaroos **are** mammals]). Temporal reference, like episode breaks and speech allocation, is left deliberately vague in *L'Opoponax*, obliging the reader to play a more than usually active part in creating narrative coherence.

Speech and Deixis

Deictics, both personal and temporal, usually play a large part in distinguishing narrative from reported speech, a distinction of great importance in assessing whether a given passage represents the internal monologue of a character or the assertions of the narrator. In order to discuss the use of citation in *L'Opoponax*, it is useful to look at some examples. In some cases, reported speech is formally distinguished from narrative by the use of a *verbum dicendi*. Contrary to the usual custom, however, the phrase is much more frequently postposed than preposed. In this way, an utterance can be allocated to a speaker after the speech has been recorded, rather than used as an introduction to speech. The effect of this postposition is similar to the use of cataphora instead of anaphora, where a pronoun is introduced first and only later resumed in a full noun phrase. Readers are obliged to invest a certain amount of energy in working out whom the pronoun refers to; thus, the referent, when eventually clarified, will stand out in their minds more than one introduced first by a proper name or definite descriptor. In a similar fashion, the effort expended in attributing direct speech to the correct character invests that speech with greater importance.

In the following passage, only one introduction to speech is used, immediately after the first sentence of direct speech, and it is left to the reader to work out where the conversation begins and ends, how many turns it takes, and who the participants are.

5.14.   Tu l'aimes toi ta mère? La petite fille qui s'appelle Josiane Fourmont **dit** ça. J'aime ma mère, oui j'aime ma mère. Tu l'aimes comment? Comme ça. (23)

Do you love your mother? The little girl called Josiane Fourmont **says** this. I love my mother, yes I love my mother. How much do you love her? Like this.

In this example, the first sentence is formally attributed to Josiane Fourmont by the phrase "Josiane Fourmont dit ça," indicating that it is direct speech. In the seven turns that follow, however, the *verba dicendi* must be understood. The personal deictics *tu*, *toi*, *ta* and *je*, *ma* indicate that whoever was addressed as *tu* replies with suitably altered pronouns. Thus the eight turns of the conversation relate to each other in a tightly cohesive fashion, but not to the surrounding text, since the referent for Josiane's *tu* is not formally indicated. The reader assumes that the addressee is Catherine Legrand, but this is because she has been established as the focalizer and therefore the default deictic center.

Similarly, in the middle of an episode describing how Valerie Borge's attention is claimed by the other girls, leaving her indifferent to Catherine Legrand, a long passage of what appears to be direct speech suddenly intervenes. Since this incident occurs toward the end of the novel, the reader has become used to interpreting the use of personal deictics as indicators of the speech of the characters. It does not become clear until the end of the passage, however, who the referents of *je* and *vous* are. *Vous* (which functions both as a formal second-person singular pronoun and as a second person plural) is especially puzzling since the schoolchildren address each other, and are addressed by adults, as *tu*. It therefore initially appears to be a second person plural, addressed to a group of referents rather than singling out one. The passage is not introduced by any *verbum dicendi*; instead, its narrative status is explained only after its presentation.

5.15.   On voit en se retournant . . . qu'Anne-Marie Brunet a lâché la main de Valerie Borge. . . . **Je suis** *L'Opoponax*. Il ne faut pas le contrarier tout le temps comme **vous faites**. [The passage continues thus for six more sentences]. **Vous** lui **écrirez et vous pourrez** mettre la lettre derrière le piano. . . . **Je suis** *L'Opoponax*. Valerie Borge tourne dans tous les sens le papier qu'elle vient de trouver. (230)

Turning round one/she sees/I see that Anne-Marie Brunet has dropped Valerie Borge's hand. . . . **I am** the opoponax. You should not vex it/him/her all the time like **you do**. . . . **You will write** to it/him/her and **you can** put the letter behind the piano. . . . **I am** the opoponax. Valerie Borge turns the paper she has just found over and over in her hand.

The reader learns at the end of this passage that it is not direct speech as such, but rather a note addressed to Valerie Borge, the writer of which must be Catherine Legrand, since she has been commenting on the number of Valerie's admirers and is the only character who has been *contrariée* (vexed). In the note, Catherine addresses Valerie in the formal *vous* form to underline the importance and solemnity of her message. She takes on the persona of the mysterious opoponax, who assumes no schoolgirl intimacy with Valerie. Even here, however, Catherine alternates between first and third person reference with regard to the opoponax, declaring "je suis l'opoponax," but switching to the third person immediately afterwards: "Il ne faut pas le contrarier."

Although there is always some indication that direct speech has taken over from ordinary narration (otherwise we would be unable to make this distinction), these signs may amount to no more than the polyphonic effect of two voices speaking at once. In a section describing a nature walk the schoolchildren take in the local forest, the voice of the teacher explaining features of geographical interest mixes with that of the seven-year-old narrator and becomes incorporated into her speech (see Ducrot 1984). The narrator reports, for example:

5.16.   Les parties herbues alternent avec de larges sentiers de terre battue argileuse qui se craquelle quand il fait chaud selon des réseaux compliqués, des losanges élargis tendant à la circonférence et tangents les uns aux autres. Quelquefois ça fait comme des brèches on peut presque apercevoir le feu qu'il y a à l'intérieur de la terre. (67)

The grassy parts alternate with wide footpaths of well-trodden clayey earth which cracks when it's hot according to complicated networks, diamond-shaped patches widen out and stretch toward the circumference and tangents of other patches. Sometimes it makes a kind of gap one/we can almost see the fire that's inside the earth.

The vocabulary of the first sentence—*herbues, argileuse, circonférence, tangents*—is that of an adult, and a learned adult at that. The knowledge it expresses, of the kind of soil upon which they are walking and the patterns formed by cracked earth, is far beyond the common stock of information young children usually possess. This erudition comes in stark contrast to the belief expressed in the following sentence that if the gaps were wide enough you could see the fire in the middle of the earth. It is the contrast between the two, in terms of vocabulary, knowledge, and world-view, that gives away the presence of the teacher's voice coming out of the child's mouth. A moment's reflection will show that this kind of parroting is very common among children. Textually, it serves to limit the perspective to that of Catherine Legrand, who can thus quote the lesson she is learning from her teacher without being obliged to give up the floor.

Episode Boundaries

In other cases, the appearance of personal deictics marks the beginning of a new episode boundary. For a novel that eschews the traditional paragraph breaks, such indications are of enormous importance. During an account of a game of tennis, the reader suddenly encounters the first person deictic *je*, in a sentence that sounds at once too poetic and too megalomaniacal to be attributed to the little girls playing.

5.17.   Noémie Mazat . . . se met en extension pour frapper la balle . . . ni Suzanne
        Prat ni Nathalie Deleu ne peuvent contrer. . . . Je suis maître de moi comme
        de l'univers je le suis, je veux l'être. (221)

        Noémie Mazat . . . stretches out to hit the ball . . . neither Suzanne Prat
        nor Nathalie Deleu can hit it back. . . . I am master of myself as of the uni-
        verse I am, I want to be.

The last sentence could represent the thought of the triumphant Noémie, but this would suggest a focalizer separate from Catherine Legrand, one who is able to enter the minds of the other characters. Since it has been clearly established that focalization is through Catherine, who mostly focuses on the external world around her, with very occasional glimpses into her own mind, but never into that of anyone else, readers, who are trained to interpret deictics as indicating direct speech, will assume that this odd ending to the game is a quotation, as in the example concerning the opoponax discussed in the preceding section. Subsequent sentences prove this assumption right, for the next character referred to is a Madame Doullier, and after a brief description of her attempts to gain the students' attention, the reader is told that we are in a French class. Although the narrator never explicitly states this, the reader assumes that "je suis maître de moi" is a quotation from the literature the girls are studying in this class, though it is not attributed to any particular author.[3]

In their work on episode boundaries (discussed briefly in chapter 2), Teun van Dijk and Walter Kintsch (1983) list seven markers of topic change:

1. Change of possible worlds: X dreamt . . .
2. Change of time or period: The next day . . .
3. Change of place

4. Introduction of new participants
5. Full noun phrase reintroduction of old participants
6. Change of perspective or point of view
7. Different predicate range (change of frame or script) (204)

Only four of these devices are used in *L'Opoponax* to mark a change of episode: change of place, introduction of new participants, full noun-phrase reintroduction of old participants, and different predicate range. Some examples may help elucidate:

Change of Place: Véronique Legrand est encore occupée à broyer de la brique. [episode boundary] Dans la buanderie les bacs sont gris. (52)

Véronique Legrand is still busy scraping brick. [EB] In the laundry the basins are gray.

Introduction of New Participants: Mademoiselle dit que l'encre c'est du poison. [episode boundary] Monique Respiaud vient chercher les élèves les unes après les autres. (55)

Mademoiselle says that ink is poison. [EB] Monique Respiaud comes and gets the pupils one after the other.

Change of Predicate: On s'appuie sur le papier pour former des lettres. On fait même des trous. [episode boundary]. On joue au bateau. (26)

One leans /we lean on the paper to form the letters. One even makes/we even make holes. [EB] One plays/we play boats.

These three devices are the most frequently used markers of a new episode and cause few problems in recognition for the reader. The reintroduction of old participants with a full noun phrase may, however, fail to be recognized as a signal of a new episode, since, as we have already elaborated, the children are systematically referred to by their full names, which are pronominalized only by the all-encompassing *on*. Two mentions of the same name frequently occur in the same sentence and are therefore unlikely to signal an episode boundary, as may be seen in the following:

5.18. Véronique Legrand et Catherine Legrand ont les couteaux ouverts dans les paumes des mains, Véronique Legrand le tient ouvert dans la main gauche. (114)

Véronique Legrand and Catherine Legrand have their knives open in the palms of their hands, Véronique Legrand holds hers open in her left hand.

There are no changes of point of view or of possible world to signal an episode break, since the angle of focalization and therefore the worldview remain the same throughout. As for change of time or period, there are extremely few indications of time in the novel, a fact related to the use of the present as the main tense for narration. Catherine is not given to looking ahead to the future nor to ruminating on the past, and those passages that do feature tense switching are not placed at episode boundaries but are first anchored by present-tense predicates, as we will see.

Given this rather restricted set of devices for formally marking changes of episode, it is not suprising that Wittig relies on the reader's real-world knowledge to show both the passage of time and a change of frame. At the beginning of the novel, Catherine is taken to school for the first time, and one imagines her to be about four; by the end, her best friend Valerie has grown breasts and is therefore probably eleven or twelve. These events represent a time lapse of eight or nine years. The chapters of the novel (unnumbered and untitled) are sequenced according to what subject the children are learning at school and who dies in that period. In chapter 1, the children learn to count and Robert Payen dies; in chapter 2, they learn to read and write and Marie-José Venant dies; in chapter 3, they learn the history of Charlemagne and Anne-Marie Losserand's little brother dies; in chapter 4, they learn the Latin gerundive and *mon oncle* Fromentin dies; in chapter 5, they learn Old French and one of the nuns dies; in chapter 6, they learn classical French poetry and the bishop dies; in chapter 7, they read and act the *Odyssey* and one of their lay teachers dies. This dating by school curriculum is something of a wry French joke (sequencing by funeral has a graveyard humor to it too), given the many complaints about the rigid uniformity and centralization of the French education system (a proud bequest of Napoleon).

What Wittig has done is provide external and objective criteria by which the reader may assess the children's age in each chapter—a task made easier for the French reader since popular legend insists that at any hour of any school day the minister of Education in Paris knows what any child at any level is learning in any *département* of France. Apart from these broad guidelines, however, readers must rely on their ability to interpret focalization to determine episode boundaries, since so many of the formal cues are either absent or potentially ambiguous.

Tense

Although the principal tense for narration is the present, in keeping with a story that is seen and told at the same moment, other tenses do occur throughout the text for specific purposes. The only past tense used is the *passé composé*, which relates events and actions immediately preceding the moment of telling and whose consequences have a direct effect on the present. The *passé composé* used in this novel could equally well be defined as an aspectual marker, indicating anteriority, rather than a tense marker. When the children attend the funeral of the bishop, they are given hot coffee to drink to keep them warm and improve their voices.

5.19.   On **a bu** du café debout dans le réfectoire on **a posé** les tasses sur les tables
        blanches. On **entend** le métal des cuillers. (204)

        One **has/we have drunk** coffee standing up in the refectory **one has/we
        have put** the cups down on the white tables. One **hears/we hear** the metal
        of the spoons.

This scene is described immediately after the drinking of the coffee, while
the children still hold the teaspoons in their hands, so the consequence of
this past action is considered from the point of view of the present. The
effect of immediacy is enhanced by the fact that there are never more than
two past-tense predicates before narration returns to the present tense, as
in the case above. Thus, even tense switches are drawn into the service of
focalization: a switch into the past indicates backgrounded information,
while the present tense narrates in the foreground.

   This use of the *passé composé*, composed of the auxiliary *avoir* and a past
participle, is very similar, in both structure and function, to occurrences of
être in the present tense with a past participle used adjectivally. Technically,
the former (involving *avoir*) is a past tense, whereas the latter (involving *être*)
is a present tense, but as we will see, they can function in strikingly similar
ways. The narration of the coffee drinking functions like description, as can
be seen from its formal similarity to phrases like that in example 5.20 below.

5.20.   On **est arrêté** à la hauteur d'une des chapelles. (206)

        One **is/we are stopped** at the level of one of the chapels.

This occurs in the episode concerning the bishop's funeral. The adjective
describes a state that has been achieved by an immediately preceding action and shows vestiges of that action, as may be seen in the adjective *arrêté*,
the result of the action of stopping. In a similar vein, the children are still
warm from the coffee they have just drunk.

   Elsewhere, the *passé composé* is used in the manner of a sports commen-
tator, to give one the impression of a blow-by-blow account of an event as
it happens.

5.21.   Denise Joubert **a presque dépassé** la limite du champs. Elle dépasse la limite
        du champs. (32)

        Denise Joubert **has nearly crossed** the boundary of the field. She crosses
        the boundary of the field.

Again, sandwiched between predicates in the present tense, the *passé composé*
functions more to highlight the action in the present—the crossing of the
boundary of the field—than to arrange events along a time line.

   The future is used most often to relate events foretold by someone with
greater authority than the narrator, usually the nuns.

5.22.   Quand on **sera** grand on **pourra** lire sans la règle. (23)

When one **is**/we **are** big, one/we **will be able** to read without the ruler.

The narrator reports using the future as a marker of *irrealis*—it is hard for a child who is still having difficulty making out letters on a blackboard to imagine a future where she will read without needing to line up the letters along a ruler. The future frequently represents an unreal, hazy time that is not of the present, as may be seen by the use of this tense to predict the coming of the opoponax, an entity Catherine has invented to claim Valerie's attention.

5.23.   C'est à l'aube qu'on **verra** assise sur l'appui d'une fenêtre la forme de *l'opoponax*. (240)

At dawn one/we **will see** the form of the opoponax sitting on a windowsill.

The future tense serves as a modalizing device, indicating the narrator's desire to believe in the events she recounts, though she is unable to tie them concretely to the present.

From this analysis of the interplay of pronouns, tense, deictics, reported speech, and episode boundaries, it is clear that each of these textual elements works to reinforce the sense that Catherine Legrand is not only the focalizer of the novel, but also the narrator. It is this unusual coincidence, internal to the story, that gives readers the impression that the individual, at times idiosyncratic point of view of the little girl has become a universal perspective. It is impossible to judge the success of the epicene *on* without also examining the other features that create its meaning in the text; to do otherwise is to mislead the reader and misread the novel. Readers such as the two French writers quoted at the beginning of this chapter (Marguerite Duras and Claude Lorrain) observe that the individual point of view of one young schoolgirl appears to become a universal, even generic perspective. This effect is caused in large part by the fact that, due to restricted focalization, reinforced by a blurring of episode boundaries, temporal distinctions, personal deictics, and the difference between narration and quotation, readers can only see the world through one perspective, and in order to follow the text, it must become their own.

The extraordinary effects of *L'Opoponax*—its immediacy and sense of immersing the reader in the events described—are usually imputed to the use of *on*. However, the use of *on* is merely the most attention-grabbing aspect of the novel. As we have seen from our examination of other texts in earlier chapters, meddling with pronouns tends to have a big impact on both the reader and the text. But these effects do not stop at the pronouns, nor are they produced exclusively by them. It is not hip in these days of high postmodernism to quote structural clichés with anything but ironic intent. Hipness notwithstanding, it is a fact that language is a system in which "tout se tient" (everything holds together). Change one part of the system and you change the system.

It is not coincidental that in each of the literary works discussed here—
L'Opoponax, Les Guérillères and *Le Corps lesbien*—Wittig's most obvious
innovation involves pronominal choice. Neatly ordered and easily defined
semantic systems such as the kinship system, color terminology, and pronominal forms were an obvious starting point for linguists aiming to extend the discoveries of phonological structuralism into the fields of syntax
and semantics. Experiments conducted to prove or disprove the Sapir-Whorf
hypothesis have also centered round such ordered systems as color terminology and perceptions of color by speakers of different languages (see Berlin
and Kay 1969, Kay and McDaniel 1978, Kay and Kempton 1983). In the
same way, Wittig has taken the pronominal paradigm as a template for her
exposition of the oppressive nature of language.

Elles *in* Les Guérillères

Before I conclude this chapter on Monique Wittig's use of pronouns, it will
be useful to look briefly at the pronouns that feature in her subsequent novels, *elles* in *Les Guérillères* and *j/e* in *Le Corps lesbien*. Although interesting
in their own right, neither has the same far-reaching effect on almost every
level of the text as *on*. This is not simply because *on* neutralizes the traditional opposition between masculine and feminine in the third person, but
because it gives no indication of number or person either. As was demonstrated in chapters 2 and 3, empathy, or "the speaker's identification . . . with
a person who participates in the event that he describes," according to Kuno
and Kaburaki's definition (1977, 628), is a key element in focalization. The
discussion of *Sphinx* made it clear that empathy for A***, a third person
character whose gender is never formally given, is highly influenced by the
impossibility of using pronominal reference to designate him/her. In
L'Opoponax, in which the most commonly used pronoun is also epicene (and
has been chosen for that very reason), empathy is likewise affected, only to
opposite effect. Instead of losing empathy with Catherine Legrand, as happens
with A***, the narrator empathizes with her to the point of coincidence. The
reader cannot but see the world through Catherine's eyes. Although there is
a complex interplay between the different uses of the gendered pronouns
il/s and *elle/s* in *Les Guérillères*, and some questions as to the exact value of
the '/' in the j/e of *Le Corps lesbien*, these features only marginally affect
reader or narrator empathy.

It is the feminine plural pronoun *elles* that carries the story of *Les
Guérillères*. Wittig intends it to convey a universal point of view, as *ils* (mas-
culine plural) is commonly said to do and as *on* is so successful in doing in
L'Opoponax.

> Il y a universalisation du point de vue à partir du pronom "elles" comme
> on a coutume de le faire à partir du pronom "ils." C'est une démarche qui
> a pour but de rendre caduque les catégories de sexe dans la langue. (Wittig
> 1985b, 10)

There is a universalization of point of view from the pronoun *elles* as is customary with the pronoun *ils*. This move aims to make the categories of sex redundant in language.

In order to establish the point of view of *elles* as that of the "sovereign subject," Wittig eliminates *il* and *ils* from the first two parts of the book. When the masculine pronouns emerge toward the end, the reader has become so used to seeing *elles* as universal that it is *il* and *ils* whose perspective seems marginal. This, at least, is Wittig's intention. The war waged by *elles* (the *guérillères*, or soldiers, of the title) on *ils* (they_m)—or, more grammatically, on *eux* (them_m)—is a linguistic war, not a war between men and women but a war between pronouns, a battle for "absolute subjecthood," in Wittig's terms. "The goal of this approach is not to feminize the world, but to make the categories of gender obsolete in language," she writes (1986, 70). Toward the end of the work, a lone *il* comes to join *elles*, who rejoice and praise the young man for joining them.

5.24.   Elles apprennent au jeune homme qu'il est le premier à les avoir rejointes. (203)

They_f inform the young man that he is the first to have joined them.

The masculine singular *il* is now included in the pronoun *elles*, as we see at the end of the sentence where "il" (he) is described as the first (premier_m) to have joined (rejointes_f) them, a reversal of the grammatical requirement that where there are both masculine and feminine referents, the masculine plural *ils* should be used.[4]

Although it appears on elementary grammar tables as simply the feminine equivalent of *ils*, *elles* is far less frequently used in French, not only because *ils* covers the masculine plural, the generic, and a combination of male and female antecedents, but also because descriptions of all-female groups are less common than descriptions of all-male or mixed groups. As the psychoanalyst Luce Irigaray has pointed out:

Jusqu'à présent, il est nécessaire que les femmes restent exclusivement entr'elles pour qu'un pluriel soit féminin: elles s'aiment, elles sont belles, etc. (1990, 459)

Up till and including the present it has been necessary for women to remain exclusively in each other's company for a plural to be feminine: they_f love themselves/each other, they_f are beautiful_fpl, etc.

Irigaray here emphasizes not only grammatical but also cultural independence.

Wittig habitually uses *elles* (and, less often, *elle*) without any nominal antecedent and with no subsequent clarification of the referent. The pronouns are thus neither anaphor nor cataphor, but take their meaning from the verbal predicates ascribed to them. *Les Guérillères* opens with the statement

"Quand il pleut elles se tiennent dans le kiosque" (when it rains they$_f$ stay in the kiosk) (9); the reader expects *elles* to be defined later when linked to a proper name or lexical noun phrase, but no such designator appears in the text. *Elles* are simply the ones (female) who remain in the kiosk. At the next appearance of this pronoun, therefore, it is impossible to state definitely whether it refers to the same group. Are the *elles* in "elles se font peur en se cachant derrière les arbres" (they$_f$ frighten each other by hiding behind the trees) (9) the same *elles* who shelter in the kiosk? The question goes unanswered save in the English translation, in which *elles* is translated as *the women*, providing a definite referent and thereby losing the generic sense of *elles*.[5]

The same strategy is used in *Le Corps lesbien* and provides a strong intertextual link to the earlier work. The first appearance of *elles* in this text appears to be a traditional generic, with the sense of "people in general," except that it is feminine in form instead of masculine: "ce qu'elles nomment l'affection" (what they$_f$ call affection) (7). However, *elles* reappears almost immediately with what seems to be more specific reference. Explaining that there is no name for what is happening, the narrator declares that "pas une ne l'ignore" (not one$_f$ is ignorant of this fact) (7). This suggests that the first use of *elles* is not generic, since it is made up of quantifiable parts (*une*). When the narrator then turns to a subjunctive apostrophe, "qu'elles le cherchent si elles y tiennent absolument, qu'elles se livrent à de belles rivalités" (let them$_f$ look for it if they$_f$ absolutely insist, let them indulge in battles of fine rivalry) (7), it becomes clear that *elles* must have a definite referent. As in *Les Guérillères*, however, this referent is never formally specified.

Another tactic Wittig employs in both *Les Guérillères* and *Le Corps lesbien* to ensure that the feminine plural comes to take the place of the masculine in expressing a universal voice is to highlight the use of *elles* by placing adverbial phrases between the pronoun and the verb it commands. In *Les Guérillères*, one finds such phrases as

5.25.   Elles alors applaudissent. (152)

Они They$_f$ then applaud.

Elles, à ces paroles, se mettent à danser. (73)

They$_f$, at these words, begin to dance.

Eles alors pressent Sophie Ménade de questions. (73)

They$_f$ then ply Sophie Ménade with questions.

In *Le Corps lesbien*, this tactic is used with even greater frequency, and the amount of intervening matter is increased.

5.26.   Elle en silence se tient. (138)

She in silence stands.

Elles portant des torches s'agenouillent. (103)

They$_f$ carrying torches sit down.

Elles en t'apportant un rince-doigts et des fruits glacés t'apprennent. (118)

They$_f$ bringing you a finger bowl and some glazed fruit inform you.

Subject pronouns in modern French are considered to be clitics, or bound morphemes, because they are unable to stand alone and will tolerate only a very restricted range of items, such as the negative particle *ne* and the direct object pronouns (*me*, *te*, *le*, etc,), between them and the verb they command. Indeed, Martin Harris labels the pronoun + verb unit a "polymorphemic word" composed of subject-prefix + stem (M. Harris 1988, 232; see also M. Harris 1978, 111–26, for an overview of the historical development of the cliticization of pronouns in French). It is thus all the more striking to observe the amount of material Wittig places between pronoun and verb. While the position of the adverb *alors* in "elles alors applaudissent" might pass unnoticed, in the last two examples given a whole participial phrase is set between pronoun and verb. The second of these, with its dual objects *rince-doigts* (composed of verb + noun) and *fruits glacés* (noun + adjective), themselves reasonably complex in structure, is so flagrant a breach of the traditional rules that it provokes laughter.

It might seem at first that if one wished to create an unmarked feminine which could replace the masculine in its generic use, the feminine should simply be slipped in and used generically, without calling any particular attention to this inversion of the usual gender hierarchy. Such a tactic might, however, be misinterpreted. As Wittig has been at pains to point out, she intended not a simple tit-for-tat in which masculine pronouns are overthrown and feminine pronouns set in their place, but to make the categories of sex redundant. If either the masculine or the feminine can have a generic meaning, neither one presides. In the examples in 5.25, where the normally bound pronoun is placed farther and farther from the verb, its gender becomes increasingly salient.

A similar effect is achieved through Wittig's use of masculine pronouns. In *Les Guérillères*, although the masculine *il/s* is witheld until three-quarters of the way through in reference to human subjects, the forms *il* and *ils* both appear frequently in reference to inanimate and nonhuman referents. I will give but a selection. In the following examples, *ils* in "ils ressemblent à de gros poulets" (they$_m$ look like big fat chickens) refers to *les crapauds* (the toads) (44); in "ils leur semblent démodés" (they$_m$ seem old-fashioned to them), to *les vieux textes* (the old texts) (68); and in "ils se blessent les yeux, le museau, ils s'arrachent les poils dans le cou" (they$_m$ wound each other's eyes and muzzle, they$_m$ tear out the hair in each other's neck), to *trois chats* (three cats) (47). In this way, the reader becomes accustomed to seeing masculine pronouns, both singular and plural, but in reference to nonhumans only. The masculine pronouns contrast markedly with the feminine pronouns, since the latter overwhelmingly refer to human beings. As we have seen from Comrie's work in chapter 2 on language universals, because of the hierarchy of animacy, it is much less common for items lower down the scale, including animals and objects, to be pronominalized. Wittig is clearly subverting the traditional order.

Wittig combines this tactic of lowering the animacy status of the masculine pronoun with an usually high frequency of expressions involving *il* as a dummy morpheme, or place marker.[6] According to Grévisse (1970), this neutral *il* is a

> procédé de style qui permet de donner plus de valeur à l'action exprimée par le verbe, en diminuant d'autant l'importance du sujet ou même en l'éludant tout à fait. (557, §606)

> stylistic device that allows one to place more emphasis on the action conveyed by the verb, thereby lessening the importance of the subject or even avoiding it altogether.

Nonreferential *il*, which has the same form as the masculine singular pronoun, eclipses the subject, focusing the reader's or hearer's attention on the predicate instead. Its attraction for a novelist intent on derailing the generic masculine is evident, for readers who come across the form will become used to interpreting it as an empty place marker. Nonreferential *il* is found throughout the text in expressions pertaining to such areas as:

Meteorological Expressions: il pleut (it's raining)

Existentials: *il en existe* (there exists); *il se crée* (it is created); *il s'y forme* (it forms); *il s'y tient* [*des génisses*], (there are [heifers]); *il en trouve* (there are); *il ne reste que* (there remain only); *il tient lieu de* (it takes the place of)

Presentatives: *il s'agit de* (it is about); *il comprend* (des pages), (it includes [some pages]); *il arrive que* (it happens that); *il ne se passe pas* [*de moments*], ([certain moments] do not take place); *il est écrit que* (it is written that); *il est question de* (it is about); *il en a été ainsi* (it has been like that); *il provient* (it results)

Epistemic Modals: *il n'est pas possible* (it is not possible); *il se peut que* (it could be that); *il faut* (it is necessary); *il semble* (it seems); *il est nécessaire de* (it is necessary to)

Discourse Expressions: *il est parlé* (it is spoken); *il est dit que* (it is said that); *il est répondu que* (it is replied that); *il ne sort pas* [*une phrase logique*] ([no logical phrase] comes out)

Expressions of Difficulty and Utility: *il est difficile de* (it is difficult to); *il est inutile de* (it is useless to); *il est aisé de* (it is easy to)

Most of these expressions are relatively common, though some, such as *il est parlé*, are marked as a literary register. What is unusual in *Les Guérillères* is the overall frequency of such devices. The absence of men from the first three-quarters of the novel allows the women's perspective to become the dominant one. It is, however, the combination of the absence of human masculine referents and the frequency of inanimate, nonhuman, and non-referential uses of the masculine pronouns that causes the masculine to be deprived of its usual universalizing perspective.

J/e *in* Le Corps lesbien

Having explored the possibilities of the epicene third-person *on* and the feminine plural *elles*—the former neutralizing the sexual distinction, the latter championing the feminine—in *Le Corps lesbien* Wittig turns her attention to the first person singular, *je*, written *j/e*, a neologism she has created. The slash between the first letter of the first person pronoun and the second is repeated throughout the paradigm: *me* is spelled *m/e*, *ma*, *m/a*; *mon*, *m/on*; and *moi*, *m/oi*. The exact meaning of the slash is unclear, or rather, it is polysemic. In the author's note to the English translation of 1975, Wittig states that *je*, as a feminine subject, is obliged to force her way into language since what is human is, grammatically, masculine, as *elle* and *elles* are subsumed under *il* and *ils*. The female *je* who writes must use a language fundamentally alien to her. Wittig explains that the slash in *j/e* is intended as a graphic representation of the problematic status of the feminine as subject: "J/e is the symbol of the lived, rending experience which is m/y writing" (English in the original) (1975, 11). The slash is a visual reminder of women's alienation from, by and within language.

Ten years later, however, in her discussion of grammatical gender, Wittig claims "the bar in the *j/e* of the *Lesbian Body* is a sign of excess. A sign that helps to imagine an excess of 'I,' an 'I' exalted" (English in the original) (1986, 71). This new explanation suggests that, far from signaling the difficulty for women of taking up the subject position in a linguistic structure in which the masculine is both the unmarked and the universal term, the slash in *j/e* has the positive value of an exuberance so powerful it is "like a lava flow that nothing can stop" (1986, 71). Within ten years, *j/e* has evolved from a mark of alienation to a mark of exuberance. Dare one suggest that its creation succeeded, Whorf-like, in changing the societal perception of woman from victim to victor? Or is the change in meaning merely reflective of an ideological development from the 1970s to the 1980s? The answer seems to be that Wittig had, by 1986, forgotten her argument of eleven years before and had since been influenced by comtemporary feminist arguments against seeing women purely as victims of an oppressive patriarchal system. Nevertheless, the neologistic pronoun *j/e* may be celebrated for its protean powers and the question it poses to each new reader.

In this chapter on *on*, *elles*, and *j/e* in the work of Monique Wittig, I have shown that the main elements disturbed by the use of a marked pronoun set are textual cohesion, focalization, and narrator empathy. In turning to an analysis of Anglophone texts, we will see how far these effects are language dependent and whether they may be shared with another language. In the next chapter, I examine a corpus of novels written in English featuring epicene neologisms in place of the traditionally gendered third person pronouns *he* and *she*.

6

"Na sat astride Three, na hands on nan throat"

Epicene Neologisms in English

"I utterly refuse to mangle English by inventing a pronoun for "he/ she." "He" is the generic pronoun, damn it."

Ursula K. Le Guin, "Is Gender Necessary?" 1979

"I dislike the so-called generic pronouns he/him/his which exclude women from discourse . . . they/them/their/ should be restored . . . and let the pedants and pundits squeak and gibber in the streets."

Ursula K. Le Guin, "Is Gender Necessary? Redux," 1987

As we have seen, the question of pronouns has been a recurring theme for feminist novelists working in both English and French (as well as a number of other languages). In chapters 2 and 3, I looked at novels that avoid pronominal reference, creating genderless characters whose sex is not revealed by the usual grammatical means. In chapter 4, I examined the lexical innovations Monique Wittig employs in three of her novels to subvert the gender binary, while in chapter 5, I investigated her use of epicene *on* and the effects this has on the surrounding text. From this investigation, a cultural division emerges among the different novelists and the methods they have chosen to expose or replace the masculine bias. While the British novelists discussed in chapter 3—Brigid Brophy, Maureen Duffy, Sarah Caudwell, and Jeanette Winterson—pick the solution adopted by Anne Garréta, that of avoiding pronominal reference, the American novelists discussed in this chapter—Ursula K. Le Guin, Dorothy Bryant, June Arnold, and Marge Piercy[1]—have invented their own pronouns or used the traditional pronominal paradigm in unusual ways, in the manner of Monique Wittig.

Science fiction, especially feminist science fiction, lends itself well to experimentation. It is not surprising that three of the American texts studied in this chapter on invented pronouns are science fiction novels. Le Guin and Piercy are two of the best known and most widely read feminist science fiction authors. The origin of science fiction as a genre has been traced to the work of another woman author, Mary Shelley's *Frankenstein, or the Modern Prometheus*, published in 1818 (Aldiss and Wingrove 1986); some authors have argued, however, that it had its roots even earlier in the eighteenth-century gothic (Lefanu 1988, 2–3). Interestingly, many of the characteristic traits of mystery novels may be traced back to the same origins—see, for example, Edgar Allen Poe's gothic mysteries such as *The Murders in the Rue Morgue* or Sir Arthur Conan Doyle's *The Hound of the Baskervilles*. Although we now think of science and detective fiction as very different genres, with their own conventions, the fiction of the telescope, fixed on the vast expanse of space, and the fiction of the magnifying glass, fixed on minute traces left in the drawing room, do have points in common. Where science fiction turns to other planets and imagines what life must be like on them, mysteries put the routine of daily life into sharp focus. Feminist science fiction mostly avoids the hard sciences of physics and astronomy for the soft sciences of sociology, anthropology, and linguistics, trying out new social systems or new ways of organizing daily life. It is in the context of this new dailiness that the epicene pronouns appear.

The feminist theorist Elaine Morgan notes that if you use the pronoun *he* in a book about the history of man, "before you are halfway through the first chapter a mental image of this evolving creature begins to form in your mind. It will be a male image and he will be the hero of the story" (1972, 2; quoted in Spender 1980, 151). Morgan comments that the use of *he* is "a simple matter of linguistic convenience," which, given the context of her remark, a consideration of the masculine bias in scientific thought, is clearly intended ironically. The use of generic *he* is neither simple nor convenient. Nor is it clear that "linguistic convenience" would cause one to choose the pronoun *he* to anaphorize *man*. This choice is more a matter of gender concord, since singular *they* is the pronoun of preference in informal speech (where convenience might be said to outweigh elegance), as in "everyone loves their mother." Morgan goes on to say how she longs to find a book that begins, "[W]hen the first ancestor of the human race descended from the trees, she had not yet developed the mighty brain that was to distinguish her so sharply from other species" (1972, 2; quoted in Spender 1980, 151). If the feminine pronoun in Morgan's imaginary textbook produces a sense of shock, this indicates that the reader has, despite the lack of overt markers of masculinity, imagined a man. This shock underlines the fact that the feminine is rarely generic. Despite Morgan's lament, most theorists have rejected the substitution of the female pronoun for the male, believing that this would merely turn the problem around without solving it.[2]

In some cases, the epicene but formal *one* is used in official documents in preference to generic *he* or singular *they*, still considered ungrammatical by purists and contemporary linguistic watchdogs such as high school English teachers.[3] In such contexts, the proscription against *they* may be so strong that even plurals are avoided. In a 1993 fellowship application form, the Townsend Center at the University of California, Berkeley, advised,

"Graduate *students* . . . should submit . . . a curriculum vitae indicating whether *one* is a legal resident of California" (my emphasis). The anaphorization of plural *students* by singular *one* strikes the eye as more incongruous than the anaphorization of singular *student* by plural *they*, which it was no doubt intended to avoid despite its grammaticality.

As we have seen, Monique Wittig makes epicene *on* the hero/ine of *L'Opoponax*, where, in keeping with standard spoken French, it takes the place of all three persons, both singular and plural, at different times, depending on context. While this strategy works admirably in French, in English, *one* (*on*'s nearest equivalent) sounds stuffy and scholastic. Wittig complained that Helen Weaver, the English translator of *L'Opoponax*, would not use *one* to translate *on* (1986, 68; see note 3 in chapter 5). She admits that English *one* "sounds and looks very heavy" but, she adds, "no less so in French" (1986, 68). This is simply not the case. French teachers tell their pupils not to use *on* in writing because it sounds colloquial, uneducated, marked for the spoken language. The *Le Monde* journalist Jacques Cellard, for example, reports on a speech class in a French primary school, in which a young student was corrected for saying "on a fait un projet d'aller en Corse" (we planned to go to Corsica) (1978; quoted in Mühlhäusler and Harré 1990, 185). The teacher considered *on* inappropriate for classroom use and more suited to the informality of the playground. An extensive corpus of transcriptions of conversations with nine-year-olds made in 1964 contained no examples of *nous* (we) used as an unstressed subject pronoun: in each case where a first person plural marker was required, the pronoun chosen was *on* (Söll 1979). In English, however, *one* may be encouraged in formal writing as having a more impersonal and scholarly and therefore more authoritative voice. It is hard to imagine a British or American nine-year-old (whose parents were not upper class) using the pronoun *one* with any frequency. In terms of register, *on* and *one* are not equivalents, but opposites.

Epicene pronouns in English have experienced something of a renaissance recently with the rise of the Internet. They are particularly popular on MUDs (Multi-User Domains) and MOOs (Multi-User Domains Object Oriented), text-based online interactive environments in which members create descriptions for themselves and have the option of creating rooms and other objects to use in their fantasy scenarios. LambdaMOO, created by Pavel Curtis of Xerox Park and perhaps the best known of the MOOs, offers members a choice of ten different gender assignations. The default is set at neuter (it); the other choices are: male (he), female (she), either (s/he), Spivak (e), splat (*e), plural (they), egotistical (I), royal (we), or second (you). [4] (The third person pronouns used by the MOO program to refer to the different genders appear in parentheses after each mention). Most players choose between the two traditional genders, male and female, but the fact that the default is neuter forces them to make a choice, even if it is only to represent their real-world gender. Only two of the set, Spivak and splat, involve neologistic pronouns; the others use different parts of the existing pronominal paradigm such as the first person singular and plural, the second person, and the third person neuter. LambdaMOO, owing to its pioneering status and user-friendly design, has served as the model for MOOs used in instructional settings, such as English as a second language and foreign language classrooms. In my experience, students also most often opt for a representation of their own real-life gender, but the necessity of choosing and the range of choices available occasion much animated discussion of sexism in language and the generic masculine in English.

Writing of the century-long search for an epicene (common-gender) third person pronoun, of which he gives over eighty examples from more than 200 sources between 1850 and 1985, Dennis Baron dismisses the whole endeavor as "The Word That Failed," the title of the tenth chapter of his *Grammar and Gender*. Indeed, he states explicitly, "[T]he creation of a common gender pronoun to replace the generic masculine 'he' . . . stands out as the [linguistic reform] most often attempted and the one that has most often failed" (1986, 190). This condemnation of failure is interesting. If success is to be measured only by the entry of one of these pronouns into everyday language, then the attempt has indeed failed. Singular *they* has shown a dogged resistance to the attempts of conservative grammarians to eradicate it, while the various invented pronouns such as *ne, nis, ner; ho, hom, hos;* and *shis, shim, shims, shimself* exist only in the articles exhorting their use. However, Baron's own impressive list of contenders is testimony to the depth and longevity of concern. Indeed, postings on the Linguist electronic discussion list during 1993 and 1994 recommending the use of epicene *hann* attest that replacements for the generic masculine are still being sought. (see Linguist List 1993a and 1993b).

Baron was concerned not with literary uses of epicene pronouns, but with their uptake in the language at large. This is of course a perfectly reasonable distinction. The carefully selected, gracefully balanced phrases of fiction often bear little resemblance to spontaneous speech, with its vivid lexicon and distinct syntactic structure. One cannot make valid claims about the spoken language by considering the literary texts produced by its speakers. Nevertheless, the role of literature in introducing, promoting, and popularizing specific words and phrases cannot be dismissed. Where would we be without the term *malapropism*, derived from Mrs. Malaprop of *The Rivals*, whose every second word was *mal à propos* (not to the point, out of context)? Would the phrase "Big Brother is watching you" ever have seemed sinister without George Orwell's *1984*?

Let us turn to a consideration of the work of feminist novelists who took up the challenge of replacing the generic masculine, creating ingenious responses to the masculine prerogative in their own novels. In *The Kin of Ata Are Waiting for You* (1971), Dorothy Bryant proposes *kin*, unmarked for either gender or number; in *The Cook and the Carpenter* (1973), June Arnold introduces *na, nan*, and *naself;* in *Woman on the Edge of Time* (1976), Marge Piercy uses *person* as subject pronoun and *per* as object pronoun and possessive. Ursula K. Le Guin's science fiction novel *The Left Hand of Darkness* (1969), which features the generic masculine *he* for the ambisexual Gethenians, caused such a storm that she was obliged to reply. Her responses will be discussed at length later.

Since three of these novels—*The Left Hand of Darkness, Woman on the Edge of Time*, and *The Kin of Ata Are Waiting for You*—have been continuously in print for almost twenty years, and all four together have sold hundreds of thousands of copies, they can hardly be said to have failed. Each time a reader encounters the neologism *kin*, *na*, or *per*, he or she is obliged to grapple with the ideological motivation behind these terms. Why have these pronouns been invented? What is wrong with the traditional pronouns they replace? What purpose do the neologisms serve? What effect do they have? Insofar as the aim of the author was to raise these questions, the neologistic pronouns work, and keep working each time the book is read. Consider the epigraph of this chapter: "Na sat astride Three, nan hands on nan throat" (Arnold 1973, 113). Who has their hands on Three's throat, a man or a woman? What gender is Three? The old trick still works. If we imagine the two characters as a man and a woman, we probably see the man with his hands on the woman's throat, the woman subdued, trying to scream, and we assume we are witnesssing a scene of domestic violence. If we imagine them as two men, we probably think of them fighting each other, perhaps in a barroom brawl, and expect some swift retaliation from Three. If we imagine that na is female and Three male, we might picture the scene as sex-play. If we imagine them as two women, we may dismiss the scene as lighthearted fun.[5] Readers encountering Marge Piercy's *person* and *per* for the first time remark initially on the jolt these new forms produce, requiring them to question their own gender bias, and then on the effect the pronouns have after they put the book down. Nancy Henley reports, "I found myself going around thinking in the new pronoun *person*, and others have recounted similar experiences" (1987, 16). Andre Ciecierski, a contributor to the Linguist list, notes, "It was confusing at first, but by the end of the book I found myself wanting to use it in conversation" (28 April 1995).

Baron uses a quotation from Mary Daly as an epigraph to his chapter on epicene neologisms: "It is a mistake to fixate on the third person singular." In the context of a chapter titled "The Word That Failed," this quotation will probably be understood to mean, it's a mistake to be obsessed with the generic *he*, as there are other more important problems to be solved in the feminist struggle. However, in *Gyn/Ecology*, the book from which the quotation comes, Daly continues by referring to Monique Wittig's description of how not only the third person but also the first person singular also excludes women: "The pronoun *I* conceals the sexual identity of the speaker/writer. The *I* makes the speaker/writer deceptively feel at home in a male-controlled language. When she uses this pronoun she may forget that *she* is buried in the false generic *he*" (Daly 1978, 18). Daly is saying not that it is a mistake to point out the sexism of pronouns, but that the third person singular should not be singled out for criticism. It is an important point, for all the writers discussed in this work aim to highlight, each in her own way, the linguistic derogation of women and to redress the balance to some extent by the effect their fiction has on the reader. None "fixate on the third person singular" in isolation.

Ambisexual Gethenians

Plot Summary: The Left Hand of Darkness

On the planet Gethen, the ambiguously sexed Gethenians live in arctic temperatures year round. The kingdoms of Karhide and Orgoreyn are in conflict. Genly Ai, an interplanetary ambassador, arrives on this planet to encourage its leaders to join the Ekumen, a federation of planets, only to get caught up himself in the battle for power between the two kingdoms.

In the mid-1960s, Le Guin recalls having been caught up in a "groundswell of feminist activity" (Le Guin 1976) and feeling a need to define for herself the meaning of gender and sexuality in language. This was a period in which women were questioning all their previous assumptions about the relationship between the sexes and the role of women. Consciousness-raising groups were mushrooming, and new solutions to old issues such as childbearing, child rearing, and family life were being discussed with extraordinary vigor and energy. It was in this political climate that Le Guin wrote *The Left Hand of Darkness* (1969), a novel set among the androgynous people of Gethen, whose bodies, for two-thirds of each month, are ungendered. During the last third of the month they enter "kemmer," the human equivalent of being in heat. Male or female genitalia develop when they come in contact with another Gethenian in kemmer, but they never know in advance which genital formation they will exhibit. A Gethenian who has borne three children may sire two more, for example. As this chapter's epigraphs show, the creation of Gethen brought with it the thorny problem of which pronouns to use to refer to such sexless/duosexual beings. In 1979, Le Guin's championing of the generic masculine and refusal of feminist inventions was adamant. A mere eight years later, in 1987, however, she announces just as strongly felt a dislike of the generic masculine. With her usual keen ear for metaphor, Le Guin remarks, "*The Left Hand of Darkness* is haunted and bedevilled by the gender of its pronouns, a wild, fierce and intractable tribe" (1995, personal communication).

Le Guin's initial solution, in 1969, was to use the masculine generic. In "The Question of Sex," chapter 7 of *The Left Hand of Darkness* (66–71), an investigator from the Ekumen (an observer with both a political and an anthropological function) voices the author's views on pronouns. As in any work of fiction, author and narrator are separate entities, often with distinct or opposing worldviews and their own ethos. In the following passage, however, Le Guin's 1976 view of the role of the generic masculine (as seen in Le Guin 1979) may be heard in the voice of the narrator. "You cannot think of a Gethenian as 'it'. They are not neuters. They are potentials or integrals." Instead, the investigator asserts, "I must use 'he,' for the same reasons as we used the masculine pronoun in referring to a transcendent god: it is less defined, less specific, than the neuter or the feminine" (70). The investigator remarks further that the use of the masculine or generic pronoun leads her to think of Gethenians as men rather than as menwomen. However, her presumption of masculinity goes beyond the ambisexual Gethenians, for when she speaks of the as-yet-unappointed envoy from the Ekumen, she again uses the masculine pronoun: "unless he is very self assured his pride will suffer" (70). She assumes the envoy will be masculine, predisposing readers of her dispatch to appoint a man. The problem of the generic masculine and its totalitarian habits does not exist in the language of the Gethenians, apparently. They, we are told, rejoice in a "human pronoun" (encoding information regarding number and animacy but not gender).

In another telling passage in the novel, Le Guin shows that she was at some level aware that masculine pronouns prompt a masculine reading. In the opening scene, the envoy from the Ekumen is reporting on a parade. He introduces an unknown member of the crowd as "the person on my left" (11). The character is subsequently referred to as "this person," the demonstrative *this* providing a referential link to the first mention. In the next sentence, the anaphoric *his* is used to refer to the person's forehead: "Wiping sweat from his dark forehead the man—*man* I must say, having said *he* and *his*" (11). If the pronoun *he* had truly been generic, there would have been a choice of masculine or feminine designation, but the envoy insists that he has no choice but to call the person a man. Given the description of the person's actions (wiping off sweat), this usage cannot be generic.

Le Guin was roundly criticized by feminist readers and reviewers in the late 1960s and 1970s for her use of the generic masculine. In 1979, in response to this criticism, she published "Is Gender Necessary?," the article from which the first epigraph to this chapter comes. In this piece, she argues, echoing Harvard University's Calvert Watkins and others (as discussed in chapter 1), that while the generic masculine is problematic, it is nonetheless less restricted than either the feminine *she* or the neutral *it* and far preferable to the invention of clumsy neologisms. The story, however, did not end with this statement, and neither did feminist criticism. The groundswell of feminist activism launched itself upon the language, and Le Guin, being part of that groundswell, produced a piece of informed self-criticism in an essay written in 1987 (from which comes the second epigraph to this chapter). This essay would be interesting for its structure alone—a *sous-rature* approach that preserves the original 1979 essay but adds a commentary bracketed off in italics. This procedure allows the reader to see the development in Le Guin's thinking, a reminder that "one had to go there to get here." The 1987 voice argues with its earlier self. The earlier voice states that pronouns were not the real issue, and that had she made the female side of the Gethenians more prominent, these androgynous beings would not have struck readers as masculine, despite the use of *he*, *him*, and *his* in reference to them. The later voice turns this statement around: "If I had realized how the pronoun I used shaped, directed, controlled my own thinking, I might have been cleverer." By 1987, LeGuin had absorbed contemporary feminist reworkings of the Sapir-Whorf hypothesis[6] and applied them to the novel.

Le Guin's commentary poses the thorny question of what a novelist can do when she realizes twenty years later that she disagrees with herself, especially when her former position has been quoted "with cries of joy" (1987, 7) by adverse critics. Well, she can write a public recantation, as Le Guin did, but it was too late to revise the novel itself. Le Guin found an ingenious two-pronged literary solution to this problem of having one's past remain alive in one's present. Her first response was to reprint "Winter's King" (1975), another story that set on the planet of Gethen that actually predated *The Left Hand of Darkness*. In this story, she used feminine pronouns throughout, though she was (at the time of the 1975 reprint) still adamantly opposed to invented pronouns: "I find made-up pronouns, 'te' and 'heshe' . . . dreary and annoying" (93). To refer to indefinite antecedents, Le Guin retained the use of the generic masculine, however: "lunch is served from a buffet and eaten standing up perhaps so that *one* will not feel *he* has spent the entire day sitting at table" (94).

The semantic clashes that result from the unvarying use of feminine pronouns in "Winter's King" are highly amusing, especially when juxtaposed with those caused by the use of masculine pronouns in *The Left Hand of Darkness*.

The Left Hand of Darkness	"Winter's King"
My landlady, a voluble man (38)	Prince Emran is well. She is with her attendants (99)
The king was pregnant (73)	The young king had her back against a wall (94)
A paranoid pregnant king and an egomaniac regent (82)	The ex-king of Karhide knew herself a barbarian (110)
It certainly was difficult to imagine him as a young mother (85)	She sired six children (117)

In the novel, men get pregnant; in the short story, women sire children. It is hard to believe that these early exercises in gender bending and blending provoked only righteous anger when their comic aspect is so apparent. Indeed, "the king was pregnant" has made it into *Bartlett's Familiar Quotations*, so striking is the image conveyed.[7] The laughter produced by the clash between the generic masculinity or femininity of these examples and the biological or cultural traits usually restricted to the opposite sex point to the subversiveness of Le Guin's pronoun choice.

The second solution Le Guin devised was to introduce invented pronouns in the 1985 screenplay of *The Left Hand of Darkness*. She remarks that these pronouns were modeled on a British dialect and therefore were not entirely her creation (1987, 15). The pronouns in question, *a*, *un*, and *a's*, replacing *he* or *she*, *him* or *her*, and *his* or *hers*, were accepted quite happily when read aloud, though some members of the audience commented that the subject pronoun *a* sounded too like an American Southern *I*. Le Guin was, however, still uneasy with the use of grammatical neologisms. While these pronouns might be acceptable in a screenplay, a guide for oral performance, they would, she hypothesizes, "drive the reader mad in print" (1987, 15).

This distaste for written neologisms is interesting in an author famous for her contribution to science fiction, a genre that revels in neologism. Indeed, her 1985 novel *Always Coming Home* includes a twelve-page glossary of words of the Kesh, an imaginary native northern California culture. In her introduction to this glossary, Le Guin informs the reader that she had intended to include only those words that occur in the book (or accompanying recording) but had in the end added a number of others "for the pleasure of my fellow dictionary readers and adepts of what an illustrious predecessor referred to as the Secret Vice" (509). It is unclear why the invention of individual lexical items, or indeed of a whole language, should be a source of pleasure, while invented pronouns elicit the adjectives "dreary" and "annoying." Even in the 1987 commentary on her earlier condemnation of invented pronouns, Le Guin writes only that she dislikes them less than the so-called generic. It might be that her distaste stems from a recognition that lexical items are an open class and are therefore not central to the structure of a language, whereas pronouns, as we have seen in chapters 2 and 5, are a closed class, having a morphosyntactic function; they are fundamental to the grammar and ought therefore to pass unnoticed, as crucial and unconscious as breathing.

But we have not quite finished with the twists and turns of Le Guin's pronouns, for the matter remained a source of concern into the 1990s. The publication of a special twenty-fifth anniversary edition of *The Left Hand of Darkness* in 1995 presented a new opportunity to tackle the problem. In an entertaining and insightful afterword, which was written but never published, Le Guin explains the evolution in her thinking, condemning as "logobullies" those who would banish singular *they* but pointing out that *they* will not do for definite, specified antecedents (personal communication).[8] *He or she, she or he, he/she*, and *s/he* Le Guin dismisses as "laborious little monstrosities employed by the conscientious," observing that they imply referents who are not genderless but of either sex. Her search for the right pronouns to use for her ambisexual beings she terms "the Great Gethenian Pronoun Problem." A problem that has persisted over twenty-five years, despite energetic attempts to elucidate and resolve it, justifies such an impressive title. Le Guin explains that although she played with using some of the experimental pronouns used in other feminist works, such as Marge Piercy's *per*, which I will discuss later, she ended up inventing her own—an interesting move for an author who had earlier declared that made-up pronouns were "dreary and annoying" (1975, 93) and would "drive the reader mad in print" (1987, 15).

The pronouns Le Guin proposes, for use in her own work, are *e* for *he or she*; *en* for *her or him*; *es* for *her, his, hers*; and *enself* for *herself, himself*. She was, she says, looking for something "that didn't look weird, didn't look foreign, looked like and sounded like plain English" (1995, 5). In similar fashion, she praises the creation of *Ms.*, to replace *Miss* and *Mrs.* because it was "not a thin-air invention, but a new spelling of the old, honorable Southern usage *Miz*" (personal communication). Le Guin insists on neologisms that follow English phonological and morphosyntactic rules, believing (correctly) that they will be more easily assimilated. In this, she follows Wittig's neologizing in *Les Guérillères* and *Le Corps lesbien*. Having chosen a set of pronouns, Le Guin rewrote the first chapter of *The Left Hand of Darkness* using these epicene items and presents it at the back of the book as an alternative to the original opening chapter, a process she terms "repronouning." The reader may therefore compare the two versions, and, indeed, a third, in which Le Guin has replaced the masculine pronouns of the original with the feminine, changing the gender of nouns such as *king* to *queen* and *lord* to *lady*. Players on LambdaMOO who set their gender to Spivak, splat, or either are merely following in Le Guin's wake.

The twenty-five-year history of the different versions of *The Left Hand of Darkness* and the explanations its author has given for her changes of mind, parallel the changing opinions of feminist writers as concerns the generic masculine. As Le Guin remarks, "I've never seen so clearly how I was controlled, when I wrote the book, by the hidden force, the real dominance, of that false-generic 'he'" (personal communication). Although Le Guin was the earliest of the writers in this study to grapple with questions of language and gender (apart from Monique Wittig, writing in French), by the mid-1970s American novelists participating actively in the women's liberation movement were putting feminist ideas to work in their fiction.[9]

Kin

Plot Summary: The Kin of Ata Are Waiting for You

An unnamed novelist murders a young woman and while fleeing from the crime crashes his car down a steep slope. He awakens on Ata, where all people are kin and work together, guided by their dreams, in an egalitarian paradise. After living in this peaceful community, he decides to return to the world and face his trial for murder, which he will use as a platform to speak about Ata.

In the language of *The Kin of Ata Are Waiting for You* (Bryant 1971), we are told, there was "no pronoun but kin." In the world inhabited by the kin, inanimate objects are carefully divided into masculine and feminine, heterosexually paired in all arrangements from building to planting to eating, but there are no pronouns for *he* or *she*. This subverts the usual hierarchy of animacy by which, according to Bernard Comrie, pronominal reference frequently correlates with a higher degree of animacy, as does case marking for agent and patient in transitive constructions (1981, 179–80). Since the Atan pronouns vary in form only when they refer to inanimates, the roles of agent and patient are marked only for referents lower down in the animacy hierarchy. There are discrete lexical items for the concepts *man* and *woman*, but these are seldom used, and there is only one pronoun for human beings, a word that makes no distinction of gender or number. The Atan personal pronoun is used both in the second person, ("people called to one another by this word when not using someone's name" [50]) and in the third person ("they referred to one or more people by it" [50]). It is used "the way most people use brother," except that *brother* is specifically masculine and singular. The only person it does not seem to cover is the first; there is no suggestion that Atans refer to themselves as speaking subjects by this pronoun. Since "the language lacked all sense of the singular, the individual" (50), this is perhaps not surprising. In many ways, *kin* appears to function like *on* in Monique Wittig's *L'Opoponax*, depending on context to disambiguate reference.

The motivation for this breaking down of the usual boundaries of person, number, and gender is the desire for a society that is socialist in conception, based on collective enterprise rather than individual effort. If the grammar of the language does not require the speaker to conceptualize people as men or women; speaker, addressee, or nonparticipant; or singular or plural, then these distinctions will be less salient. Combined with the lack of a singular/plural distinction in the pronominal paradigm is the lack of temporal distinctions. Our textual informant, a stranger to Atan society who plays a role similar to that of Genly Ai on Gethen, does not explain whether Atan is one of the many languages that encode temporal information by adverbial modifiers rather than morphologically in the verb. But he does note a "lack of a sense of time," which may mean that aspect is of more significance than tense. Bryant provides these indications of the nature of the Atan language for the reader to ponder. She gives no examples of it, for it has, she explains, no written form. A writing system is, in fact, the special gift of the unnamed novelist who lives among the Atans.

Aspects of *kin* are to be seen in the pronominal systems devised by other novelists discussed in this book. Although *kin* itself is unique to Bryant's work, ideological homogeneity, egalitarianism, and the absence of sex-role segregation are ideals dear to June Arnold and Marge Piercy. Whereas Bryant merely describes the pronoun of Ata, Arnold and Piercy both employ their epicene neologisms in their novels, allowing us the opportunity for a more extensive analysis. They do not, however, banish the traditional pronouns, but create a complex interplay between the two systems. The moments when the systems combine or collide are of great significance in each book. The epicene pronouns must be considered in terms of the whole pronominal system of each novel because they cause a redrawing of the distinctions made by all other pronominals. Whereas Le Guin opposed the introduction of grammatical neologisms because their unfamiliar forms render them so noticeable, Arnold and Piercy use this foregrounding effect to emphasize their respective ideological points.

Na *and* Nan

Plot Summary: The Cook and the Carpenter

A women's group establishes a commune in an elementary school in Texas, only to be evicted by the local sheriff and his deputies. The story revolves around the women's discussions about how to create a feminist community and their attempts to involve the local people in their endeavor. It focuses on *The Cook and the Carpenter*, lesbian lovers who are attempting to bring up the Cook's children in a nonsexist way.

June Arnold's *The Cook and the Carpenter*, unlike the other novels discussed in this chapter, is not set on a science-fictional world, but in a small town in Texas. This choice of setting removes ideas of gender and language from the arena of the fantastic and places them in the dust of everyday life. The story begins when a woman arrives to warn a group of people who have just moved to town that local residents plan to throw them out. Without explanation or preamble, the narrator uses the pronouns *na* and *nan* to refer to the newcomers. This strategy is employed to naturalize the pronouns, so that the lack of gender distinction appears as an unproblematized status quo. *Na* is both subject and object pronoun, replacing *her* and *him* as well as *she* and *he*. It thus collapses the morphological distinction in written English between subject and object. Although readers know the sex of the person who came to warn the group, since this information is formally revealed by the clearly feminine designator "the woman," they do not yet know the sexual composition of the group of newcomers. Although she does not herself belong to the group, the woman who tells them about the townspeople's attitude toward them uses the epicene neologisms that characterize their speech. The narrator also uses the neologisms to refer to her [For ease of recognition, all uses of the epicene neologisms are set in boldface in the examples given here. It should be noted that the author does not highlight them in any way.]:

6.1.   The stranger had come that morning at eight with a basket of eggs on **nan** arm. (5)

Although her husband, Will, is addressed as "boy" by one of the men he is serving with drinks at a private party and thus identified as male, epicene pronouns are also used by his wife to refer to him:

6.2.   "Didn't take Will long to figure out what they was talking about, but **na** didn't let on **na** heard anything." (5)

In contrast, at a bar in town (and therefore on the townsfolks' home ground), in a scene involving the carpenter, a character from the newcomers' group, and one of the townspeople, the epicene *na*, *na*, and *naself* are reserved for the carpenter, while no pronouns are used for the townsperson:

6.3.   A person sitting two stools down spoke to the carpenter.
       The carpenter had seen the speaker come in.
       The carpenter looked on the floor and then at the speaker.
       "It look like a wallet or a checkbook," the person said.
       The carpenter knew **na** had neither a wallet or checkbook with **na**. (7)

As can be seen from example 6.3, *the carpenter* is pronominalized after the third mention, once the referent has been activated and the contrast established between this character and the townsperson. The latter, on the other hand, is never accorded pronominal reference, instead being designated by a range of epicene lexical items: *a person* in the first sentence, *the speaker* in the second and third, and *the person* in the fourth. The move from indefinite to definite determiner observed between the first and fourth sentences demonstrates that the referent is now specific. Later on in this episode, the speaker is referred to as "the white-haired one" (8), still without pronoun or proper name, markers of high animacy. Although the person who addresses the carpenter proceeds to conduct a four-turn conversation with her, he is referred to only by description, showing that the narrator refuses to empathize with him. This is both a deliberate effect created by the author and the consequence of pronoun avoidance.

The contrast between the referring expressions used to designate the newcomers and those used for the townspeople is not the only salient one in this novel. There is also a difference between the referring expressions used to designate those who are sympathetic to the newcomers and those who are hostile. *Na*, *nan*, and *naself* are not only epicene, they also encode information with regard to empathy. In the case of Will and his wife, the egg woman, who comes to warn the newcomers, the neologistic pronouns are used not so much because they are epicene, since the reader is already aware of the genders of the referents, but as a method of demonstrating the narrator's empathy. Will and the egg woman are tolerant of and helpful toward the newcomers, so they share the same pronominal system. As we have seen in earlier chapters, the characters most frequently pronominalized are the ones with whom the narrator empathizes and through whom the action is focalized. The story of how Will learns of the planned attack on the newcomers is told through his eyes and using the epicene pronouns.

In some cases the epicene pronouns prove themselves somewhat unwieldy, particularly in environments in which a change of reference is required in the same sentence. In contrast, this system works reasonably well in shorter sense units, as may be seen in example 6.4:

6.4.   The cook took **nan** arm, **nan** shoulder, held **nan** face with **nan** own. (47)

The first three occurrences of the possessive *nan* refer to the carpenter, whereas the fourth refers to the cook, a switch reference aided by the addition of the reflexive adjective *own*.

6.5.   **Na** ducked behind **nan** companion and hugged **na**. (67)

In example 6.5, the first occurrence of *na* refers to the subject, as does the possessive *nan*, while the second occurrence of *na* refers to the object. Although slightly harder to process, since the English morphological distinction between subject and object has disappeared alongside gender information, this sentence is still relatively easy to understand since the direct object immediately follows the verb, respecting the canonical word order of English. The sequence in example 6.6, on the other hand, is notably awkward.

6.6.   The carpenter shook **nan** brain . . . and listened: the cook's voice was pointing at the carpenter's head and was hoping that the other person did not mind **na** (the cook) saying this, that **na** (the cook) was sure the other person (now clearly the carpenter) did not. (22)

The carpenter is twice referred to as "the other person," while the pronoun *na* is reserved for the cook. If the neologisms had encoded case, as their traditional English counterparts do, the problem might have been avoided, for the first occurrence of "the other person" would be in the nominative case (corresponding to *she* or *he*), while the first occurrence of *na* would be in the accusative (corresponding to *her* or *him*). In this way, at least two of the clumsy parentheses would have been eliminated. Similarly, in example 6.7, the repeated neologisms are clumsy and cumbersome.

6.7.   **Na** felt split down the middle. It's timing **naself** told **naself**. (107)

The odd, pseudo-Irish-sounding phrase "herself told herself" or "himself told himself" looks even stranger when translated to the neologistic forms. Arnold has deliberately chosen a conspicuous form in order to draw attention to the battle of the pronouns in her novel. While Piercy's pronouns *per* and *person* are clearly related to the epicene noun *person*, and Le Guin's *e* is homophonous with the Cockney pronunciation of *he*, Arnold's *naself* stands out, not readily assimilated.

Elsewhere in the novel, Arnold has tried out other solutions, such as repetition of the noun phrase instead of pronominalization.

6.8.   Andy's gum was juicy fruit—it was the first taste of juicy fruit that told me it was Andy's gum. . . . I can't believe I'm chewing Andy's gum. (89)

In example 6.8, this repetition works reasonably well because the referent is not a human being but a piece of chewing gum. One might have expected the name *Andy* to be pronominalized after its first mention, but since the point of the sequence is to express the strangeness of having someone else's gum in one's own mouth, the three occurrences of *Andy* serve to underline that strangeness.

Arnold also occasionally uses the neuter pronoun *it* instead of her own neologisms, as in example 6.9:

6.9.   A parent with a self of its own. (29)

In this case, the implication of nonhuman status inherent in the use of *it* works well, as the sentence itself is an ironic testimony to parental independence. The irony is only enhanced by the hint that the referent is commonly considered less than human: independence usually collocates with high animacy. Mothers are meant to be devoted to their children, giving up their sense of self in the process, but the epicene "parent" allows greater freedom from social sanction.

A much more remarkable pronoun change occurs three-quarters of the way through the novel. The carpenter's group occupies Shadyside Elementary School, and plans to use its ample rooms to provide health, education, and other services to the local population. Inevitably, the police come and arrest the occupiers. During the scene of the arrests, the epicene pronouns prevail. In the following passage it is impossible to tell by grammatical means the gender of the deputies or of Leslie, a member of the carpenter's group.

6.10.   A hand covered Leslie's nose and mouth, pushing into **nan** face; one deputy
          easily dragged **na** to the car; another followed . . . whacking Leslie's body
          wherever **nan** stick could land. (139)

Furthermore, the name *Leslie* is given to both girls and boys, and sheriffs' deputies may be male or female. After the group has been thrown into holding cells for the night, however, the traditional third person pronouns assert themselves for the first time in the novel, and the neologisms are discontinued.

6.11.   The sergeant pushed Three to the floor and, with **his** foot on **her** back,
          told the policewoman to take off **her** shoes, pull down **her** pants. (139)

In example 6.11, one is not obliged to search the context for cultural clues in order to work out the gender of the sergeant, the police officer, or Three, since this information is formally provided in the pronouns *his* and *her* and in the gendered noun *policewoman*.

The question of why the epicene pronouns are used for two-thirds of the novel and why traditional pronouns take over is thus planted implicitly in the text. The reader discovers, after the group has been thrown into prison, that they are in fact all women, since all now have female pronouns assigned to them. It is with the telling phrase "with his foot on her back" that every-thing changes. The nongendered pronouns cannot hold out against such an onslaught; the men have won. Gender is indeed central, if it means one sex has its foot on the other's back.

Likewise the scene in which the deputy beats Leslie up is reprised when a newspaper features a photograph of the beating:

6.12.   The deputy's face as **he** beat **her** [was] a contortion of hate. (147)

The reader may well have surmised that Leslie was a woman, since the name is often spelled *Lesley* when borne by a man, and that the deputy was male, since most sheriff's deputies are men, but these would have been no more than guesses based on the unmarked case. Now there is no mistaking the sex of each protagonist. "He beat her" leaves no room for doubt about either the sex or the role played by each character.

The epicene pronouns are backed by a battery of epicene noun phrases: the women's liberation movement is referred to as *people who share the group's politics* (45) or their *own group* (10); men as *those others* (61); mothers as *parents* (29); husbands and wives as *partners*, distinguished as the ones "who work for money" versus the ones "who work for so-called love" (94). Occasionally this usage sounds a little stilted, as in "[y]ou let that one look, now let me" (35). Instead of the demonstrative *that one*, a pronoun would have seemed more natural—"you let her/him/na look, now let me"—since *that one* singles one unit out from a group. But no group has been estab-lished; there are only the speaker and the referent. The traditional pronoun *he* or *she* would, of course, have revealed the gender of the referent, and only the group occupying the school and their sympathizers use the epicene *na* and *nan* in their own speech. *Na* is a mark of in-group status, which the narrator shares but not most of the townsfolk. To use the neologisms *nan* and *na* is to place oneself inside the women's group, to declare one's iden-tification with feminist ideology. Since readers, in order to understand the text, are obliged to make the conceptual link between separatist practice and gender-neutral pronouns, they too are required to identify with the women's group, or at least to read from the women's position.

We later discover that the person who says "You let that one look," in-sisting on seeing a diagram of female genital organs, is the deputy sheriff, to whom epicene pronouns are unknown. The connection between the use of epicene pronouns and the possession of a feminist consciousness is under-lined by two incidents during which the prevailing status quo is overturned. The first occurs early on in the novel, when the women's group is still flour-ishing unhindered and the epicene pronouns prevail. One day, while the children are playing, their cries become highly charged and sex specific. At this point, instead of the epicene term *children*, they are referred to as *boys* and *girls* as their make-believe game degenerates into ugly name-calling:

6.13. "I am a tiger!" a boy cried.
       "I am a lion!" a second boy said.

       . . .

       "Bitch!"
       "Bitch!"

       . . .

       "Pussy!"
       "Pussy!"
       "Cock!" (55)

Even in the women's group, sexual divisions come to the fore when the little boys begin to act like grown men. It is then not possible to refer to them as an undifferentiated group of *children*. This scene makes apparent on the linguistic level conflicts that have also begun to emerge on the political level, as seen in the fraught relations between the women's group and the outside world. The women are trying to bring up nonsexist children in a nonsexist environment, of which the nongendered pronouns are an integral part. But they cannot control all aspects of the children's lives any more than they can control the land they have occupied. The group exists within, and only with the tolerance of, a wider, sexist society whose values and hierarchies also exert an influence on the children and their speech patterns. This is evidenced by the ease with which the children divide themselves into a warring group of boys versus girls and their immediate appropriation of the sexed terms "pussy" and "cock."

A counterpart to this incident occurs after the women have been arrested and the reign of gendered pronouns has resumed. A large crowd has gathered ouside the courthouse to support the women. Someone throws soap powder all over the street and sidewalks; someone else turns on a fire hydrant; anarchic billows of white foam float over the police cars, and the officers seem to be moving on clouds. The police try to clear away the foam, but for some time their efforts are in vain. It seems that the women are again in control. At this point the epicene terms make a brief reappearance. A clump of soapsuds lands

6.14. On the hat of a **police** who knocked it away so vigorously **na** stirred up the suds at **nan** feet. (148)

The term "a police," albeit awkward, since *police* is usually considered a collective noun, has been used to avoid gender specificity, and the pronouns *na* and *nan* show that the women's language has won a brief victory.

Is Arnold implying that in a group composed only of women gender is meaningless, or that police aggression forces a gender split? The members of the group are called by nontraditional or epicene names such as *Nicky, Stubby,* and *Chris,* and their roles are not stereotypical for women; the carpenter, for example, is sanding the porch in the opening scene, and the cook and the carpenter become lovers. Are gendered pronouns unnecessary since sex differences are apparent from cultural clues? Different readers will interpret the novel in different ways, though its frame of social realism, its setting in small-town Texas in the mid-1970s, and its feminist slogans do make a radical feminist reading more compelling than others. The neologisms are so eye-catching and incongruous, given the realism of the rest of the text, that an obvious interpretation would be that they are intended to focus the reader's attention on what is missing—on the pronouns they replace and the reasons for grammaticalized gender distinctions.

In the preface to her novel, Arnold writes: "Since the differences between men and women are so obvious to all . . . the author understands that it is no longer necessary to distinguish between men and women in this novel. I have therefore used one pronoun for both, trusting the reader to know which is which." This statement would seem to provide the key to the text. If the neologisms work, if readers can tell who is male and who is female without having this information grammatically coded, then one must conclude that indeed the differences between men and women are obvious and further coding is unnecessary. If, on the other hand, readers are surprised by the return of the gendered pronouns and the sexual identities they reveal, then sexual difference may not be taken for granted. Readers who discover only by the use of *he* and *she*, two-thirds of the way through the novel, that the group that occupies the school is composed of women, while the people who oppose them are men, demonstrate by their own discovery that gender cannot be identified from people's actions. From this perspective, the preface is deliberately ironic.

Even without the preface, however, this point is made within the novel itself. The epicene speech of the women's group is utopic; it cannot sustain the onslaught of male violence to which it is subjected. The language is defeated at the same moment as its speakers. While the book itself may end with the defeat of the women's cause, its publication points to a triumph of a different kind. *The Cook and the Carpenter* was published by one of the earliest feminist presses in the United States, Daughters, Inc., a company June Arnold founded in 1972 to publish books by and for women. Arnold has in fact argued for the exclusion of men from the whole printing and publishing process: "we should wear headbands which state: My words will not be sold to 'his master's voice'" (1976, 24). While Daughters, Inc., flourished, Arnold maintained a separatist preserve. The great pronoun war turns out to be merely a battle, fought on many fronts, a strategy among others for creating and maintaining women's autonomy.

Person *and* Per

Plot Summary: Woman on the Edge of Time

This book is an ingenious mixture of science fiction and social realism. Connie, a twentieth-century psychiatric patient, escapes from her own time period for a series of much-needed breaks in the twenty-second century, an egalitarian utopia. The peace and security of the later era is threatened, however, by outside aggression, and Connie is forced to return to her own time, where the doctors are waiting to perform a brain-control operation. In the last scene, she performs her one act of violence as she poisons the doctors' coffee, killing four people.

The epicene pronouns Marge Piercy has created operate rather differently from those of Arnold. The third person pronouns map Connie's movement between the time periods: the narrator and characters in the present time use traditional pronouns, whereas characters in the future time use the epicene neologisms *person* and *per*. Unlike Arnold's novel, in which the characters' gender is not linguistically given until two-thirds of the way through the text, Piercy's futuristic characters are introduced by the narrator with the pronouns appropriate for their gender.

   The novel opens as Connie gets up from her kitchen table and thinks to herself,

6.15.   Either I saw **him** or I didn't and I'm crazy for real . . ., **she** thought. (9)

Connie is referred to by the feminine *she*; the person she is thinking about, Luciente, one of the characters from the future, is referred to by the masculine *he*. (Like Arnold, Piercy does not highlight the pronouns she uses. I have set in boldface third person pronouns in examples for emphasis). Epicene *per* is not introduced until forty-seven pages later, in the speech of Luciente, in reference to a friend from the future world. Gendered pronouns are clearly established as the status quo, while the epicene forms are an egalitarian development. Since events are focalized by twentieth-century Connie, her pronominal system prevails in narration, except for events recounted in the direct speech of the futuristic characters.

   Connie uses the semiotic system and the social values of her own time to judge the gender of the people from the future, but her initial assumptions are sometimes proven wrong. This causes a clash between Connie's twentieth-century preconceptions of correct gender appearance and behavior and the futuristic codes, a clash played out in the pronominal system as well. Because Luciente is well muscled and self-confident, Connie thinks of *him* as a man, as we have seen in the opening line of the novel quoted above. However, when she embraces *him*, she realizes her mistake:

6.16.   She felt the coarse fabric of **his** shirt and . . . breasts! (66)

She searches her vocabulary for the correct term for such a person.

6.17.   You're a woman! No, one of those sex-change operations. (67)

The term *woman*, which would signify a person with breasts, is rejected in favor of the inhuman designator *a sex-change operation*, which describes the person who has undergone surgery in terms of the surgery itself. Connie is unable to accept without some mental transition that the person she believed to be a man is actually a woman. At the pronominal level, the same process of transition occurs. Connie cannot simply shift from masculine to feminine pronouns, for this would suggest that the shift from male to female was a common, accepted occurrence. Instead she invents a new pronoun to describe this transitional state: *him/her*. This new pronoun demonstrates the strain placed on the grammar of twentieth-century English by the egalitarian future. When the narrator next refers to Luciente, following Connie's change of consciousness, she uses feminine pronouns: "**she** moved with . . . authority" (67). The transition is complete, and the gap in the system—a pronoun appropriate for a person of ambiguous gender—is sealed over. For the moment.

Accompanying the neologistic pronouns are many epicene lexical items that refer to artifacts and concepts specific to the society of the future: *mems* (family members, though there may be no biological link among them), *kidbinder* (a person who looks after people's children), and *pillow friends* (people with whom one has a sexual relationship). This gender-neutral vocabulary causes Connie frequent difficulty since she speaks a language that encodes sex differences systematically. She notices "people who must be women because they carried their babies on their backs" (71), guessing at the correct pronoun from cultural information regarding sex roles that relate to her own time rather than the society of the future. Since the proper names are frequently epicene too, Connie manages as best she can, as may seen from this sequence:

6.18.   The tall . . . person was staring at her. Jackrabbit, Luciente had said: therefore male. **He** . . . (77)

Connie cannot tell Jackrabbit's sex simply from looking at him, hence the neutral term *person*. Then she remembers that his name is Jackrabbit and is relieved to settle her dilemma with the masculine pronoun, which would be appropriate to refer to a male—or "jack"—rabbit.

The interchange between the present and future in Piercy's novel is much more fluid than that between the woman-only and mixed communities of *The Cook and the Carpenter* and causes frequent shifts in the pronominal system. During the sequences set in the future society of Mattapoisett, the two pronominal systems, traditional and epicene, coexist. Events described by the future-time characters feature the epicene system; those described by the narrator feature the traditional system. In passages where Connie is speaking to futuristic characters, the differences between the two cultures are paralleled by the pronominal system used. On being told that Connie's niece has a boyfriend-pimp who beats her up, Luciente translates this to the language of her own time, using the epicene pronoun *per*, which Connie immediately corrects:

6.19.   "Your mem has a sweet friend who abuses **per**."
        "**Her** pimp." (63)

In a society in which prostitution flourishes and men live off their girlfriends' earnings, epicene pronouns make no sense. A similar clash between the two different worldviews may be seen in an episode in which Luciente tells Connie that the children of Mattapoisett spend a week in the wilderness as part of the rite of transition between childhood and maturity. Pointing to one of the children in question, Connie asks in horror if the girl is really abandoned alone in the wilderness. The reply is most unreassuring, from Connie's point of view. Not only must the child stay out overnight, she remains in the wilderness for a week. This time it is Connie's turn to be shocked by the barbaric customs of the future, and the shock is again registered in the change of pronouns used to refer to the young girl. Where Connie uses the feminine *she*, the people of Mattapoisett use *per*.

6.20.   "Does she stay out there over night?"
        "For a week. Then the aunts return for per." (116)

The dissonance between the two social systems appears most clearly in a scene in which a female character from Mattapoisett, Erzulia, takes on the essence of one of the male characters, Jackrabbit, a blurring of gender boundaries impossible in the more sexually segregated twentieth century. The futuristic characters have a biological sex; they are anatomically men and women, but their gender status is equal. At Jackrabbit's memorial ceremony, Erzulia, who is leading the ritual, takes on Jackrabbit's personality, while Bolivar, who had been Jackrabbit's lover, watches and finally joins in.

6.21.   **She** danced Jackrabbit. Yes **she** became **him**. . . . Bolivar's head . . . lifted
        from **his** chest. Suddenly Erzulia-Jackrabbit danced over and drew **him**
        up. . . . Bolivar began to dance with **him/her**. . . . . Bolivar jumped back.
        "I felt **per**!" **he** cried out. (316)

The traditional pronouns show the scene from Connie, the time traveler's, point of view. The gender shock of "she became him" is the more apparent since the phrase itself defies the usual possibilities of the twentieth-century pronominal system, and a new pronoun has to be introduced: *him/her*. We have seen this pronoun before, in reference to Luciente, after Connie discovered she was a woman, but here it refers to a genuinely duo-sexed being, rather than to a masculine-seeming woman. Bolivar's use of the epicene "I felt **per**" offers another solution, a system that avoids mention of gender. The language of the more advanced time forces changes in that of the earlier century.

Mattapoisett is not, however, the only possible future, for the reader glimpses another alternative when Connie tries to find her way to Jackrabbit and Luciente's time but gets lost. While the society of Mattapoisett is an egalitarian utopia, Gildina's life in a futuristic New York is a nightmarish dystopia. Luciente had explained to Connie that in Mattapoisett "we've reformed pronouns" (42), but in Gildina's version of the future people still use the traditional gendered ones, representing the extreme pole of a sexually segregated and sexist culture. Speaking of her mother who had been in a geriatric unit and may now be dead, Gildina notes that *she* was over forty and so may have been cremated (290). In this future, the feminine pronoun refers to a person who has no control over her life, is old at forty, and may be disposed of at will. In contrast, the masculine pronoun designates someone with enormous social power who controls his female companion. Gildina's husband, Cash, locks her in their apartment all day out of jealousy. With horror, Connie reads some of the listings in Gildina's catalog of "Sense-all" films. The one entitled *Sorrinda 777* tells a story of forbidden love between a doctor and the futuristic equivalent of a medical orderly who is asked to give up her own heart to replace the doctor's wife's own defective organ. The repetitive use of the feminine pronoun *her* reinforces the sense that this future is as far as one can get from egalitarian Mattapoisett:

6.22.   **her** faithfulness, **her** suffering, **her** shining love: will **she** give the ultimate
         sacrifice of **her** heart? (293)

The film presents a futuristic twist on the old nurse-in-love-with-married-doctor story, in which the gendered pronouns encode maximal power differences between the sexes.

Occasionally the characters in Mattapoisett use gendered pronouns:

6.23.   I have a sweet friend . . . and **her** tribe is Harlem-Black. (103)

There seems to be no textual reason for this, it answers no necessity of the plot, and one is inclined to conclude it is simply a mistake. Piercy seems at times reluctant to use the epicene pronouns she has invented and often avoids them, employing other techniques such as proper name repetition or ellipsis. In some episodes this produces a disjointed effect, as may be seen in example 6.24, which constitutes Arthur of Ribble's memorial speech for his dead son, Jackrabbit, formerly called Peony. This passage is characterized by a high occurrence of ellipsis and proper names and relatively little use of pronouns, although there are only two animate referents in the discourse (Arthur and Jackrabbit), and only one of them, Jackrabbit, may be referred to in the third person. Since the whole episode is a eulogy to the recently dead Jackrabbit, this referent should remain active throughout the discourse, yet his proper name is given seven times, often where there is no intervening matter or where none of the intervening matter would deactivate the referent—that is, there are no references to other characters. The continual use of his name instead of a pronoun is therefore doubly marked.

6.24.

a.	Jackrabbit [PN] was my child. [El] Gave me joy . . .	PN →El
b.	Person [Pr] was running in seven ways at once . . .	Pr
c.	Jackrabbit [PN] wanted to do everything. Person [Pr] could not, [El] would not choose.	PN →Pr →El
d.	Instead Jackrabbit [PN] would begin to weave . . . , [El] would launch . . . an experiment, [El] would begin studying spiders, [El] would start glazing a nanelon, [El] would demand to be taught how holies function, [El] would begin cartography.	PN →El→El →El →El →El
e.	Person [Pr] would know a bit about spiders, . . . [El] would have had three cartography lessons and [El] abandoned the experiments.	Pr →El →EL
f.	Person [Pr] drove me wild!	Pr
g.	I would yell . . . and my child [LS] would sulk . . . But person [Pr] would forgive me.	LS → Pr
h.	My child [LS] would forgive me and [El] tell me how person [Pr]—then named Peony[PN]—wanted to learn theory of wind power, [El] construct a mill, [El] learn lithography, [El] study Japanese	LS → El →Pr →N →EL →El →El
i.	I comped Peony [PN] to choose something.	PN
j.	When Peony [PN] began to think . . . of shelf diving, I bound per [Pr] into making a commit.	PN → Pr
k.	I obsessed Peony [PN] into being ashamed of flightiness. (309–10)	PN

PN = Proper name   El = Ellipsis   Pr = Pronoun   LS = Lexical substitute

An analysis of the nature and number of expressions used to refer to Jackrabbit in this passage reveals that of a total of fifteen expressions, seven are epicene pronouns (*person* 6, *per* 1), six are proper names (*Jackrabbit* 3, *Peony* 3), and two are lexical substitutes (*my child* 2). The device used most frequently, however, is ellipsis—a series of verbs headed by the same referring expression—of which there are thirteen occurrences in Arthur's speech. As I demonstrated in chapter 2, there is a hierarchy in both cohesion and empathy among the different referential devices. According to this hierarchy, ellipsis creates the tightest cohesive link and, at the same time, implies the highest level of empathy from the narrator. Anaphoric pronominal reference comes after ellipsis, followed by lexical substitution, with proper name repetition evincing the least cohesion and the lowest degree of empathy. I have divided the sentences in example 6.24 into eleven lettered groups, according to the sequence of referring expressions in each group. Observing the hierarchies of cohesion and empathy outlined above, a sequence ends when a device lower down the scale follows one higher up the scale. Since ellipsis is the highest element on the scale, a change to lexical substitution, or proper name repetition will end the sequence. In 6.24a, the movement is from a proper name (Jackrabbit) to an ellipsis (gave me), indicating that the referent is active. In 6.24b, Jackrabbit is referred to by pronoun "person," which because it is higher up the scale of cohesive devices, increases both cohesion and empathy. In 6.24c, however, the repetition of the proper name "Jackrabbit" serves both to block empathy and terminate the sequence.

What is remarkable, then, about example 6.24 is both the number and the nature of the switches between the different devices. Once a topic has been established, one expects the movement of referring expressions to go from less cohesive, less empathic to more cohesive and more empathic. A switch from lower to higher empathy demonstrates that a referent has become active, and the viewpoint of that character may become the point of focalization. A switch in the opposite direction, from higher to lower empathy, usually accompanies the introduction of a new referent or a change of episode (as we have seen from the analyses of *Sphinx* in chapter 2 and of *L'Opoponax* in chapter 5).

Once the topic of Jackrabbit—his character and flightiness—had been established, one would have expected him to be referred to pronominally for the most part, with occasional excursions into ellipsis for strings of predicates serving the same purpose, for example, to exemplify his short attention span. Instead we get a puzzling mixture of devices that make Jackrabbit appear first familiar, then like a new character. In example 6.24d and e, the string of ellipses suggests an accessible referent whose way of looking at the world affects the narrator's recounting of the tale, often a sign of focalization through that character. Thus Arthur reports that Jackrabbit "would know a bit about spiders" and "something of how holies [holograms] function." Since Arthur has made clear his exasperation with his son's continual changes of interest, he would be more likely to claim that the boy had learned nothing whatever. The phrases "a bit about" and "something of" express Jackrabbit's own appreciation of his progress. Yet in 6.24g and h, Jackrabbit is referred to by lexical substitution, *my child*, and by an entirely new proper name, *Peony*, launching another series of ellipses. This dizzying fluctuation in levels of empathy might reflect Arthur's own changing sentiment toward his recently deceased son, now seeing things from the child's point of view, now from his own, rather more jaundiced eye. Or it could indicate a lack of ease with the neologistic pronouns on the part of the author.

In marked contrast with Jackrabbit, Connie is often referred to using a subject pronoun even where her name does not appear in the passage. In one notable episode (194–95), Connie is referred to twelve times as *she* or *her* although her proper name is not given once. Of thirty-five expressions used to designate animate referents, there are a total of twenty-two pronouns (nine of which refer to persons other than Connie, principally the doctors or other patients); six proper names (*Dr. Morgan, Redding,* and *Luciente* [4]); three lexical noun phrases (*the doctors, the patients,* and *outpatients*); two indefinite pronouns (*others*); and two ellipses.

Even taking into account the fact that this passage is narration rather than reported speech, the number of ellipses as compared to anaphoric pronouns and use of proper name is significantly different in the two passages. In Arthur's speech, the proper name accounts for six out of twenty-eight items referring to Jackrabbit (nearly a fifth); pronouns account for seven items (a quarter of the total), while ellipses account for thirteen items (almost half). In the passage concerning Connie, on the other hand, there is zero mention of her name and no use of ellipsis, while more than half of the total number of referring expressions (thirteen out of twenty-two) are pronominals referring to her. Since Connie is the principal focalizer and all events are seen through her eyes, the narrator may safely assume she remains active in the reader's mind throughout the novel, hence the absence of her proper name in the passage in question. But, one could point out, Jackrabbit is just as salient in the scene of his memorial service. It is the choice of ellipsis over pronominalization that is most distinctive in Arthur's speech, followed by the abrupt return of the proper name. It seems that, like Le Guin, Piercy finds morphosyntactic neologisms cumbersome to use, even when they are her own invention. The preference for ellipsis over pronominalization appears to be motivated by a desire to avoid overburdening the text with neologistic forms.

Although the strategy creating epicene or common-gender pronouns is the same in both Arnold's and Piercy's novels, the intentions of the two authors are rather different. Piercy intends her novel to reflect the egalitarian future world of Mattapoisett, a world in which sex-role differentiation has been reduced to the point where fetuses are brought to term in giant "brooders," where three mothers, of either sex, volunteer to rear the baby, and where men are able to lactate just as women do. Indeed, Piercy affirms, "I use the common gender pronouns to reinforce the egalitarian nature of that society" (personal communication, 13 December 1993.) Gender distinctions are not an issue in Arnold's short-lived women's community, because in this separatist environment, there is only one gender present among the adults. Although the children of the women's community include both girls and boys, they play a minor role in the novel and are only distinguished by gender in the brief episode analyzed earlier (see example 6.13). It is significant that the children's genders are revealed in a moment of explicit hostility between the boys and the girls.

Many readers have assumed that the traditional pronominal system is entirely replaced by the epicene neologisms in Piercy and Arnold's novels. Dennis Baron states, for example, "June Arnold uses *na* and *nan* . . . for all the third-person pronouns in her novel *The Cook and the Carpenter* (1973), whereas in *Sister Gin* (1975) she silently reverts to conventional pronoun usage" (1986, 209). This description suggests that Arnold created her epicene pronouns, tried them out in her first novel, found them unsuccessful, and dropped them in favor of traditional pronouns in her subsequent works. The phrase "silently reverts" implies a sheepish return to the fold prompted by failure. But we have seen, although the epicene neologisms, and the ideology for which they stand, are defeated during the course of the novel, the defeat itself is used to underpin the author's message. As for Piercy's pronouns, they are the arrowheads of a future utopia that both point the way to go and stand as evidence that utopia is achievable.

Both Arnold and Piercy use their neologisms as a supplement and a contrast to the masculine/feminine dyad of the more conventional *he/she*. Because of this, the neologisms achieve great significance, since they can be used to point out gaps and inequities in the traditional system. As we have seen, juxtaposition of the two systems makes the clash much more apparent than if only epicene pronouns were used. The unfamiliar nature of the pronouns themselves calls attention to their presence. This is something of a mixed blessing. While *na, nan, person*, and *per* are remarkable enough to require the reader to pause and ponder their appearance and significance, their novelty value makes them unwieldy, causing their authors to avoid them at times in favor of low-empathy, low-cohesion devices such as proper name repetition and lexical substitution.

Far from condemning such experiments as failures that "mangle English" and "drive the reader mad," I would suggest that this "wild, fierce and intractable tribe" (to use Le Guin's expression) points the way to future developments and shows up the inadequacies of the existing system. In the next chapter we will see how the traditional systems function for more liminal groups, such as transsexuals and hermaphrodites, and how they deal with its inadequacies.

7

"Avant j'étais un transsexuel, maintenant j'étais une femme"
Linguistic Gender and Liminal Identity

So far in our discussion of the linguistic gender system in French and English, we have mainly considered literary texts in which the gender identity of the characters is itself unproblematic. Many of the novels studied are by or about lesbians or bisexual women, adding sexual orientation as an axis of inquiry, but the characters themselves are not usually described as sexually ambiguous. Exceptions to this are Natalie Clifford Barney's *The One Who Is Legion*, Brophy's *In Transit*, and Ursula K. Le Guin's *The Left Hand of Darkness*. The first two are narrated by figures whose gender identity is unorthodox: the narrator of the former is a hermaphrodite, while that of the latter is either-male-or-female. However, the conventions of the genre in which each novel was written—the first symbolist, the second parodic— prevent the reader from taking this gender ambiguity at face value. In Barney's novel, the intention is obviously metaphoric, a breaking down of the self into constituent parts, while Brophy's parody depends on the reader's recognizing the gender conventions. Only Le Guin grapples with, and expects her readers to believe in, truly ambisexual beings, but the science-fictional setting serves to divorce the beings described from everyday reality.

All the writers whose work has been examined here play with linguistic gender, teasing the reader with neologistic pronouns or the complete absence of pronouns. However, each in her own way is still focused on the idea of femininity even while trying to redefine it. Even Monique Wittig, despite her famous declaration "Lesbians are not women" (1992b, 32), proposes a female who is neither defined by nor dependent on men for her existence, rather than repudiating the very idea of femininity. In her fiction, she does not question the validity of female designators but exploits and reinforces them. In this chapter I will consider a rather different use of the gender system and a different constituency, at times at odds with but mostly indifferent or impervious to the authors discussed so far and the ideology they reflect. I turn my attention to figures who find themselves not on the losing side of the gender binary, as women do, but invisible to it: male-to-female transsexuals, hermaphrodites, and drag queens. The hermaphrodite body, being at once both male and female, and the transsexual body, being at one time male, at another female, pose an obvious conundrum for the linguistic gender systems in French and English, organized as they are around the unmarked/marked dyad of masculinity/femininity. Yet the reiterated desire of transsexuals for the anatomical and hormonal configuration of the opposite sex, their belief that they cannot live a life of dignity and self-respect unless their body is surgically altered so that they may inhabit the world of the gender with which they identify, poses an even larger problem for theories of gender fluidity.

Ecriture féminine: *Writing the Body*

Before examining the function of grammatical gender in French accounts of transsexual, hermaphrodite, and gay male figures, we will look briefly at some of the statements made concerning gender identity and the body by French feminists. These statements form something of a bridge between feminist theory about gender dualism and the physical and anatomical transgression of transsexuality and hermaphroditism. In an interview with Marie-Dominique Lelièvre in *L'Evènement de jeudi* (May 1986), Anne Garréta champions an androgynous gender fluidity, demanding, "Quand vous mixez un homme et une femme qu'est-ce qui vous reste?" (when you mix a man and woman together, what's left?). The question is interesting for its confusion of addition and subtraction. If it were possible to create a being made up of a man and a woman, there would of course be nothing left—everything would have gone into the new dual-sexed being. But if the question is really about the mixing together of traditionally masculine and feminine attributes, then the residue would be composed of the unisex elements, those that are considered neither masculine nor feminine but common to both sexes. In an explicit attack on the *écriture féminine* school of French feminism (as seen in the works of Hélène Cixous and Chantal Chawaf), Garréta remarks, "Part of the fun with *Sphinx* was to destabilize the easy identifications, the asinine reductions and simplifications around 'la différence des sexes' and 'le Féminin,' these new essentialist sacred cows" (personal communication, 18 November 1993; English in the original). By 1986, *écriture féminine* was hardly new, having seen its heyday in the mid-1970s, but essentialist it certainly was. Nor is it surprising that the adamantly postmodern Garréta should oppose it so strongly.

Chantal Chawaf launches her essay "La chair linguistique" with the rhetorical "[l]'aboutissement de l'écriture n'est-il pas de prononcer le corps?" (is not the aim of writing to articulate the body?) (1976, 18), while Hélène Cixous exhorts, "Ecris! L'écriture est pour toi, tu es pour toi, ton corps est à toi, prends-le. . . . Les femmes sont corps. Plus corps donc plus écriture." (write! Writing is for you, you are for you, your body is yours, take it. . . . Women are bodies. More body so more writing) (1975, 40, 48).

Cixous's command is more than a little puzzling: of what does the greater corporeality of women's writing consist? Elsewhere she goes some way toward elucidating the question, explaining that she believes women's writing to be more concerned with the material than men's ([1976] 1992, 91). This insistence on the physical nature of women's writing has been taken up by more than one feminist writer. Françoise Collin, the founder and director of the Belgian feminist magazine *Les Cahiers du Grif*, complains of a kind of fascism in men's language, which she said was cut off from the body and material reality: "[o]n est bien loin du corps vivant: on est dans les signes qui ne se réfèrent à rien" (we are far from the living body; we are among signs which fail to refer) (1992 [1976], 23). Like Cixous, Collin suggests that women have a more material relationship to language than do men, who tend toward abstraction. In the language of men, signs tend to point to other signs rather than to real-world entities. Annie Leclerc claims that language may be called feminine insofar as it could only have been written by a woman: "[d]ans la mesure où ça ne peut naître que de nous, parce qu'on est restées acrochées au corps" (insofar as it can only be born of us, because we have remained attached to the body) (1976, 18). She adds, however, that a man too may write the feminine on the condition that he goes back to his body.

Leclerc's perspective is already less essentialist and more grounded in constructionist materialism, the theory that gender distinctions are constructed in and by societal pressure. Julia Kristeva expands on the theme, returning to Lévi-Strauss's theory of the exchange of women and its relation to language. For her, the *effet femme* (feminine perspective) comes from the knowledge of the underdog, or, as she puts it, "l'esclave en sait plus que le maître" (the slave knows more than the master) ([1974] 1992, 59). Whereas Cixous, Chawaf, and Leclerc speak, somewhat vaguely, of women's language, Kristeva speaks of the semiotic system, the cultural meaning of symbolic codes, including language. She states that "[o]n peut dire aussi que cet 'effet femme' peut être assumé par un homme et c'est même ce qui démontre l'homosexualité masculine" (one can also say that this *effet femme* can be displayed by a man, which is in fact what indicates male homosexuality) ([1974] 1992, 59). The command by Cixous and others to "write the body" must be interpreted in its metaphorical sense. It invokes a return to material concerns, anchored in the physical reality of the writer's life, rather than in the falsely universalizing abstraction deemed typical of men, who, being the unmarked sex, may regard their own physicality as a prototype that may therefore go unmentioned. Kristeva's point is that homosexual men, being marked out as different because of their sexual orientation, may be more aware of their own physicality.

The Transsexual Challenge

Cixous and others have frequently been accused of essentialism, and there is an obvious gender essentialism in the idea that one has been born in the wrong body. If gender is a continuum, related only partially to the biological facts of the body, as Garréta would have it, then a sex-change operation is no more than cosmetic surgery, while the anatomy of the hermaphrodite should be irrelevant to his/her destiny. The specific challenge posed by transsexuals has been taken up, and sometimes bitterly opposed, by American theorists and radical feminists. Part of the ensuing discussion has centered around the use of gendered pronouns. Janice Raymond's *The Transsexual Empire* (1979) is subtitled *The Making of the She-Male*, a phrase that, says the author, illustrates her belief that while transsexuals may be fundamentally masculine or feminine, they are not fundamentally men or women. With this distinction, Raymond is drawing a line between the biological trappings of femininity (and masculinity, though she is principally concerned with male-to-female transsexuals) and "true womanhood," which, though culturally based, is inculcated from birth onward and cannot be replicated in voice workshops and afternoon sessions on how to speak like a woman.[1] When referring to male-to-female transsexuals, Raymond refuses to use the pronouns *she* and *her* unmodified, putting them in scare quotes—"she," "her,"—instead to emphasize their anomalous status. Femininity is not, according to Raymond, simply a question of anatomical configuration. Feminine pronouns confer a status on the referent that existential statements such as "you are a woman", comforting though they may be, cannot. The use of a feminine pronoun presupposes the femininity of the referent; it does not assert it. The important difference here between an assertion and a presupposition is that the truth of an assertion can be questioned or denied simply by putting the clause containing it in the interrogative or the negative, as has been demonstrated in chapter 3. Cooperative speakers do not question presuppositions, and social commerce relies on cooperation.[2] Raymond is explicitly refusing to cooperate with the transsexual worldview, believing that the transsexual project displaces and denaturalizes women.

This refusal to understand or accept is prefigured in Connie's shocked and antagonistic reaction to Luciente in Marge Piercy's *Woman on the Edge of Time*, published in 1976, three years before Raymond's book. As we observed in chapter 6, when Connie first encounters this character from the future, she is unable to process the perceived contradiction between Luciente's self-confident manner and feminine gender and, striving for an appropriate designator, calls her "a sex-change operation." As she comes to know Luciente, she begins to see her apparently unfeminine behavior as another way of being a woman. Even the term "sex change operation" is considered pejorative nowadays. The transsexuals I have spoken to in the San Francisco Bay Area feel that "sex reassignment surgery" is more appropriate, suggesting that the person's sex has not been changed but rather made to fit their self-perception.

The fight over the right to pronominally feminine (or masculine) status has not been restricted to theoretical works. A heated debate arose in the gay, lesbian, and transgender communities over the correct way to refer to Billy Tipton and Teena Brandon, two people who were anatomically female but lived their lives and were accepted by their community as men. Billy Tipton was a jazz musician who married a woman and adopted and brought up children with her. At his[3] death in 1989, it was revealed that he was anatomically female. While the gay community has claimed Billy Tipton as a lesbian and a passing woman, the *Transsexual News Telegraph* (*TNT*), a transgender 'zine of the San Francisco Bay Area, claims Billy Tipton as a transsexual man. Whereas the gay community uses the pronoun *she* to refer to Tipton, *TNT* uses *he*: "Billy Tipton was transsexual. He lived and died as a man. . . . Hands off! He's one of ours!" (*TNT*, summer 1993).

Feelings are even more heated when discussion turns to Brandon Teena. The *San Francisco Bay Times* (a gay paper) ran an article on the murder of Teena Brandon headlined "Queers Have No Right to Life in Nebraska" (13 January 1994). It tells how Teena Brandon, calling herself Brandon Teena, passed as a man in Falls City, Nebraska, dating girls and playing pool "just like any straight man would." On Christmas Eve in 1993, Brandon was raped by the ex-boyfriend of his female lover and a friend of the ex-boyfriend; on 31 December, Brandon and two friends, including his lover, were found murdered. The *Bay Times* of 27 January 1994 ran two letters criticizing the portrayal of Brandon's life. Gail Sondegaard, the editor of *TNT* complained, "[y]ou kept referring to Brandon Teena as 'she' and as a 'cross-dressing lesbian' . . . Brandon went to a lot of effort to be taken seriously as a male. I think you should have respected that choice and referred to him as he obviously wished to be addressed: as a man." Max Wolf, another letter writer, makes a similar point: "it appears Brandon had made the choice to live his life using the male pronoun to refer to himself. . . . Mindy Ridgway [the *Bay Times* journalist] should . . . respect his choice by referring to him not as 'she' but as 'he.'" The wording of this letter is telling. Wolf equates the assignment of male pronouns with living as a man, as though it were the pronoun itself which conferred manhood.

Five years later, it seems, the transsexual lobby has won this particular skirmish along the gender border. In an article about *Boys Don't Cry*, the director Kimberly Peirce's film of the Brandon Teena story, the *San Francisco Chronicle* (20 October 1999) refers to Brandon as "a cross-dressing woman" and uses the anaphoric pronoun *him* at the second mention. It quotes Peirce as saying, "I instantly fell in love with him." Both director and interviewer accept Brandon as a man, apparently. However, this naturalization proves to be imperfect, for later on in the article the *Chronicle* puts the masculine pronoun in quotation marks: "'[h]e,' as friends referred to Brandon." If Brandon's gender were unproblematically established, there would be no need for either quotation marks or explanation. Furthermore, the director who was earlier quoted declaring her love for her (masculine) subject and who demonstrated her sympathy for the transsexual cause by attending the trial of Brandon's murderers in the company of a group of transsexuals from the activist group the Transsexual Menace, herself switches pronouns when talking about Brandon's youth: "[h]ere was a girl growing up in Nebraska . . . with no role models for her emerging identity." A 1996 biography of Brandon is titled *All She Wanted*, the feminine pronoun ironically making clear that however sympathetic the biographer may be to Brandon's desire to be accepted as a man, readers are expected to consider Brandon female.

In a provocative argument, Susan Stryker, a male-to-female transsexual, has said that transsexuality is a linguistic problem: "transsexual genders, by virtue of their temporality, exceed language's static capacity to represent them" (unpublished abstract, 1997). A change of grammatical gender is a mark not of a change of identity, but of a lack of identity, if we take the term "identity" to mean "the quality or condition of being the same," as my *Shorter Oxford English Dictionary* has it. Put this way, we see that the question of how identities can change is a problem not only for transsexuals but for everyone. How, Stryker asks, does one speak of the pubescent experience of a female-to-male transsexual, of the periods she used to have as a woman, but, as a man, is incapable of having? "When he got his period"? "When he got her period"? Or, to give a French example, how does one speak about the pregnancy of a female-to-male transsexual? Does one use the anatomically incorrect "quand elle était enceinte" (when she was pregnant)?[4]— one is after all speaking of a person with male genitalia—or the grammatically incorrect "quand il était enceinte" (when he was pregnant)?

The *théorie de l'énonciation*, the French school of discourse analysis, has come up with two useful terms to distinguish between the speaker of an utterance and the persona, or ethos, of the speaker as created by that utterance. Oswald Ducrot coined the terms *locuteur-L* (the speaker as such) and *locuteur-λ* (the speaker as a being in the world) to articulate the difference between the person narrating a story (*locuteur-L*) and the identity that person creates for themself in the story (*locuteur-λ*). He applies these terms, for example, to Rousseau's *Confessions*, in order to explain how the Rousseau writing (*locuteur-L*) constructs the younger Jean-Jacques (*locuteur-λ*) as brash and even vulgar (peeing in a saucepan) in order to gain the reader's belief in Rousseau's honesty, at the expense of Jean-Jacques's reputation (or ethos). An archconservative of fifty may tell a story about herself as an eighteen-year-old radical; someone who has lost a leg may tell a story from before the accident, using the same pronoun, *je*, without fear of being misunderstood, narrating in a historic present tense feats of athleticism of which he is visibly no longer capable. The contrast between oneself at the time of speaking and oneself at a previous time is immediately apprehensible, the gap between the two resolved by a concept of the self changing through time, whereas a change in the gender of the narrator causes a rupture, a sense of discontinuity, as though a second person must be involved. Time is understood as inherently changeable, while gender is stable and immutable. Both English and French have complex morphological tense and aspect systems by which distinctions of anteriority, simultaneity, and posteriority, as well as past, present, and future, may be made. Gender, in contrast, is for the most part encoded morphologically as a binary.

The discourse of transsexuality points out the gaps not only in the linguistic system, but also in the common perception of gender. In an article on male-to-female transsexual Kate Bornstein's book *Gender Outlaw*, the reviewer prefaces her remarks with an account of her own reaction to reading about and seeing photographs of intersexed infants for the first time. "There was pure terror in the idea that someone might be born neither male nor female. So central to my understanding of the world was the natural bipolar division of human beings by gender that it was as if gravity had stopped working" (Gordon 1994, 18). (The reviewer's use of the term *gravity*, with its image of strong pressure exerted on the human body to keep it in its place and prevent it soaring upward, is telling). Perhaps we need to add to our set of analytical terms the possibility of a (masculine) *locuteur-L* speaking about a (feminine) *locutrice-λ*. To the subscript notations i, j, k, and so on, denoting the same or different referents, we should add i_f, i_m and j_f, j_m to denote coreference with change of gender.

The question of how to refer to transsexuals was considered so important that the publishers of *Appelez-moi Gina* (1994), the autobiography of Georgine Noël, a Belgian male-to-female transsexual, placed the arresting question "Il ou Elle? *Il* puis *Elle*?" (He or She? *He* then *She*?) at the top of their cover blurb. The fact that the question may be asked is eye-catching in itself, whatever answer is given. Another male-to-female transsexual, Sylviane Dullak, titles her 1983 autobiography *Je serai elle*, signifying her determination not only to be accepted as a woman, but to pass as female without question, her gender presupposed, not asserted.

The technological advances in this controversial area have been accompanied by a flurry of lexicographic activity, as may be seen from the plethora of terms that have been used to refer to a person who grew up as one sex but who now manifests another and to the various transitional stages in between. Jane Hervé and Jeanne Lagier offer an impressive list containing no fewer than eighteen lexical items gathered from a study of transsexuals:

> un transsexuel, une transsexuelle, un transsexuel mâle, un transsexuel femelle, un transsexuel masculin, un transsexuel féminin, un transsexuel primaire, un transsexuel secondaire, des transsexuels H → F, des transsexuels F → H, un homme transsexuel, une femme transsexuelle, ni un homme ni une femme, un homme et/ou une femme, un homfemme, des hommes-femelles [this last from the French translation of Raymond's *The Transsexual Empire*], les trans, les T. S.; les femmes Tarzan ou Rambo, les hommes Sissi ou Vénus. (1992, 13–14)

> a transsexual$_m$, a transsexual$_f$, a male transsexual, a female transsexual, a masculine transsexual, a feminine transsexual, a primary transsexual, a secondary transsexual, M → F transsexuals, F → M transsexuals, a transsexual man, a transsexual woman, neither a man nor a woman, a man and/or a woman, a manwoman, female-men, trans, T. S., Tarzan or Rambo women, Sissi or Venus men.

Of these items, twelve (two-thirds) are grammatically masculine. Even in this liminal domain, where one might have expected a reversal, or at least an upheaval, in the traditional order, we find that the masculine once again has the unmarked value, allowing zero, minus, and plus interpretations with regard to femininity: *un transsexuel* (zero); *un transsexuel mâle* (minus), *un transsexuel femelle* (plus). The last two items on the list, *les femmes Tarzan ou Rambo* and *les hommes Sissi ou Vénus,* are remarkable for their appeal to cultural stereotypes of hypermasculinity and hyperfemininity as designations for transsexual women and men (see Livia 1995a for discussion of images of masculinity as prototypes for butch lesbian speech).

Hervé and Lagier offer a second list of six items that have been used to refer to the transsexual phenomenon itself (p. 16): *transsexualisme* (a medical and psychoanalytical term), *transsexualité* (a legal term), *holodysmorphie* (indicating that the whole body has a form at odds with the self-presentation), *hétérosomie* (the body is other [than it should be]), *xénosomie* (the body is a stranger [to itself]), and *antimorphisme* (the body has a form contrary to the usual). Though a rich vocabulary may indicate intense interest in and high cultural value placed upon the referent concerned, in this case it seems rather to be born of confusion and political disagreement, a grasping to name and thereby claim disputed territory. As the authors explain, the transsexuals in their survey also are trying unsuccessfully to find terms for themselves based on incontestable semantic, linguistic, and grammatical criteria (16). The key word here is "incontestable": as we have seen from the above lists, the terms themselves exist, but only when they are uncontested will the referents be accepted without question.

An analysis of the way one male-to-female-transsexual refers to herself in her autobiography will demonstrate the versatile uses to which the linguistic gender system may be put. I concentrate here on *Appelez-moi Gina* (Call Me Gina), by Georgine Noël, but my research data show similar results for four other autobiographies of male-to-female transsexuals writing in French: *Né homme, comment je suis devenue femme* (Born a Man, How I Became a Woman), by Brigitte Martel (1981); *Alain, transsexuelle* (Alain, transsexual_f_), by Inge Stephens (1983); *Diane par Diane* (Diane by Diane), by Diane (1987); *Je serai elle* (I Will Be She), by Sylviane Dullak (1983); and two biographies, *Histoire de Jeanne transsexuelle* (The Story of Jeanne, a Transsexual), by Catherine Rihoit (1980), and *Le Combat de la mère d'un transsexuel* (The Struggle of the Mother of a Transsexual), by Marie Mayrand (1986). In each case, although the transsexual asserts that she has been female since birth, she alternates between masculine and feminine gender concord with regard to herself, indicating that the situation was in fact far more complex. The two third person accounts (Rihoit 1980 and Mayrand 1986) also switch gender reference. Mayrand, for example, whose son changed from a masculine to a feminine identity, describes her offspring in the masculine until the moment she herself accepted that *he* was a *she.* After this point in the narrative she uses feminine concord, except when describing a photograph of her child at her second wedding, where she writes of *him* in the masculine, because for this occasion *he* was wearing a man's suit (60).[5]

Plot Summary: Appelez-moi Gina

This is the autobiography of a male-to-female transsexual who grew up in rural Belgium during the Second World War. Born Georges, Gina fights to be accepted as the woman she believes herself to be. After training to be a doctor, Gina goes to work in Rwanda and the Congo, then returns to Europe, where she finally meets other transsexuals and undergoes sex reassignment surgery.

As the following investigation demonstrates, the changes of grammatical gender in *Appelez-moi Gina* are complex, suggesting that Gina's gender identification is not stable but varies according to social situation and role. Since she presents herself as always having been female, despite the facts of her body, Noël might have referred to herself in the feminine throughout her autobiography. Or, since her sex change operation gave her anatomically correct female genitalia, she might have used masculine concord up to that point and feminine thereafter. Nine years after the operation, her sex was legally changed on her birth certificate from "male" to "female," another possible demarcation point between masculinity and femininity. Though she insists that her sex reassignment surgery, which took place when she was thirty-nine, merely reestablished the correspondence between her body and her mind (1994, 10), Noël uses the binary opposition of the French linguistic gender system throughout her autobiography to express or underscore many of her changes of mood, attitude, and identification, an expressivity that goes far beyond the simple polar opposites of "binary thinking." *Appelez-moi Gina* demonstrates how a structural binary may be subverted into expressing many more than one single opposition.

The reader first sees Noël *allongée* (lying down$_f$) (9) on her hospital bed in Lausanne after her operation.

7.1.   Avant j'étais **un** transsexuel, maintenant j'étais une femme. (10)

Before I was a transsexual$_m$, now I was a woman.

Noël uses the masculine form of the noun *transsexuel* to emphasize that it was as a male that her gender identity was abnormal. However, the use of the imperfect to describe both masculine and feminine states militates against a progressive reading of the changeover. The imperfect is typically used in French to express temporally unbounded states in the past; since it does not place them sequentially along the time line, it conveys no notion of one event preceding or following another. Thus, the temporal adverbs *avant* (before) and *maintenant* (now) claim a reality the verb tenses dispute. We will see in the following analysis that although Noël says that she always considered herself feminine, in fact masculinity and femininity overlap, compete, and alternate with each other throughout the narrative.

Before recounting, in chronological order, the main episodes of her life, Noël describes the life that might have been hers had she had sex reassignment surgery at age fifteen.

7.2. Placée dans un environnement scolaire exclusivement féminin [j'aurais pu] participer normalement aux sports. (11)

Placed$_f$ in an exclusively feminine school environment [I could have] played my part in sports in the normal way.

7.3. Heureuse d'être femme et épouse, j'**aurais aimé** adopté les enfants. (11)

Happy$_f$ to be a woman and a wife, I **would have liked** to adopt children.

The contrary-to-fact conditional of example 7.3 is used for the experience she would have liked, in contrast with the imperfect of example 7.4, which describes the events she lived through.

7.4. Comment le petit garçon pouvait-il un jour se révéler dans la femme adulte? Il **allait** vivre bien des souffrances. (22)

How could the little boy show himself one day in the adult woman? He **was going to/would** experience much suffering.

This pattern of imperfect for past lived events and conditional for future, hypothetical time is repeated to underscore the tenuousness of both positions. In addition to its use for habitual and durative events in the past, the imperfect is also used by children playing make-believe to establish *irrealis* conditions: "moi j'étais le médecin et toi tu étais la petite fille" (I'll be the doctor and you'll be the little girl; lit., I was the doctor and you were the little girl). There is a tinge, then, of the unreal in Noël's description of herself in the masculine. Noël recounts:

7.5. J'ai appris ce qu'on enseignait à qui j'étais et à qui je deviendrais. (32)

I learned what was being taught to the person I was and to the person I would become.

The impermanent nature of the person she was, and the uncertain character of the one she was to become, underline her precarious sense of identity. The *je* of "qui j'étais" (the person I was) and the *je* of "qui je deviendrais" (the person I would become) seem at odds with each other, as though they referred to different subjects.

In a lengthy introduction, Docteur Georgine Noël, as she is called on the title page, explains to the reader the medical facts of transsexualism, establishing herself as an authority rather than a victim by virtue of her medical expertise. The autobiography begins with Georges's birth. At first

Noël's choice of tense allows her to fudge the gender issue. For the announcement of her birth she uses the *passé simple* (simple past), avoiding the *passé composé* (composed past), which would have identified her as male: "je naquis " (I was born) (26). The *passé simple* also conveys a lack of connection to the present, categorizing the event as firmly part of the past with no relevance to the moment of utterance, downplaying the link between the baby boy who was born and the sixty-year-old woman who is telling the story.

Recalling how, during the dangerous years of the Nazi occupation, she and her mother were left at home while her father went off to work, Noël describes them as "seuls toute la journée" (alone$_{mpl}$ all day long) (27), using the masculine plural form of the adjective as is customary with mixed-gender referents. Since Noël's mother is clearly a woman, it must be Noël's own masculinity that prevents the adjective from taking the form of the feminine plural. Although for most of the narrative, she will insist on the isolation and loneliness of being a girl trapped in a male body, there are moments when Noël sees a certain heroism in her masculinity. She and her mother cannot be described as two females alone at the mercy of wandering German soldiers, for she at least has the body of a boy, hence the adjective *seuls* in its masculine form. When her father learns that the Gestapo have set out to arrest her cousins for refusing to work in a German arms factory, it is she who pedals furiously on her bicycle to warn them and almost certainly saves their lives. Noël reports how she jumped heroically onto her bicycle, using the historic present which, not requiring gender agreement, does not make clear whether she performs this action as a boy or a girl (35). The bicycle has, however, been introduced in some detail in the previous paragraph as an instrument for masculine independence: "je pourrais aller seul à l'école" (I could go to school alone$_m$) (35), preventing Noël from walking home from school in the company of her girlfriends, picking flowers, chasing butterflies, and reveling in other girlish activities. At first Noël resents the gift of the bicycle, because it reinforces her masculinity and autonomy at the expense of her camaraderie with the girls. It becomes heroic, however, when it enables her to go, boyishly, to the rescue of her cousins. Throughout the autobiography, Noël's alternation between masculine and feminine forms encodes subtle changes of attitude.

From this point in the narrative until she begins to write a secret diary, Noël describes herself solidly in the masculine, as may be seen in examples 7.6a–e.

7.6a.   J'étais un enfant souffreteux. (27)
          I was a sickly$_m$ child.

   b.   Elève absent . . . assis au dernier banc. (29)
          a distracted$_m$ pupil . . . sitting$_m$ on the last bench.

   c.   J'étais bon élève. (29)
          I was a good$_m$ pupil.

d. Engoncé dans mon costume trois pièces. (40)
   stuffed$_m$ into my three-piece suit

e. J'étais encore trop jeune et maladroit. (43)
   I was still too young and clumsy$_m$.

The adjective *seul* (alone$_m$) is used to describe her seven times in thirteen pages, always in the masculine, emphasizing Noël's unease with her gender status and suggesting that had she been accepted as a girl, she would not have been so isolated. Indeed, she asserts that the feminine side of herself was struggling to be born, as though the original birth, that of Georges, was inauthentic because no conscious thought was involved.

7.7. La fille cherchait à naître isolée au milieu de tant de garçons. (46)

   The girl was struggling to be born, isolated$_f$ amongst so many boys.

The feminine form of the adjective *isolée* (isolated), after a litany of *seul* in the masculine, underlines the fact that Noël is alone despite the companionship of other boys because she is fundamentally different from them.

With the idea not only of writing a diary but of writing it in a secret code decipherable only by herself comes the possibility of talking about herself in the feminine. Noël records that she did not trust her parents to respect her privacy. She describes herself as estranged from her body and states that she would have liked to transport her soul into one that fitted her better (51). The noun *étrangère* (stranger) appears in the feminine form, as does *une autre* (another). Even though she is speaking of her own alienation, this is the first time in the story of her childhood that Noël uses feminine markers for herself in a sustained sequence. Creating her own private code with which to recount her thoughts and feelings, a code very different from the one in which she is obliged to live her life, gives her sufficient distance from the masculine persona forced upon her that she could begin to tell her story differently. Her journal recounts how she followed her male friend Edgard into the playground, using the feminine form of the past participle *revenue* (came back) to underscore the fact that for her this was a heterosexual relationship.

7.8. Je suis revenue dans la cour avec Edgard. (51)

   I came back$_f$ into the playground with Edgard.

She tells of watching the little girls from the local boarding school and feeling that her place was among them. Unfortunately, her mother finds her diary and reads it aloud to her father, commenting (using masculine grammatical agreement, of course) that her son is scribbling down absolute garbage (51). The two parents laugh scornfully at the idea of their son writing in code, while Noël, now described in the feminine, listens in the dark. The contrast between the parents' use of masculine concord and the narrator

Noël's own use of the feminine emphasizes the lack of comprehension between the generations.

After this violation of her privacy, Noël realizes that the journal can no longer provide solace; her secret code is useless. She returns to the masculine, resolving never to share anything with her parents. So that she will not be tempted to give away her secret, she is determined to block everything out; the adjective *bloqué* (blocked) is in its masculine form (52). The narrative now continues with masculine concord, and, as though striving once again to make the best of her enforced masculinity, Noël informs the reader that she joined the Boy Scouts, using the masculine form of the past participle *entré* (entered/joined). For a while masculine gender and masculine exploits seem to achieve a concord that is more than merely grammatical. As before, during her heroic race to save her cousins, Noël's masculinity allows her to do things and go places forbidden to girls. The description of her delight in the scouts' blue uniform, group loyalty, and esprit de corps, as well as their speleological adventures, are summed up in a phrase full of youthful grandiosity.

7.9.   On en rentrait marqué du sceau de l'absolu. (54)

We returned marked$_m$ by the seal of the absolute.

Noël's own participation is consistently narrated in the masculine in this sequence, demonstrating that here at least the use of masculine grammatical gender coincides with her own self-concept.

The next change in grammatical gender occurs when Noël's friend Edgard is expelled from school for reading Baudelaire's *Les Fleurs du mal*.[6] Throughout her autobiography, Noël insists that transsexuals are not homosexual, stating authoritatively that transsexuality is fundamentally different from transvestitism and homosexuality (15). When deciding which cases are right for treatment and surgical reassignment, she argues, the medical practitioner must automatically exclude three groups: transvestites, homosexuals, and professional transsexuals (21). This last term refers to male-to-female transsexuals who take hormones in order to grow breasts and work as prostitutes. Added to this list of undesirables are psychopaths and sexual deviants of all hues; Noël has little patience with other oppressed social groups and shows no solidarity for others whose gender nonconformity sets them apart. To express her own attraction to Edgard and her sadness at his expulsion, Noël has to switch to a feminine self-presentation; otherwise her feelings might be dubbed homosexual.

7.10.   J'étais attirée par cet ami, ne voyais que ses yeux, mais je ne lui en fis jamais l'aveu. (58)

I was attracted$_f$ by this friend, could see nothing but his eyes, but I never let him know it.

Throughout her account of the events of the next few years, the narrative shifts between masculine and feminine gender marking. It is not until Noël moves away from the confining isolation of her village school and the little cottage in the middle of the forest where she has lived with her parents and siblings and enters the sophistications of Louvain, where she will study to be a doctor, that a feminine identity becomes stable and the masculine markers disappear. Until then she must be content with her secret wardrobe of women's clothes, which, like the coded diary of her childhood, permit her the trappings of another sexual identity. She recalls her happiness as, dressed in a woman's blouse, skirt, and shoes, she walked in the middle of the forest, far from the eyes of her family and schoolmates. Here the adjective *heureuse* (happy) is in the feminine. The adjective *seul* (alone), which dominated the account of her childhood, reappears, but this time it is in the feminine and has an entirely positive meaning.

7.11.   (Je) savourais le plaisir d'être enfin pour moi seule. (59)

I savored the pleasure of finally being alone_f for myself [being for myself alone_f].

For Noël in her feminine persona, solitude means not isolation but peace and freedom. At the end of the book, after she has achieved both a sex reassignment surgery and the rectification of her civil status, she will reflect on how being alone does not need to entail feeling ostracized and abandoned but can produce feelings of calm and even joy:

7.12.   C'est seule avec moi-même que j'étais dans la joie. (157)

It was alone_f with myself that I felt joyful.

Lonely and isolated as a boy surrounded by other boys, as a woman alone she feels complete.

In the scene of Noël's lone wandering in the forest, the adjective *seules* is picked up from "je savourais le plaisir d'être pour moi seule" in example 7.11 and repeated in the following sentence, this time applied to the wild animals who roam, unafraid, amongst the trees.

7.13.   Seules les biches et les sangliers passaient par là. (59)

Only_fpl the does and the wild boar passed by there.

Of particular interest in example 7.13 is the fact that the adjective seul**es** has the feminine form. While it is grammatically correct for the adjective to take the gender of the nearest noun it qualifies (*les biches* [the does] is feminine), this rule is often overlooked in favor of a competing one that states that where both masculine and feminine nouns are qualified by the same adjective, the masculine should prevail. Since *les sangliers* (the wild

boars) is masculine, one might have expected *seules* to show masculine concord. Instead, the feminine form is used to imply a sense of fellowship—or
rather sisterhood—in solitude between Noël and the animals, emphasizing
the naturalness of Noël's femininity. A stark contrast to this bucolic scene
is the description of Noël's return home in "normal clothes." Now the
adjective *seuls* reappears in the masculine:

7.14.   Seuls les fleurs, les champignons . . . méritaient attention. (59)

        Only_m the flowers, the mushrooms were worth attention.

Where before *seul* has agreed with the gender of the nearest noun, here,
though it immediately precedes the feminine *les fleurs* (the flowers), it shows
masculine concord, for Noël is no longer dressed as a girl. A sense of pathetic
fallacy unites Noël's feminine identity with the innocence of nature and is
recorded in the choice of grammatical gender. Her return to the masculine
is marked by the masculine form of the adjective *sûr* (sure_m) in an expression
of disgust at the conformation of her body: "sûr que ce n'était pas à moi ce
machin-là" (sure_m that it was not mine, that thingummy-jig there).
     When Noël reads of a British fighter pilot who became a woman, the
feminine forms of the adjectives fleetingly reappear, as she notes that now
she was no longer alone when she appeared in cross-gendered clothes (60).
Even though she has never met the pilot in question, just knowing of her
existence is enough to comfort Noël and reassure her that there are others
like herself. The possibility of realigning her physical make-up so that it
coincides with her own conception of her gender allows Noël to describe
herself once again in the feminine. She is, however, still only a teenager
without money or contacts, and upon her return to school the masculine
reappears—"j'étais petit et mince" (I was small_m and thin) (61)—reflecting her feeling of being formed by her surroundings.
     At last Noël leaves home. The narrative, which recounts her medical
studies in Louvain and her establishment in Rwanda and then the Congo,
stabilizes in the feminine. The adjectives and past participles that describe
her life in Africa are all in the feminine form; it is notable that even here the
adjective *seule* recurs four times.

7.15.   Engagée, attristée, habituée, innocente, gênée, happée, prête, seule, égarée,
        seule, envoyée, seule, voisine, seule, démunie, estimée, affectée, étonnée
        (100–114)

        Hired_f, saddened_f, accustomed_f, innocent_f, embarassed_f, snapped up_f, ready_f,
        lost_f, alone_f, sent_f, alone_f, neighboring_f, alone_f, running out of_f, esteemed_f,
        transferred_f, astonished_f

Suddenly, in the middle of this thoroughly femininized environment, the
masculine returns, only to disappear again immediately. The point at which
it makes its reentry into the text is highly significant. In the course of a small
dinner party with another doctor and his wife, as well as some of the local

white farmers, Noël gets drunk, disappears into her room, and returns wearing a dress. This is the only time she shows her feminine self to other people during the whole of her stay in Africa. From her account of this incident, she turns to a series of racist reflections on the "hypersexual" habits of the Congolese men she has to treat and the observation that their promiscuity has led to the spread of AIDS. It is at this juncture that she describes herself in the masculine once again.

7.16.   Né homme, je devais continuer à manifester ma supériorité sociale et sexuelle. (114)

Born_m a man, I had to continue to show my social and sexual superiority.

The revelatory past participle *né* appears here in its masculine form, so carefully avoided at the outset of the narrative by the use of the *passé simple* in "je naquis," which, though gender neutral, is hardly colloquial. Masculine gender is needed to vouch for Noël's superior status and claim her birthright. Anxious lest her appearance in feminine garb has caused her to lose face among the white people she respects, she scornfully derides what she perceives to be the African sexual libido, emphasizing her own status and authority as a sexually abstemious white male. As soon as the moment of fear has passed, she presents herself as feminine once again. When Noël feels her back is up against the wall, a return to masculine gender presentation and masculine privilege is always possible.

Upon her reintegration into Belgian life, Noël speaks of herself in the masculine. The temporary license she had to present herself as she wanted in the exoticism of her African adventure is rescinded by her need to find her way through the bureaucratic process of reentry into the European way of life. It is not until she again finds a context in which to rethink her femininity that Noël begins to describe herself in the feminine. It is, ironically, in the newspaper account of the death of "Peggy," who died of an embolism ten days after sex reassignment surgery, that Noël discovers the address of an organization for transsexuals in Paris, the Association d'aide aux malades hormonaux (A.Ma.Ho.), an assocation for aid to people with hormonal problems. In a little group of transsexual friends that meets regularly in the suburbs of Paris, she finds a community. The other male-to-female transsexuals are described in the feminine plural as *amies* (130). The grammatical feminine makes a comeback, and for the first time in the narrative, it is in the plural, for Noël has finally found other transsexuals like herself. Never before in Noël's account has there been any thread of mutuality, of activities undertaken together, that would generate a feminine plural. Indeed, as we have seen, Noël has tended to despise others like herself, rather than seek common cause with them.

After her account of her own sex reassignment surgery in Lausanne, though her sexual status is not changed on her birth certificate for another nine years, Noël endeavors to retain feminine gender concord for the rest of her life story. There are, however, two events described in the masculine before the operation is finally carried out. After painstakingly assembling all the documentation she needs, including psychiatric, psychological, and medical reports, provided at no small cost by Belgian professionals, she is told by the Swiss surgeon, "C'est très bien tout ça, mais ça vient de l'étranger" (That's all very well, but it's foreign) (134), and is obliged to start over again with Swiss officials. Recounting her frustration and disappointment, she resorts to her masculine persona, recalling that "je suis retourné plusieurs fois" (I went back$_m$ several times) (134). It seems that, as before in her return to Europe, she finds her masculine identity best suited to deal with the harassing bureaucracy.

Noël resumes the use of feminine qualifiers for the preparations that immediately precede the operation, but on the great day itself she recounts being "réveillé tôt le matin" (woken up$_m$ early in the morning) (136) and walking into the operating theater. As she leaves her bedroom, she notices a sign on the door saying "Monsieur Noël." After the operation, she decribes herself in the feminine, "couchée sur le dos" (lying$_f$ on my back) (136); the sign now reads "Madame Noël." Noël has identified as a woman for the last twenty-five years, but she reintroduces the masculine the day of her operation to underline the difference between the person who woke up that morning and the one who lay in bed that night.

It is evident from Noël's skillful manipulation that the grammatical gender system may be utilized as a rich resource for expressing and exposing the inadequacies of the concept of natural gender. The meanings of the masculine and feminine forms of the adjectives and past participles used to qualify Noël at different stages of her life vary enormously. They depend for their significance on the context in which they are found, and it is their contrastive, oppositional nature that makes them so useful in expressing Noël's changes of mood, attitude, and mental state. At times the switch from the masculine to the feminine is indicative of a sense of triumph or success, as when she manages to carve out a territory that will be wholly hers where she may try out her chosen identity. It can also imply more negative emotions, however—fear of homosexuality, for example. While the opposite movement, from a feminine to a masculine persona, often conveys a sense of frustration or failure, as when her diaries are read by her parents, or when she is forced to deal with the endless demands for official documents upon her return from the Congo, this is not always the case. Masculine concord can also express an enjoyment of the authority and superiority of masculinity, as well as a simple, if temporary, appreciation of the sexual identity she was born with, as when she goes potholing with the scouts. The gender binary of *il/elle*, and *assis/assise* has been used, most successfully, to support a wide range of meanings, many only tangentially connected to gender.

Hermaphroditic Discourse

It is not only in transsexual discourse that one finds a significant movement between the use of masculine and feminine qualifiers to describe the same

person. A similar pattern may be perceived in three accounts of hermaphrodites, the first autobiographical, the second two fictional: Herculine
Barbin's *Mes Souvenirs* (1868), Lucie Delarue-Mardrus's *L'Ange et les
pervers* (1930), and my own *Bruised Fruit* (1999). Barbin's memoirs, which
garnered renewed attention after Michel Foucault's (1978) discussion, tell
the story of how s/he was classified among the female sex at birth and grew
up in the all-female worlds of a girls' orphanage, a convent, and a girls'
school (of which she was the *maîtresse*, school mistress), only to be reclas-
sified as a male in early adulthood. Mario/Marion, the hero/heroine of
L'Ange et les pervers, in contrast, after an isolated childhood growing up as
a boy, has his/her civil status changed by his/her uncle to that of a girl in
his/her early twenties. Sydney, one of the three protagonists of *Bruised
Fruit*, grows up as a girl until early adolescence when her/his anatomical
ambiguity is discovered. Sydney is sent to a boys' school, but no surgery is
undertaken to make him/her conform to one gender or another. He/she
lives the rest of his/her life alternating between male and female personas.

Broadly speaking, Camille (Barbin's textual persona) refers to himself/
herself most often in the feminine until the occasion on which s/he first
makes love to Sara, his/her fellow teacher, after which she switches to the
masculine. Mario/Marion, in contrast, changes gender identity each time
s/he crosses the Seine from *her* Right Bank apartment to *his* bachelor digs
on the Left Bank, and despite the legal declaration of her femininity, it is
s/he who decides which identity to wear each day. In descriptions of Sydney,
third person pronouns alternate, depending on how she/he is seen by the
other characters around her/him. Since all three texts demonstrate the same
point—the versatility of the apparently rigid binary of the gender system—
we will concentrate on the first, referring to the other two only to provide
comparison.

As in the transsexual texts, the gender system in hermaphroditic texts
is used to represent not so much the anatomical facts of the body, but more
complex and changing sociocultural information. It is important to note
that the French gender system encodes rather different information for male
and female referents. Camille's and Marion's attitudes to their change of
gender assignment are also markedly different. Camille, moving from a
female identity to a male, sees this change of status, at least in the early days,
as the source of freedom and adventure. She recalls that her lover, Sara's,
eyes seemed to say, "tu as soif d'une existence libre, indépendante" (you
are thirsty for a free, independent existence) (92), and Camille himself reports, "ce vaste désir de l'inconnu me rendit égoïste" (this vast desire for
the unknown made me egotistical) (92), while her mother "était radieuse"
(was radiant), seeing her daughter's change of gender as "l'aurore d'un
avenir radieux" (the dawn of a radiant future) (106). Masculinity offers the
possibility of freedom and autonomy, a passport out of the confines of
the girls' school, and opens up the world for exploration. For Marion, on the
other hand, who moves from male to female status, the alteration of her
birth certificate is "la suprême offense" (the supreme insult) (60). He had

been his father's only son and heir, the only hope of continuing the aristocratic family name of de Valdeclare, and he now sees himself demoted to
the level of a dependent and unmarriageable girl. Femininity means restric-
tion and enclosure. For Sydney, one of the many refugees in San Francisco's
sexual underground, almost all social roles are open to either sex. It is in
the choice of a sexual partner that problems arise, for Sydney cannot decide whether he is a gay man, or she is a lesbian.

The moment of transformation from one gender identity to another
comes for Camille after she has reflected upon the act of making love with
Sara. She reports having been "heureuse" (happy$_f$) (61) that Sara consented
to share her bed, and was "folle de joie" (mad$_f$ with joy) to feel her friend
lying beside her. Realizing that after their passionate embrace "Sara *m'appartenait* désormais!!" (Sara belonged to me from now on!!) (61)—the phrase
m'appartenait (belonged to me) is in italics in the original—she refers to
herself in the masculine immediately thereafter. It is her sexual orientation
and her sexual behavior that make her masculine, not her physical make-
up, for this has not changed. After the first sexual embrace, Camille declares that instead of her masculinity separating her from Sara, it has in fact
united them physically.

7.17.   Ce qui . . . devait nous séparer . . . nous avait un**is**!!" (62)

        What ought to separate us . . . had united$_{mpl}$ us!!

The masculine plural concord of *unis* reveals the transgression she has com-
mitted. As two girls together, Camille and Sara need not be separated, for
they cannot physically unite. Yet they have indeed been sexually intimate
and therefore ought never to have been in the same bed. In the next sentence, Camille's use of the masculine plural "notre situation à tou**s** deux!"
(our mutual situation, or the situation for both$_{mpl}$ of us) belies the singular
nature of the noun *situation*. Since they no longer have the same gender
identity, the situation is radically different for Camille than for Sara. A similarly ironic contrast is marked in the phrase that follows, which opposes
the doubly feminine *deux soeurs* (two sisters) with the masculine plural
adjective *destinés* (destined).

7.18.   Destin**és** à vivre dans la perpetuelle intimité de deux soeurs. (62)

        Destined$_{mpl}$ to live in the perpetual intimacy of two sisters.

The intimacy that seemed predestined is denied by the form of the adjective which describes it.

The sexual act is, however, not the only defining moment, for, from
the first page of the memoirs, Camille's gender identity switches between
masculinity and femininity. In the second paragraph, which is also the second sentence of the text, Camille describes herself in the masculine.

7.19.   J'ai souffert seul! seul! abandonné de tous! (9)

I have suffered alone$_m$! alone$_m$! abandoned$_m$ by all!

Moving on to a description of herself in in her early years, she begins in the masculine "soucieux et rêveur (anxious$_m$ and dreamy$_m$), but ends in the feminine "j'étais froide, timide" (I was cold$_f$, shy). The movement from masculine to feminine concord here represents a move back in time. The solipsistic masculine qualifiers *soucieux* and *rêveur* apply equally to the Camille of the time of writing and the Camille of long ago, while the socially oriented feminine *froide* and *timide* apply only to the earlier Camille, implying as they do attempts at socialization that, in her isolated state, the older, masculine Camille has abandoned.

Although Camille refers to herself in the masculine once again after she and Sara have made love, the feminine returns at significant points in the narrative. When Sara's older sister, who had been running the school where both Sara and Camille teach, moves away with her husband, Sara's mother suggests that Camille take the older sister's place. Camille explains, however, that she was not old enough to take up these duties officially.

7.20.   Je n'étais pas encore majeure.

I was not yet of age$_f$ (77)

The feminine form is given because it is Camille's civil status that is at issue, and she was, at this time, still legally a girl. She asks the school inspector for special permission to assume the functions Sara's sister had filled until she is legally of age to carry them out, adding that she was confident the inspector would support her application.

7.21.   J'étais sûre de l'appui du préfet. (78)

I was sure$_f$ of the prefect's support.

The feminine is used here because Camille's certainty of support is linked to the prefect's good opinion of her as a woman, a support that would certainly have been lost had the man known of her physical peculiarity.

Before the masculine takes over completely, there is one last return to the feminine, which occurs just after Camille has been examined by the local doctor. She and Sara go to bed together as usual, and Camille recounts that once they were settled in bed, Sara tells her that the doctor had had a long talk with her mother concerning his examination of Camille. The description of them lying in the same bed uses feminine concord for the past participle:

7.22.   Quand nous fûmes couchées

When we were in bed$_{fpl}$ (80)

Camille is made anxious by the news that the doctor has informed Sara's mother of her own ambiguous gender, and she knows that she and Sara will soon be parted. She describes herself and Sara in the feminine to re-unite them, albeit temporarily. It is the last time she will have any control over how the world sees their relationship.

Through her use of the French linguistic gender system, Camille lets the reader know of her painful gender ambiguity from the first page of the nar-rative. In the English translation, the gender discrepancies are not as appar-ent, and it is not until page 58 that reference is made to the grammatical ambiguity of Camille's identity: "She took pleasure in using masculine quali-fiers for me, qualifiers which would later suit my official status." The French reader is given more information than the English reader, and therefore greater understanding of Herculine's position. Richard MacDougall, the English translator, himself concedes, "[I]t is difficult to render the play of masculine and feminine adjectives which Alexina applies to herself" (Foucault 1980, xiii n 1; Alexina is the name by which Herculine Barbin was known by friends and acquaintances until her civil status was changed). MacDougall adds that Alexina's system is "an ironic reminder of grammatical, medical and juridi-cal categories that language must utilize but that the content of the narrative contradicts" (Foucault 1980, xiii n 1). I would suggest that Camille's (Alexina's) use of language is far from ironic. Irony suggests confidence and sophistication, which run counter to what we know of Camille's simple reli-gious upbringing. The twentieth-century reader, informed by Foucault's presentation of the case and contemporary theories of gender fluidity, may well find the alternation between masculine and feminine concord ironic, but I believe it was intended to express the complex and varied states of Camille's psyche. Far from rebelling against the system or trying to expose its contra-dictions, Camille was using it to explain her perplexing situation.

In similar fashion, nearly sixty years later, Lucie Delarue-Mardrus de-scribes Mario/Marion, the protagonist of *L'Ange et les pervers*, as alternately masculine and feminine. Here the changes in gender concord are intended to produce a sense of shock, requiring the reader to work out how the gram-matical system relates to Mario/Marion's personality and mental state. The first chapter introduces us to young Marion de Valdeclare and his tormented childhood in a glacial chateau in the beet fields of Normandy. After he has finished his schooling among the Jesuits, he discovers that the chateau has been bombed and he is an orphan.

7.23.   Il avait toujours été seul au monde. Amèrement, il se mit en route pour la
         vie avec son double, son étrange et néfaste double,—sa tare native. (19)

         He had always been alone$_m$ in the world. Bitterly, he set off on the road to
         life accompanied by his double$_m$, his strange, ill-starred double$_m$—the taint$_f$
         of his birth.

In example 7.23, Mario himself is described in the masculine, but we are told he has a double, and this figure is referred to both in the masculine as "son double" and by the grammatically feminine designator "sa tare native." In this subtle way, the narrator prepares the reader for the revelations of the second chapter, where it becomes apparent that the feminine gender of the noun *tare* is more than a mere grammatical formality, for Mario's double is culturally feminine as well.

Chapter 2 opens in Laurette Wells's bedroom in Neuilly, a rich suburb of Paris, where she is scolding her friend Janine for annoying a third, as yet unnamed, character, described in the feminine.

724.   Ce n'est pas la peine de l'embêter. Elle n'aime rien ni personne. (21)

It's no use bothering her. She loves nothing and no one.

There is, apparently, no continuity between the two chapters, for place, mood, setting, and character have all changed. It is the use of the cataphoric pronoun *elle* that holds the key. As we have seen, while anaphoric links, which introduce referents first by their proper name and subsequently refer to them by pronoun, are common, cataphoric links in which the pronoun precedes the proper name are rarer and therefore more remarkable. Who, then, is this *elle* who, we are told, loves nothing and no one? The only character who might fit that distinction is a sad young man we seem to have left behind in the previous chapter. The reader will be able to tie the enigmatic *elle* definitively to Marion de Valdeclare only after several more paragraphs. By making no explicit declaration, relying instead on the subtle introduction of the unassuming pronoun *elle* and the grammatically feminine *la tare* of the previous chapter, Delarue-Mardrus forces readers to make the connection between Marion's male and female personae, thereby implicating them in his/her change of gender status.

Subsequently, when Mario speaks of himself, he uses masculine concord, sometimes feeling the need to justify his maintenance of male status.

7.25.   Je ne suis pas encore allé chez Laurette, ayant cet acte à terminer . . . avant de redevenir femme. (122–23)

(I have not yet been_m to Laurette's, since I have to finish this thing before I become a woman again.)

Mario has a small, utilitarian studio apartment on the Left Bank to house his male persona, while his female persona lives in more comfortable surroundings on the Right Bank. Unlike Mario's rough work table, Marion's delicate secretaire is too fragile for any more serious work than writing letters. As Miss Hervin, Marion uses feminine concord.

7.26.   Me voilà lancée dans l'immoralité des autres. (97)

Now here I am caught up_f in other people's immorality.

Occasionally, Marion uses both the masculine and the feminine form of adjectives and pronouns to underline her aberrant gender status. As she crosses the Seine, which forms the great divide between her two gender identities, an ironic fluidity that causes Mario/Marion much suffering, we see the transformation that must be effected for *her* to become *him*. It is as a tall, hoarse-voiced girl that she whistles for a cab (the hoarse voice and the ability to whistle already marking her out as different from other young ladies in 1930s Paris). As the cab moves toward his bachelor pad, she takes a tube of petroleum jelly and begins removing her make-up. When the key is in the latch, "[l]a voilà chez elle. Le voilà chez lui" (she was home. He was home) (38). Like Noël in her autobiography, Mario/Marion plays with the masculine and feminine forms of the adjective "alone."

7.27. C'est donc parce que je suis deux qu'il me faut toujours être seul, ou seule. (88)

So it's because I am two that I must always be alone$_m$ or alone$_f$.

Here the loneliness of the double being is emphasized. Gender fluidity provides Mario/Marion with no sense of peace or contentment, but rather drives him/her to a continual search for a way to live as others do. (See Livia 1995b for a further discussion of Mario/Marion's representation of self).

We have seen that Delarue-Mardrus introduces the grammatically feminine noun *tare* to refer to Mario in order to prepare for the use of feminine pronouns to designate the same character in the next chapter. Lest this strike the reader as a very marked use of the French linguistic gender system, it may be useful to compare this strategy with that of more canonical texts. When they want to personify inanimate objects as sexed beings, French authors frequently introduce nouns that will allow the referent to be anaphorized by pronouns of the sex imputed to it. In Emile Zola's "L'Attaque du Moulin" (The Attack on the Mill), a short story set during the Franco-Prussian war, the mill of the title comes to stand for France herself (feminine pronoun intended—"France" is grammatically feminine in French). The mill is personified as "**une** fidè**le** servante vieillie dans la maison" (a$_f$ faithful$_f$ female servant who has grown old$_f$ in the household). In order to write of the mill using feminine pronouns and adjectives, Zola replaces the masculine *le moulin* (the mill) with various feminine lexical substitutes, such as, *une gaieté* (a gay thing), *la bâtisse* (the old building), and *la partie du moulin* (the part of the mill) ([1880] 1969, 85–86). He writes, for example, "[L]a bâtisse, faite de plâtre et de planches, semblait viei**lle** comme le monde. **Elle** trempait à moitié dans la Morelle" (the$_f$ old building$_f$, made$_f$ of plaster and planks, seemed as old$_f$ as the world. It$_f$was half dipping in the Morelle) (86). The use of the feminine *bâtisse* allows Zola to anaphorize the mill as *elle* in the second sentence. Evidently, if the gender of nouns were perceived as a purely grammatical phenomenon, Zola would not have had to go to such lengths to introduce feminine pronouns. *Il* and *elle* are considered first and foremost to be *personal* pronouns, in the sense that they designate *animate* referents. Their use with inanimate referents, although it appears to share equal status with animate referents, according to the traditional grammatical rules of gender concord, is in fact far less common since, as we have seen, the hierarchy of animacy in French places animate referents much higher on scales of saliency and accessibility.

Such devices are also used to designate gender-transgressive identitities. The use of feminine lexical items, feminine concord, and feminine pronouns to connote male homosexuality is a strategy used not only by gay men among themselves (discussed later), but also by heterosexuals commenting on the perceived homosexuality of men of their acquaintance. While exclamations like "la pauvre fille!" (the poor girl), said of a person who is clearly male (Pastre 1997, 372) are intended to provoke reaction by the evident dissonance between the term used and the referent described, other uses of the feminine are more subtle. In the beginning of Honoré de Balzac's short story "Sarrasine" (1830), made famous by Roland Barthes' analysis, *S/Z*, a complex pattern emerges of the grammatically masculine and feminine terms used to refer to a mysterious figure. This figure is introduced to the reader as "un personnage étrange" (a strange personnage$_m$). The next sentence asserts, "C'était un homme" (It was a man) (Barthes 1970, 230), a somewhat unusual declaration, for a character's sex is usually presented as background information, presupposed rather than asserted. In the narrative that follows, masculine pronouns are duly applied to this person: "la première fois qu'**il** se montra dans l'hôtel" (the first time **he** showed himself in the hotel), and other grammatically masculine terms are used to designate him: *l'inconnu* (the stranger$_m$), *l'étranger* (the foreigner$_m$), and *ce monsieur vêtu de noir* (that gentleman dressed$_m$ in black) (230).

Despite explicit assurance of the referent's masculinity, reassurance seems necessary, for a mere eight lines later the narrator reiterates, "L'étranger était simplement un vieillard" (the foreigner$_m$ was simply an old man) (231). From this point on, in marked contrast to this statement, grammatically feminine terms begin to be used in reference to this character: *une goule* (a ghoul$_f$) (231); *une tête génoise* (a Genevan head—a man upon whose life depends on enormous sums of money) (231); *une personne enchantée* (an enchanted$_f$ person$_f$) (232); and *cette créature bizarre* (this$_f$ bizarre creature$_f$) (232). Soon feminine pronouns are introduced, as the narrator recounts how the image he had in his head—that of the strange old man—suddenly appeared before him. The precise wording is important here, for it is the use of a grammatically feminine noun that permits feminine anaphorization: "**la pensée** . . . qui se roulait dans ma cervelle en était sortie, elle se trouvait devant moi, personnifiée, vivante, elle avait jailli comme Minerve de la tête de Jupiter" (the thought$_f$ . . . that was rolling around in my brain had come out, it$_f$ appeared before me, personnified$_f$, alive$_f$, it$_f$ had sprung like Minerva from the head of Jupiter) (233). Since the noun governing the predicates *se trouvait*, and *avait jailli* is the grammatically feminine *la pensée*, anaphoric pronouns and adjectives exhibit feminine concord. However, because the image in the narrator's mind is that of the old man, it seems to be this figure who is referred to as *elle*.

Later described as "cette espèce d'idole japonaise" (this_f sort of Japanese_f idol_f) (235), another grammatically feminine noun phrase, the stranger is again referred to in the feminine: "silencieuse, immobile autant qu'une statue, elle exhalait l'odeur musquée des vieilles robes" (silent_f, still as a statue, it_f [i.e., the Japanese idol, or the stranger] exhaled the musky smell of old dresses) (235). Since we learn subsequently that the old man was an Italian castrato, it becomes clear that Balzac is making use of the rules of grammatical gender concord to suggest an aura of femininity without giving the key to the mystery too early in the narrative.

To give a more modern example, in an article on Michael Jackson in *Paris-Match* (17 July 1987, 43-45), Olivier Royant plays with grammatical gender to underline Jackson's bizarre sexual status and way of life: Qu'arrive-t-il à mon idole? Il paraît qu'**elle** est en train de devenir raide dingue et c'est Michael Jackson . . . roi du disco. . . . C'est **elle** et **lui** mon idole" (What is happening to my idol_f? It seems **she** is going raving mad, and it's Michael Jackson . . . king of disco. . . . **She** and **he** are my idol_f). Readers may also like to look at the use of the grammatically masculine term *monstre* and the grammatically feminine *bête* in reference to the Bête of Jean Cocteau's film *La Belle et la bête* (1946; Beauty and the Beast). Discussing her new "domestic partner" with her father, Belle uses the term *bête*, anaphorized as *elle* (she) to express her sense of the beast's vulnerability and nobility. Her father, in contrast, uses the term *monstre*, anaphorized as *il* (he) to maintain his stance that the creature is evil and inhuman.

When we look at the portrayal of hermaphrodites in English, we see that there too, the linguistic gender system may be used to good effect. As well as being an academic, I also write novels. While I was doing research for *Pronoun Envy*, and translating *L'Ange et les pervers* into English, I began experimenting with my own hermaphrodite character, Sydney. Aware of how the French gender system can be used to facilitate gender portrayal, I was eager to see how far I could push the English pronominal system in the creation of Sydney as a being of indeterminate gender. In my novel *Bruised Fruit*, Sydney is first presented through the eyes of Caroline, who conveys to the reader her doubts and uncertainties about precisely what she is looking at:

7.28.   Young, black 501s, white T-shirt. Hair cut to just below the ears, no make up on face or nails. . . . How alarming not to know a person's sex at first glance. (Livia 1999, 69)

Sydney's clothes and self-presentation do not provide the necessary clues to his/her gender identity, which is in itself unusual. We have seen in the case of Noël that, feeling at odds with her anatomical sex, she works hard to present herself in her preferred gender. Sydney, in this first glimpse, makes no such effort, leaving the task of interpreting him/her entirely to the onlooker. Caroline, who is both emotionally exhausted and naturally ingenuous, quickly settles into thinking of Sydney as a gay man, although even she remains somewhat doutbful. The reader, having no other clue, is obliged to follow her lead.

The other characters make up their own minds about Sydney's gender, depending on how s/he appears to them, and the third person narration follows the same principle. Thus, in sections describing Sydney's sexual exploits with gay men, who assume he is one of them, the narrator uses masculine pronouns to refer to Sydney.

7.29.   Sometimes he would even go to bed, when the yearning or the loneliness was too much, but always in the dark, and he made sure his partner was drunk, or stoned or something. (100–101)

In order for Sydney to preserve his partners' sense of Sydney's maleness, he makes sure, out of courtesy and terror, that they are in a less than fully conscious state when they have sex with him. Elsewhere, in passages describing Sydney's thoughts and internal psychological states, pronouns change from masculine to feminine without apparent motivation in order to underscore the disorder in his/her mind. Ironically, just as he is deciding to take control of his situation when he arrives in London, the feminine pronoun returns, underlining the fact that control is not something she can take for granted.

7.30.   He was not entirely in control of other people's reactions. They called him *sir* when he expected *miss* and ordered him out of restrooms they considered inappropriate. . . . In a week he would be in London; she would pick someone up there and practice on them. (132–33)

The function of linguistic gender markers in these hermaphroditic texts varies widely, as we have seen, but what appears to be most salient for each of the ambiguously sexed individuals is how their appearance affects those around them. Mario/Marion and Sydney are able to maintain a sense of themselves as dual sexed (however unhappy it makes them), but they have no confidence that this duality will be even comprehensible to others. Appropriate gender markers help place them in one gender camp or the other, defining moments that are continually questioned and erased by the various forms of petroleum jelly with which they recommence the task of creating a stable identity. While Mario/Marion embraces the safe gender boundary created by the Seine, Sydney finds the distinction between the genders increasingly difficult to live out. It is precisely the problem of other people's reactions, and his/her inability to control them, that leads to Sydney's unhappiness. Self-definition only goes so far.

Gay Cross-Expressing

The gender status of transsexuals and hermaphrodites is itself problematic, since the former move from one sex to another, while the anatomy of the latter contains both male and female elements. There is also a third group of sexually liminal subjects, people whose sexual anatomy and gender identification are not conflicted, but who nevertheless use gender markers traditionally deemed appropriate to the opposite sex to refer to themselves and others like them. I turn now to a discussion of such cross-expressing in the discourse of gay men and lesbians.[7] The conflict expressed in this use of the gender system is between presumed heterosexuality and actual homosexuality.

At a time when, as we saw in chapter 1, gender distinctions in nouns and adjectives in French are tending to disappear, many gay men use feminine terms to address or refer to others in the community, including their lovers and themselves. A sociolinguistic survey conducted in Paris in 1994 by Geneviève Pastre (1997) lists some of the feminine epithets gay men use when speaking to or about their lovers. These range from the hypocoristic and diminutive *ma fille* (my girl), and *ma petite chérie* (my$_f$ little$_f$ darling$_f$) to the exaggeratedly offensive *folle pétasse* (crazy$_f$ whore), *mongolienne* (mongoloid$_f$), *salope* (bitch), and *conne* (cunt$_f$) (Pastre 1997, 372). Pastre quotes an article in *Exit* (a Parisian magazine aimed at a mixed audience of gays and straights) titled "Le Pédé hors ghetto" (The Faggot outside the Ghetto) (12), which offers advice on how to attract a closet queer. The article includes two suggestions about the use of the feminine in gay speech. The first, "[N]e lui dites pas que vous êtes parti en vacances avec une bande de copines hystériques" (don't tell him you went on holiday with a bunch of hysterical girlfriends), draws attention to the use of the feminine *copine* (girlfriend) instead of the masculine *copain* (mate), which, coupled with the adjective *hystérique*, a cultural reference to women's supposed predisposition toward emotional instability, positions the speaker in a thoroughly feminine, if stereotypical, context. The second, "[N]e parlez jamais au féminin" (never speak in the feminine), is a direct reference to gay men's use of feminine concord to designate themselves as radically different from other men.

As Butler has argued, feminist theorists such as Janice Raymond view "male-to-female transsexuality, cross-dressing and drag as male homosexual activities . . . and diagnose male homosexuality as rooted in misogyny" (1993, 127). This ideological stance not only lumps three different constituencies together, but also posits male homosexuality as being about women. The texts discussed in this chapter show clearly that the three constituencies are not the same, though there may be some occasional overlap. Whereas Georgine Noël reiterates her desire for an anatomically female body to coincide with her own gender identity and is clearly focused on femininity, gay men's use of feminine signifiers do not necessarily imply any interest in femininity, whether negative or positive. We have already seen how the binary of gender can be subverted to express a rich multiplicity of psychological as well as physical states.

The question of whether gay male use of feminine gender is per se misogynist is an important one. It is hard to imagine a context in which terms like *mongolienne* (mongoloid$_f$) and *folle pétasse* (crazy$_f$ whore) would not be both pejorative and misogynist, but this is not to say that the use of the feminine to refer to men is in and of itself misogynist. In French, gay men are compelled by morphosyntactic necessity to position themselves as either male or female; the choice of femininity is, at base, a choice against the masculine rather than for the feminine. I do not believe the gay men in Pastre's survey were thinking of women at all. A complete lack of interest in women may constitute a form of misogyny in itself, but this is not a topic for this work. I believe it is more accurate to say that what these men are trying to do in subverting the feminine pronouns by applying them to male individuals is to expand the linguistic gender system to speak about themselves and their community. Feeling that masculine pronouns and concord set up a system of meanings that do not convey their experience, they focus on the only other paradigm available and take it by storm. It is not surprising that these storm tactics seem like invasion, but the fact that they succeed also shows how permeable the system is. As I have already noted, in French, feminine pronouns and concord reference not only female human beings, but any grammatically feminine noun.

For similar reasons to French use of feminine terms for men, in English, gay men often use the female pronoun *she* to refer to other gay men, especially in gay-friendly environments such as gay bars.

7.31.   Speaker A: Speaking of fags, where is Miss Thing?
        Speaker B: You mean Ron?
        Speaker A: Yeah.
        Speaker B: I don't know where she is. (Rudes and Healy 1979, 61)

In example 7.31, speaker A introduces (or expands upon) the topic of "fags" and asks after a third party whom he calls "Miss Thing," a feminine designator. The terms are thus set in this first turn: fags (male homosexuals) are to be spoken about using feminine reference. The term "Miss Thing" has been borrowed from African American vernacular English and given a homosexual reading in gay circles. By using it, speaker A is himself recreating, or even imposing, a gay discourse, placing his own conversational turn in a wider context of gay men using feminine signifiers. Speaker B is unsure who is being designated "Miss Thing," since the term may be used to refer to any uppity and prominent female. It is, however, unlikely that speaker B is searching his mind for an uppity *woman* at this point in the conversation, as his question "You mean Ron?" makes clear. Speaker B's turn is more complex than it may appear at first sight. Speaker A has introduced a gay discourse that ties fags to feminine designators. Speaker B's turn does not provide a female designator, however, but the masculine first name Ron. At this stage in the dialogue it is unclear whether speaker B has accepted speaker's A's terms. His turn could perhaps be interpreted as an overt refusal of them. Except that he has been able to access a male name in response to the question-prompt "Miss Thing." By offering a male name in response to an apparently feminine signifier, in fact B is both agreeing to enter the gay discourse introduced by A and signaling his approbation. A's second turn is limited to an affirmative, which not only verifies B's suggestion for a referent for "Miss Thing," but also commends B's entry into the gay discourse domain. If we consider only the content of B's second turn, he is expressing a negative, and Ron, or Miss Thing, is not located. But more important to the relationship established in this dialogue between A and B is the fact that B has used the feminine pronoun *she* in reference to the person he previously called "Ron." B accepts as fags not only Ron, but also himself and A, who use the same linguistic system. In this short exchange, then, a community of three has been created, even though one is absent and unlocatable. (My analysis of Rudes and Healy's example.)

In example 7.31, the feminine noun phrase "Miss Thing" justifies and even preempts the use of feminine pronouns. But it is equally possible for feminine pronouns to be used without any antecedent feminine noun, as in the following exchange referring to a young man:

7.32.   Speaker A: Who's that next to George?
          Speaker B: I don't know but she's kind of cute. (Rudes and Healy
                      1979, 57)

In example 7.32, *she* is deictic rather than anaphoric that is, it points directly to the context of utterance, making a link between the person next to George and the pronoun "that" and therefore stands out as more marked. It presupposes that the referent is female—or nonmasculine—despite the fact that both speaker and addressee are looking at the person concerned, and both know "he" is a man. The point of the exchange is not only to impute male homosexuality to the person described in the feminine, but also to place speakers A and B in the same category. This strategy requires a homogeneous discourse context for reference to succeed. The use of female pronouns to refer to gay men (or of masculine pronouns to refer to women) is limited to specifically gay contexts; it can have serious social consequences if the device misfires. Brandon Teena was taken seriously as a man and was raped and murdered because of it, as are many male-to-female transsexuals, including Venus Xtravaganza, whose performance in the film *Paris Is Burning* is discussed at length by Butler (1993, 121–40).

It is important to note that this linguistic strategy is intended not to reflect a feminine persona so much as to dissociate the speaker, addressee, and any third party described in the feminine from heterosexual alliance and to create a homosexual alliance. As such, it is a statement of sexual orientation rather than of sexual identity. The men who use these feminine forms to refer to themselves or to other gay men are proudly designating themselves as well as the referents as traitors to heterosexual masculinity. The very fact of referring to another man in the feminine, even if the speaker never uses feminine designators in reference to himself, indicates participation in this countercultural, anti-heterosexual discourse mode. Speakers thereby underline their own alliance with the sissy, the nelly, and the drag queen and in fact create this alliance by their use of the feminine gender.

As Pastre points out, while *fille*, meaning a girl, or a prostitute, is used frequently by gay men to refer to themselves and each other, *femme*, meaning both a woman and a wife, is much rarer, indicating that it is not mature womanhood that is envisaged by the use of feminine terms and concord, but youth and sexual availability.

Lesbian Cross-Expressing

While Pastre's survey did produce a few masculine forms used by lesbians to address their lovers, such as "mon chéri" (my$_m$ darling$_m$) and "je suis ton petit mec" (I'm your little bloke, your little fella), none were used to refer to women in the third person; thus, the addressee was always present and the clash between her sex and the gender designation evident. It is also worth noting that while men are never addressed in the feminine unless some comment on their sexual orientation is intended, one frequently hears mothers replying to their daughters "oui, mon gran**d**" (yes, my big$_m$ [one]), "oui, mon peti**t**" (yes, my little$_m$ [one]), "oui, mon chéri" (yes, my darling$_m$), or "oui, mon vieu**x**" (yes, my old$_m$ [one]) without any suggestion of homosexuality. Because the masculine is the unmarked term, it may be used generically, that is, with a zero interpretation as regards the mark of gender, as in "les grands doivent aider les petits" (the older ones must help the little ones); with a minus interpretation, as in "les grands hommes font de mauvais pères" (great men make bad fathers); or with a plus interpretation, as in the above example of "oui, mon grand," said to one's adolescent daughter. This may explain why the lesbians in Pastre's survey reported such minimal use of the masculine: it may have been considered unmarked or generic rather than specifically masculine. The feminine, on the other hand, being the marked half of the dyad, is usually restricted to a plus interpretation and if applied to a masculine referent implies femininity or a homosexual orientation.

The use of masculine terms and concord to connote lesbianism or mannishness among women is much rarer, in large part due to the fact that the masculine may so easily be taken for a generic. Christiane Rochefort plays with the use of masculine concord to designate lesbian orientation in her description of the relationship between Céline and her fifteen-year-old sister-in-law, Stéphanie, in her novel *Les Stances à Sophie* (1963). While referring to a man in the feminine is immediately comprehensible as a suggestion of homosexuality, Rochefort has to set up a complicated game of role playing for the masculinization of Céline to be read as an implication of homosexuality and not simply a grammatical error. We have seen in chapter 1 that gender concord in French is on the wane, especially in the colloquial discourse of younger speakers.[8] Stéphanie, still a *lycéenne* (high school student), positions herself as Socrates' friend and pupil Phèdre (Phaedrus), calling her sister-in-law, Céline "Platon" (Plato), to highlight the unequal power dynamic between them. The schoolgirl declares her love for Céline but receives no corresponding avowal. After a classical commentary on the nature of love, the lover, and the loved from Céline, Stéphanie sighs and appears to accept that her love is unrequited.

7.33.   Alors, c'est moi qui aime?
         So, I'm the one who loves?

         C'est ce que tu as dit.
         That's what you said.

         Et toi qui es aimée?
         And it's you who are loved$_f$?

         Grammaticalement obligé.
         Grammatically obliged.

         Si je t'ai bien compris . . .
         If I have understood$_m$ you correctly.

         Comprise.
         Understood$_f$.

         Platon.
         Plato.

         Pardon.
         Sorry.

Grammatically, if "je t'aime" (I love you), then "tu es aimée" (you are loved), as Céline points out. Stéphanie tries to push the grammatical one step further by addressing Céline in the masculine, using masculine concord for the past participle *compris* in order to suggest a homosexual orientation: "Si je t'ai bien compris." For Céline to accept this masculinization of herself without demur would be to implicate herself in Stéphanie's declaration, rather than be its passive addressee. Instead, she immediately corrects Stéphanie, insisting on feminine concord: *comprise*. In order to defuse the situation and wave aside the rebuff, Stéphanie explains that she is speaking to Céline as Plato, an explanation Céline gracefully accepts, though, given the homosexual nature of the subject matter of the Phaedrus dialogue, this only continues the ambiguity.

    In English, too, it is less common for female referents to be referred to in the masculine than for male referents to be referred to in the feminine. Nevertheless, instances of this type of cross-expressing can be found in a range of contexts, from the novels of the Victorian Charlotte Brontë (writing in her masculine persona as Currer Bell) to the contemporary speech of drag kings and butch "brothers." In Brontë's *Shirley*, the eponymous heroine makes up a male identity for herself since, as she says, she has a man's job to do.

7.34.   "I am an esquire: Shirley Keeldar, Esquire, ought to be my style and po-
         sition; it is enough to inspire me with a touch of manhood." (1891, 180)

This persona is accepted in the spirit of fun by the rector, who proceeds to refer to Shirley using masculine pronouns. Speaking to Shirley's companion and mentor, Mrs. Pryor, the rector even suggests a few more masculine roles for Shirley to play.

7.35.   "Mrs Pryor, take care of this future magistrate, this church warden in perspective, this captain of yeomanry, this young squire of Briarsfield. . . . Don't let him exert himself too much." (182)

In nineteenth-century England, it was impossible for a woman to fulfill these roles, and seditious ideas such as woman suffrage were as yet unknown; thus, the shared joke does not threaten the status quo.

At the far end of the range of women cross-expressing as men are lesbian drag kings. Drag kings are women who dress as men, often wearing a moustache and "packing"—strapping a dildo between their legs to simulate the bulge of a penis. Drag kings refer to themselves and their buddies in the masculine (Bell 1993a). They are more likely to threaten the status quo because they are more likely to be taken seriously as men than Shirley Keeldar, in her long dress and petticoats, would have been. What is at issue for them is not taking over social roles that have been reserved for men, as was the case with Victorian squires, church wardens, and military captains, but being seen as men. However, for the drag king performance to work, onlookers need both to believe they see a man, and to realize for themselves that in fact the person before them is a woman. Only with this double identification are the cultural codes that designate manhood seriously under attack. It is in the slippage betwen the first and the second look that the appendages of masculinity lose value. They seem to index a man, yet the person wearing them is a woman. This polyphonic gaze (to coin a phrase) ironizes the use of masculine signifiers. (See also Rusty Barrett 1997 on the ironic gender performance of African American drag queens.)

While male-to-female transsexuals such as Georgine Noël aim toward a [+feminine] identification, the gay men in Pastre's survey aim toward a [-masculine] identification. There are many similarities in the verbal performance of the two groups, but their motivation is strikingly different: the transsexuals are constructing themselves around notions of femininity, the gay men around notions of masculinity. The efforts of the former are sincere attempts to sound like women; the gossip and banter of the latter are intended to establish in-group rapport, to *épater les hétéros* (shock straight outsiders), and to create a playful or parodic atmosphere. Similarly, Shirley Keeldar does not wish to be taken for a man, she merely wishes to adopt some masculine mannerisms to express her unusual status as a single young woman in Victorian England who is responsible for her own fortune. Drag kings, in contrast, wish both to be taken for men and to be understood as women.

As the preceding investigation demonstrates, the dyadic structure of the linguistic gender system in French lends itself to a multiplicity of meanings that may have little to do with biological or cultural gender attributes. It can express in-group solidarity or outsider status, sympathy or antago-

nism. Its avoidance may signify a refusal to commit or a fear of causing offense. While the linguistic marks of gender are on the decline in mainstream
French, they may be used by groups whose sexual orientation or gender
identity is at odds with societal norms. Sexually liminal communities may
use linguistic gender in ways both paradoxical and ironic; they call the very
system whose simple binary excludes them into play to generate their own
meanings and construct their own network of alliances.

While feminist writers inventing their own conventions of nongendered
language are part of a movement toward a more egalitarian society in which
distinctions of natural gender will be seen as less and less crucial, others,
describing individuals whose anatomical or psychological configuration
outlaws them from the traditional categories, make use of the very system
feminists decry. This championing of the traditional by outlaw or liminal
figures may seem at first paradoxical, or at the least a sign of false consciousness. However, because of his/her ambiguous status, the hermaphrodite,
the transsexual, or the drag king may be said to act as a troubleshooter for
gender, revealing resources available in the gender system to which more
traditional identities have scant recourse. Grammaticalized gender, which
many feel acts as a trap to limit people in their gender roles, also provides
linguistic devices for expressing gender fluidity.

8

"Pendue pour des inventions illicites"

Implications

This book started with a discussion of pronoun envy, a phrase coined by the Harvard Linguistics Department as a way of disparaging feminist concern about the social implications of a linguistic gender system based on binary thinking in which masculinity and femininity figure as the two terms in a hierarchical opposition. Having closely examined the workings of the linguistic gender system in a wide range of French and English novels and other literary works, I believe it is helpful to look again at the presuppositions with which I set out.

One of the questions I posed at the beginning concerned the current state of the gender systems in French and English and whether their redundancies were being junked as excess baggage or reanalyzed as performing new functions. As research conducted into spoken French demonstrates, gender concord for adjectives and past participles is on the wane, at least in unmarked situations. In the pronominal system, in contrast, gender distinctions remain important in both English and French. As we saw from the analysis of Garréta's *Sphinx* and Duffy's *Love Child*, the avoidance of gendered pronouns results in low cohesion and low empathy. The pronominal systems of both languages retain their traditional function: that of anaphorizing nominal antecedents, or indicating by the form of the pronoun in question whether the referent is grammatically masculine or feminine. They are also instrumental in two other discourse functions: those of conveying the angle of focalization and of creating a cohesive text. Thus the so-called redundancies of pronominal gender can be shown to serve important textual functions. We cannot term these discourse functions *re-*

analysis, however, since they have not replaced but coincide with the traditional function and may well have developed alongside it. In other words, as soon as there was a recognizable set of pronouns in place to anaphorize the noun, these pronouns also served to convey empathy and focalization and create cohesive text.

Despite the mocking dismissal of the Harvard linguists, we saw that many feminist authors in both Francophone and Anglophone countries have constructed robust armories to counterbalance perceived inequalities, either avoiding linguistic gender markers altogether or creating epicene alternatives. This does not give the whole picture, however. French (and Québécois) feminism would be seriously misrepresented if we only considered the techniques used to avoid gender markers in the fiction of writers such as Monique Wittig and Anne Garréta. The avoidance of gender has received more support from Anglophone than Francophone feminists. English and American campaigns to create and promulgate epicene forms from job titles to pronouns find no exact parallel among French and Québécois feminists. On the contrary, French feminist campaigns have focused on the feminization of job titles and an insistence on the use of feminine pronouns to designate feminine referents. The difference in the tactics employed by Francophone and Anglophone feminists is due in large part to the differing structures of the two languages. Because English lacks morphological gender, except in the pronominal paradigm, epicene terms such as *the chair* (of a committee), *the head* (of a department), or *the minister* (for education) may be used for men or women without a built-in prejudice in favor of a masculine reading (beyond the cultural weight exerted by the preponderance of men in these positions). In French, on the other hand, *le chef* (*du département*), *le ministre* (*de l'education*), or *le président* (*de la Banque Nationale de Paris*), although semantically generic, are masculine in grammatical gender and predispose the listener to imagine a man filling these positions. French feminists have therefore pushed for the creation of specifically feminine terms for use when women take these roles. This is a stronger arm to use against the hierarchical oppositions of markedness than the English preference for epicene forms.

The feminization of job titles goes against the current drift of the French language toward the gradual decline of gender concord and distinctions in nominal gender. This does not mean feminine job titles are doomed to failure. The feminist campaigns come from a strongly felt anger at women's linguistic invisibility and are as integral and organic a part of the process of language change as the gender erosion remarked in popular usage. What we are witnessing is the evolution of a morphosyntactic obligation into a stylistic choice. If the feminization of job titles and the use of gender concord markers are stylistic devices, we need to know what they connote. One connotation is a feminist perspective on the part of the speaker, but this is not the only possibility. Stylistic devices depend for their meaning not only on the immediate linguistic environment, but on the discourse context, including social setting, register, genre, and medium.

As we have seen in chapter 7, transsexuals, hermaphrodites, lesbians and gay men and gay male drag queens also manipulate gender markers for particular ends, but their ends are rather different than those of feminists such as Benoîte Groult, the French novelist and activist, who seek to create feminine equivalents for masculine terms and thus establish gender parity. Many male-to-female transsexuals are taking on symbols of femininity, such as make-up and styled hair, that women who are born women are increasingly tending to abandon. The linguistic behavior of the French transsexuals discussed here parallels this sartorial display. They employ feminine gender concord as frequently in the first as in the third person, whereas, according to Blanche-Benveniste's 1990 study, discussed in chapter 1, the majority of French speakers are coming to regard as invariable adjectives and past participles that qualify first person pronouns. (See also *Lesbia Magazine* March 1984, pp. 14–15, "Le Transsexualisme.")

The speech of transsexuals is to a large extent more carefully constructed and consciously produced than that of speakers with other gender identities. As H. Merle Knight observes, "[T]he cross-gendered . . . must consciously overcome various forms of gender interference in order to operate effectively in the target role" (1992, 312). "Gender interference" refers to the speech patterns of the dispreferred gender in which the transsexual individual has grown up. One might say that transsexual speech is characterized by a form of hypercorrection, an overgeneralization of the morphosyntactic rules of gender concord and the discourse patterns deemed suitable for each sex. Knight comments on an occasion when a female-to-male transsexual told his companions that a woman had rebuffed him after he sent her a dozen roses. His companions, both male-to-female transsexuals, were uncomfortable with the topic and made only perfunctory remarks before changing the subject (315). Knight's interpretation of this event is that each person was acting out the speech patterns of their former gender: the female-to-male transsexual was asking for an emotional response typical of women, while the male-to-female transsexuals were disconcerted by the personal turn of the conversation. Whereas another researcher might have concluded that the participants had learned to be flexible in their employment of male and female speech characteristics, Knight considers all three to have failed to project their new gender identity correctly. Many heterosexual women are asked by heterosexual men friends for advice about their love lives and choose simply not to respond, or dismiss the request with a brief "Why don't you ask her?" No loss of gender status necessarily results.

Although transsexuals work to uphold the traditional gender roles in order to pass as members of the sex in which they feel most comfortable, gay male drag queens and lesbian drag kings employ the stylistic choices of linguistic gender to project an image of themselves as not conforming to the expected role. The ludic possibilities of this nonconformity have been put to good use by novelists who play on the stereotypes of masculinity and femininity that will be recognized by their readership. The stylistic possibilities of linguistic gender allow for very different, even contradictory interpretations of the same phenomenon, depending on the discourse setting. A punctilious observance of the traditional rules for gender concord, for example, may indicate that the speaker is an old-fashioned schoolteacher, a radical feminist, a postoperative male-to-female transsexual, or a gay drag queen. In fictional discourse, it is evident that the functions and effects of linguistic gender cannot be ascertained without taking into consideration other textual features such as point of view, degree of narrator control, and range of cohesive devices employed. In the oral medium there are other considerations, such as register, social status, and the relationship between speaker and addressee.

Research by scholars into earlier French texts and the gender systems of other languages shows similar patterns regarding the use of cross-gender markers by sexually liminal groups. In his study of homoeroticism in premodern French language and culture, Randy Conner (1997) shows that at the court of the notoriously homosexual Henri III (1551–89), the king was habitually referred to in the feminine by his *mignons* (favorites and lovers), the introduction of grammatically feminine nouns such as *sa majesté* (her/his majesty) justifying this usage. Michael Jackson is not the first to have his natural gender questioned by a sly manipulation of linguistic gender. Conner notes that Michel de Montaigne's *Journal de Voyage en Italie* (1580–81), written under the reign of Henri III, includes a passage describing how a group of women dressed as men in order to find work in a nearby town. The pronouns used to refer to one of the women in question change from feminine to masculine and back to feminine. This pattern relates not to the author's knowledge of the woman's gender, but to how the woman was accepted by the people among whom she lived. Marie sets out from her home in Chaumont in masculine attire. She is described first as one of "sept ou huit filles" (seven or eight girls), then as a "jeune homme bien conditionné" (young man of good condition) who marries another woman. After she has been recognized by someone from her home town, Marie is "pendue pour des inventions illicites à suppléer au défaut de son sexe" (hanged_f for employing illicit interventions to compensate for the lack inherent in her sex).[1] The crime for which she receives such a harsh punishment was not that of impersonating a man per se, but, supposedly, for using a dildo with her partner. It is clear, however, that it was her successful drag king act that bothered everyone so much.

Evidently the twentieth-century transsexuals and drag queens and kings we have encountered in chapter 7 were not the first to test the limits and possibilities of the French and English gender systems. As Kira Hall observes, "[L]inguistic gender, in its close association with one of the most basic divisions in social organization, is used as a tool for evoking a wide range of societal discourses on power and solidarity, difference and dominance" (1997a, 33). Since pronouns in both English and French do far more than simply "stand in for the noun," they allow the speaker or writer a certain amount of license that provides him or her the opportunity to treat gender markers as stylistic devices whose meaning is to a large extent contextual.

What implications does the stylistic function of gender markers have for the system itself? We have until now considered masculinity and femininity as opposites, the two terms in a binary in which masculinity is the unmarked and femininity the marked term. As Linda Waugh observes, markedness is "the asymmetrical and hierarchical relationship between the two poles of any opposition" (1982, 299). Further, "the marked term necessarily conveys a more narrowly specified and delimited conceptual item than the unmarked" (301). In a letter to Roman Jakobson, Nikolaj Trubetzkoy remarked that although objectively the two terms of an opposition may refer to different positions in a range or continuum, "subjectively they are always transformed into an opposition" (1975, 162f; quoted in Waugh 1982, 300). Applying this statement to gender, we would say that although there may be many different positions one could occupy along the continuum from masculinity to femininity, it is nevertheless the poles that serve to define the categories. As Waugh remarks, "[A]ny opposition is an opposition of choices (not things), choices among unequals . . . , oppositions are relations (not things), and oppositions define the concepts of the system . . . through the relational network they create" (1982, 315–16). It is the network that lends meaning to the individual terms, defined by hierarchical opposition to other terms.

In linguistic terminology, the feminine is the marked term of the gender dyad. Yet if we consider medical definitions of gender, particularly those used to diagnose gender dysphoria and intersexed (that is, hermaphroditic) infants, it becomes apparent that masculinity is marked by the possession of a penis and femininity by its lack. "Never assign a baby to be reared, and to surgical and hormonal therapy, as a boy, unless the phallic structure . . . is neonatally of at least the same caliber as that of same-aged males with small-average penises" preaches John Money, an American expert on intersexuality (Kessler 1990, 18). On the other hand, should an infant with XX chromosomes (the classic female pattern) rejoice in a "perfect" penis, the doctor is advised against amputating the penis but should instead (1) remove the female internal organs, (2) implant prosthetic testes, and (3) have the *boy's* hormones regulated throughout *his* life (19; my italics). The proposed interventions are far more intrusive to the integrity of the body, and more radical in terms of the physical trauma sustained, than an infantile penisectomy. The physicians' primary concern here is with the possible psychic trauma of castration, rather than with the actual physical consequences of surgery on the internal organs and lifelong hormone treatment. This is quite a reversal of the usual medical ethics, which tends to prize organs over psyches. Suzanne Kessler, who has conducted considerable research into the treatment of intersexed infants, sums up the opinions held by the doctors she interviewed: "The formulation 'good penis equals male; absence of good penis equals female' is treated in the literature and by physicians . . . as an objective criterion, operative in all cases"

(1990, 20). Thus, in medical discourse at least, the mark of masculinity is the penis, even when hormonal, chromosomal, and other anatomical evidence points to femininity.

The French booklet on transsexuals in *Que sais-je?* (what do I know?) series notes that in talmudic law an androgyne, classified as an "either-man-or-woman" (*ou-bien-homme-ou-bien-femme*), may marry a woman but not a man. If he were a man married to another man, both partners would be transgressing the law against homosexuality. If, on the other hand, she were a woman married to another woman, the marriage would simply be void (Pettiti 1992, 118). Once again, femininity, though marked, is perceived as empty of value. A similar logic lies behind the English statutes outlawing male but not female homosexuality on the grounds that the latter did not exist, as Queen Victoria is reputed to have declared. In the case of both intersexed infants and adults, masculinity will be assumed (or even created) because the consequences of putting a person in the female category who "rightfully" belongs in the male are perceived as far more serious than those of wrongly putting a female in the male category.

Arguing against the simplistic identification of feminine with non-masculine, the Italian semiotician Patrizia Violi (1987), a collaborator of Luce Irigaray, has proposed (following Greimas) a four-part schema to replace the traditional masculine/feminine dyad. Instead of a relation merely of opposites, this quadripartite system features two relations: opposites and contradictories. According to this schema, masculine and feminine appear on the same semantic axis because they are opposites, but not contradictories. The contradictory of masculine is not feminine, but non-masculine. Feminine and non-masculine are not reducible to each other in this system; this allows the feminine to have positive defining qualities rather than simply a lack of masculinity (Violi 1987, 29–30).

If we consider the use of linguistic gender markers as to some extent a stylistic choice, then the choices involve three possibilities: not using gender markers of any kind (e.g., avoiding the use of pronouns); using the markers deemed appropriate to the gender of the character; or using the markers deemed appropriate to the other gender, that is, allowing the character to cross-express. In the texts considered here, we have seen all three possibilities explored. Garréta and Duffy, for example, avoid gender markers. Arnold and Piercy use masculine pronouns for male characters and feminine pronouns for female characters in the non-utopian sections of their novels. Authors as diverse as Charlotte Brontë and Christiane Rochefort allow their female characters to use masculine designators.

This does not, however, exhaust the possibilities investigated in this book. As we have seen, in transsexual and hermaphroditic texts, there may be no core gender identity, or it may change at some moment of ontological crisis, or it may move back and forth between male and female. To this we must add the use of epicene neologisms by science fiction writers and others, as well as Monique Wittig's innovatory style, which seeks to feminize the textual environment so that the feminine becomes the unmarked term.

The choice between *elle* and *il*, or *she* and *he*, is usually considered binary, and indeed, I have used this term so far in this book. Given the diverse and imaginative worldviews that are constructed within this binary, we would have to conclude that in itself it is about as constrictive as the binary arithmetic that underwrites the World Wide Web. From the basic high pulse/low pulse train of the electrical charge flowing though the microchip (represented as flows/does not flow), binary numbers are converted to octal (base 8) and hexadecimal (base 16), which operate as shorthand for the much longer radix 2 numbers. An old-fashioned IBM RAM (random access memory) chip, for example, contains 64,000 bits (binary digits) and allows you to store any type of information and perform whatever operations on it you like (delete, compare, add, multiply, cut, paste, etc.). My point is that although the root of this system is binary, it is not actually constituted by a zero or positive pulse, but by high and low pulse represented as zero/+ 1. Furthermore, it is on this lowly base that the complex video, audio, graphic and textual interfaces of contemporary Web sites are built. The uses to which the linguistic gender systems of English and French have been put are, arguably, even more varied than those of the Internet. An electrical pulse does not have the option of disappearing en route through the microchip: a real zero would indicate a power outage and crash the system. In contrast, as we have seen with the texts that avoid mention of gender, this procedure creates very marked discourse, but it is readable, as the comments of critics and reviewers attest. It does not crash the system; it inserts a question mark.

Having introduced this mathematical model, let us look at it more closely. In mathematical terms, gender, when conceived of as constructed of the two terms "masculine" and "feminine," is not a binary at all. Binary numbers are numbers in base 2, and the binary system uses just two symbols: 0 and 1. There is thus only one positive term: 1. When a higher number needs to be symbolized, the place value increases, not the number—that is, the symbol moves one place to the left. Thus decimal 1 is written in binary arithmetic as 0001, while decimal 2 is written 0010. Gender is a binary, mathematically, when only one of the terms is invested with positive value. Thus, if the masculine is considered universal, and only femininity is sexed (which Wittig has argued, as we saw in chapter 4), then gender is a binary in which femininity has the value 0001. Conversely, if femininity is seen as merely the negative of masculinity, as neonatologists treating intersexed infants appear to believe (chapter 7), then gender is a binary in which masculinity has the value of 0001. What we have seen throughout this analysis of literary texts, however, is that both masculinity and femininity are invested with positive value. They are, as Violi has argued, opposites, but not contradictories.

Thus far, I have considered the implications of the present study for how we conceptualize the linguistic gender systems of French and English and their functions. Cultural gender is also, of course, one of the most basic divisions in social organization, involving a complex set of power relations.

Judith Butler argues that gender should be considered performative in the Austinian sense that it calls itself into being by virtue of its own felicitous pronounciation (1990). Here she is speaking not of linguistic gender, which she sees as only one of the semiotic tools for gender citation, but cultural gender. Cultural gender cannot be seen as indexically linked to the sex of the referent; rather, it is a prescription requiring the referent to act in accordance with prevailing gender norms, norms that are thereby re-created or cited by the referent, who is obliged to enter into a set of relations she did not create and over which she has little power. Performatives work through citation, that is, they invoke and place themselves in a preexisting semiotic system. Butler states that "citationality" has contemporary political promise because it allows for a reworking of abjection into political agency (1993, 21). Speaking of the possibilities for action, she elaborates that identifying with a gender involves identifying with sets of norms with their own preexisting power and status; one is forced to identify with a norm "one never chooses, a norm that chooses us, but which we occupy, reverse, resignify to the extent that the norm fails to determine us completely" (1993, 126–27).

For Butler, therefore, and for queer theorists whose work is based on an understanding of her work, individual speaking subjects are obliged to perform gender by entering into a culturally comprehensible set of practices. Political agency is achieved only by reversing or resignifying the norm, that is, by subverting it in subtle ways. There is little space in this theory for revolutionary acts, no sense that one could hijack the prevailing norms and force them to go in the opposite or an entirely new direction. Nor is there much space for intersubjective relations. Jacques Derrida, who is widely quoted by Butler, argues in *Limited Inc.* (1988) that in his view, in contradistinction to that of Austin, performatives work not because they depend on the intention of the speaker, but because they embody conventional forms of language that are already in existence before the speaker utters them.

If both speaker intention and, to a large extent, speaker agency are removed from a consideration of gender, then we are left with a semiotic system much like that of *Alphaville*, as discussed in chapter 4 where words reign and subjects are spoken by their own sentences. While such a determinist view may be useful in philosophy or rhetoric, the fields in which Derrida and Butler work, it is hard to see how a complete exclusion of such features as hearer recognition of speaker intent or intersubjective relations could be of value to a consideration of reader hypotheses about experimental texts. Indeed, many of the features discussed in the present work, such as focus and empathy, might arguably be described as reader-based phenomena. In order for an experimental text to work, it is essential for the reader to recognize both the conventions that produced it and what is intended by them. This is especially true of the more daring uses of the gender system. The difference between the performance of a drag queen or drag king and the carefully constructed behavior of a transsexual is often primarily to be discerned at the level of intention. This difference involves the distinction between two social phenomena: parody and passing. Exactly the same discourse may be invoked, but the former is intended ironically, while the latter is sincere. Conventions must be recognized in order for them to be felicitously cited or invoked. (For more on the drag king in literature as well as real life, see Judith Halberstam's *Female Masculinity* [1998]; for more on transsexuality and gender conventions, see Susan Stryker, ed., *GLQ* 4, no. 2, Transgender Issue [1998].)

To give a couple of rather different examples: speakers may unintentionally invoke a system of racial hatred that is unfamiliar to them by using words or expressions of whose connotations they are unaware. I was at a feminist book fair in Barcelona attended by a group of African Americans, among many others. At the next table were some young Spanish women talking about a black book cover which clearly they disliked. On hearing the word *negro*, one of the African Americans turned round, her face angry and watchful, clearly wondering if the Spanish women were talking pejoratively about her and her friends. A short conversation followed, in faltering English on the part of the Spanish women, and the tension was resolved. In fact, as soon as she heard the Spanish women speaking English, the African American's face began to relax. It was clear that there was no intention to wound in the uttering of the word *negro*.

Closer to home, when my young twins were very little, their tear ducts had not yet opened, so every morning their eyes would be covered with sticky goo that needed to be wiped off. My partner, an American, would take a facecloth and coo at them, "Who's got gooky eyes?" Hearing the word "gooky," which was new to me as a British person, I would do what I thought was the same thing. "Gooky eyes," I would chant, cheerfully as I washed them. A friend interrupted me and asked me what I had said. I repeated the phrase. "Don't you know that 'gook' is a pejorative word for a Vietnamese person?" she asked. I had not. Nor did I know that my pronunciation of the word, with a long /u:/, was so different from my partner's pronunciation, with a short /ʊ/, that it had a different meaning. Realizing that my grasp of American English was imperfect, I reverted to the British term "gunky."

These two examples, involving perceived racial slurs, are easy to understand. It is also easy to see that since they were not intended, they do not in fact constitute slurs. With gender issues, the situation becomes even more complex, since gender and its cultural reproduction have been so naturalized that it is hard to tease apart intention and performance. Yet here, too, speaker intentions are important, as important a part of their message as the words themselves. Clearly, the use of linguistic gender markers that are apparently at odds with a speaker's cultural gender can have devastating consequences and involve dire retribution, whatever the user's intentions may have been. Cultural codes can be misunderstood; no one can dictate the perlocutionary force of their words, but this is not to say that perlocutionary force is irrelevant. Teena Brandon and Venus Xtravaganza were murdered for subverting the prevailing gender codes; their intentions in performing this subversion were not accepted. They have many peers in an unfortunate lineage that may be traced back as far as the sixteenth-century Marie of Chaumont and beyond. The hegemonizing power of cultural gender is indisputable. What is demonstrated by the texts examined here is that the possibilities for subverting that hegemony through grammatical gender and other means are equally impressive.

Notes

1. Introduction

The chapter title translates as "One man in two is a woman."

1. See also E. J. Dionne, "Two Women Liberate Church Course," *Harvard Crimson*, 11 Nov. 1971, 1; "Pronoun Envy," *Newsweek*, 6 Dec. 1971; and "Letters to the Editor," *Newsweek*, 27 Dec. 1971. The "pronoun envy" affair is reported in detail in Miller and Swift 1977, 75–77, 176 nn 8, 9, 10, 11, 12, 13.

2. All translations throughout this work are mine unless otherwise indicated.

3. Readers should bear in mind that Watkins et al.'s letter to the *Harvard Crimson* was written a quarter of a century ago and can hardly be taken as an expression of its authors' current opinions on the subject of language and gender. I am quoting it because it is expressive of the intellectual opposition to feminist linguistic concerns at the beginning of the second wave of the women's liberation movement.

4. The term *phallogocentric* comes out of, and has been coined in opposition to, the long Judaeo-Christian tradition of the power of naming, sanctified in the Old Testament by God's presentation to Adam of every beast of the field and every fowl of the air, for "whatsoever Adam called every living thing, that *was* the name thereof" (Gen. 2:19). As in the old saw "the winner names the age," he who has the power to name the world owns the world.

Many feminist writers, including those whose work is discussed in these pages, believe that experiences and activities for which no unique lexical item occurs in the language are undervalued and overlooked. While this may indeed be the case in many instances, it is not necessarily true. Distinction and separation are not the only functions of language and linguistic classification. In classifying languages such as American Sign Language (ASL), classifiers emphasize comparison between entities, rather than contrast. In ASL narrative, classifiers often predominate over discrete lexical items; thus, a highly sophisticated narrative may be constructed of many classifiers and only a few lexical items. The word "hummingbird," for example, may be signed using the sign "Bird," accompanied by classifiers describing its prototypical actions: beating its wings, hovering in the air, and dipping its beak into flowers. Though the English term may be finger spelled in order to pinpoint the exact referent, deaf informants tell me that non-lexicalized finger spelling of this kind smacks of clumsy translation rather than authentic ASL. I am indebted to ASL instructors and native ASL speakers at Vista Community College, Berkeley, Calif., particularly Cheri Smith and Ella Lenz, for discussion of these points.

5. This presentation of the so-called Sapir-Whorf hypothesis is necessarily cursory. It is not my aim to spell out all its intricacies and complexities, fascinating though they are. Instead, I limit myself to explaining its broad terms and its relevance to the writers whose work is under discussion. Readers whose appetites are whetted for more should see Sapir [1929] 1970 and Whorf 1956a and 1956b for the original presentation of the idea that "language is a guide to 'social reality.'" Whorf claims, for example, that "the forms of a person's thoughts are controlled by inexorable laws of pattern of which he is unconscious. These patterns are the unperceived intricate systematizations of his own language" (1956a, 252). But see also Graddol and Swann 1989, who argue that the Sapir-Whorf hypothesis was misnamed and should more accurately be called the Whorfian hypothesis (136–56), and Hill and Mannheim 1992, who present an exhaustive study of the theory of linguistic relativity and come to the conclusion that just as the Holy Roman Empire was neither holy nor Roman nor an empire, so the Sapir-Whorf hypothesis was neither Sapir's nor Whorf's nor a hypothesis (386). Hill and Mannheim also provide an extensive (242-item) list of references for work on the issue. *Rethinking Linguistic Relativity*, edited by John Gumperz and Stephen Levinson (1996), offers a thoughtful collection of articles on the subject by anthropologists and linguists that span the terrain from "the classic Whorfian issues of the relation of grammar to thought to consideration of language use in sociolinguistic perspective" (9).

6. I use the subscripts $_f$ and $_m$ throughout this work to indicate whether a French term is grammatically feminine or masculine.

7. Wayne Smith remarks, for example, that in Taiwan Sign Language the A handshape is the sign for the noun "male." The A marker is also used for singular pronominal reference (person is indicated by orientation). However, if the I handshape, which is the sign for "female," is introduced into the discourse, then the A marker will refer only to a boy or man, while I refers to a woman or girl (1990, 213–15).

8. According to Istvan Fodor (1959, 212–13), what began in Proto-Indo-European as a classification system for nouns based on their phonological endings developed into a grammatical system of syntactic concord causing an assonance-like agreement in elements such as determiners, participles, and adjectives associated with the noun. Over the years these divisions gained a certain amount of semantic motivation, with prominent animate and inanimate, masculine and feminine nouns lending their attributes to a declension as a whole. Declensions with a number of nouns referring to female animates became associated with the female sex, while those featuring a large number of nouns referring to male ani-

mates were associated with the male sex. This process was accompanied by some reclassification of nouns that clearly did not fit into the declension to which their phonology assigned them.

Philosophers and linguists from Plato to Jespersen have endeavored to show a semantic base for the gender assignment of nouns, whether their referents were animate or inanimate. Jesperson and Plato notwithstanding, the gender of French nouns referring to inanimates can, to a large extent, be predicted according to phonological rules, as the Russian linguist I. A. Mel'cuk observed in 1958, and as Tucker, Lambert, and Rigault elaborated: "In order to decide on gender the native speaker has merely to process a noun backward from its terminal phone" (Tucker, Lambert, and Rigault 1977; quoted in Corbett 1991, 61).

For animate referents, the situation is a little more complex, as gender assignment has a semantic core. During a period when flexional endings created concord between different parts of the noun phrase, such a system was used to indicate which adjectives or other qualifiers should be associated with which nouns. In contemporary French, this work has largely been taken over by a more fixed word order: adjectives placed immediately after a noun (the unmarked position) will generally be assumed to qualify that noun; no other clue is usually needed.

Fodor's theory about the origins of grammatical gender has not gone unchallenged, however. See also Muhammad Hasan Ibrahim, *Grammatical Gender: Its Origin and Development* (1973, 30–51) for a comprehensive discussion. Ibrahim's main argument is that "gender in its origin was an accident of linguistic history" (50) with no semantic significance.

2. Nongendered Characters in French

The chapter title translates as "With our sexes/sexual organs mixed together, I could no longer distinguish anything."

1. In the case of quotations from French writers such as Garréta and Wittig, if a French version is not given, the statement was originally made in English.

2. While gender in later Latin certainly had a syntactic function, this function—i.e., agreement marking in the noun phrase—was already being taken over by prepositions and a more fixed word order. For an overview of these developments, see M. Harris 1978, 30–35, and Price 1971, 258–60. There has been some controversy as to whether Latin already showed signs of a stable subject-verb-object word order; see esp. Pinkster 1991. My intention here is not to enter into the great Latin word-order debate, but to make the point that since the syntactic function of gender had already been superseded by other structures in the late Latin period, it can hardly be said to constitute the main function of gender in modern French. Instead, some other function should be looked for, unless the system has become redundant. The utility of a novel written without recourse to the linguistic gender system, at least as far as the main characters are concerned, is that if gender is redundant, nothing will seem to be missing in the depiction of those two characters, whereas if gender has taken on new functions, something will strike the reader as odd.

3. Frédérick is masculine and Frédérique feminine, but Frédéric is epicene.

4. I use the subscripts $_i$ and $_j$ to indicate nouns and pronouns that designate the same referent.

5. I am grateful to Anne Garréta for providing me with a thick file of reviews of her novel, as well as two unpublished conference papers she wrote concerning linguistic gender.

6. The seventeenth century is known in France as the period of *bon usage*, the rigorous codification of the French language, the creation of the Académie française (1635), the publication of the *Grammaire de Port-Royal* (1660), and the first *Dictionnaire de l'Académie* (1694). Despite these reforms, the language looked and sounded very different from the French of today. It is somewhat ludicrous to praise a modern author for writing pure seventeenth-century French prose. Irony must be suspected.

7. Anne Garréta was twenty-three when *Sphinx* was published, a fact that did not go unmentioned in reviews of her work. She had recently completed her master's thesis on *Les Lettres portugaises* under Julia Kristeva at the Ecole Normale Supérieure, one of the most prestigious of the Parisian schools. Given the linguistic particularity of *Sphinx*, it is interesting to note that the *Lettres portugaises* was first presented to the French public in the seventeenth century (1669) as a translation of letters written by a Portuguese nun to her lover, an officer in the French army. Soon, however, doubts were raised as to the authenticity of the document, and it was later shown to have been the work of a Parisian writer: a literary creation rather than a spontaneous outpouring, a French work rather than a translation, from the pen of a man rather than that of a woman.

3. Nongendered Characters in English

1. Although female genital mutilation is also sometimes called "female castration," this is an unusual and contemporary use of the term that was not current in the 1960s when *In Transit* was written. Moreover, a woman who has undergone this mutilation is never referred to as a *castrata*. A woman who is "unsexed" has usurped masculine social prerogatives, not suffered a hysterectomy. Lady Macbeth's cry "Unsex me here, and fill me from the crown to the toe top full of direst cruelty" (act 1, scene 4) is not a plea for surgical intervention.

4. Experiments with Lexical Gender in French

The chapter titles translates as "The female sphinx, the female bull, and the newly born she-lambs."

1. Wittig sees women as defined by heterosexuality and lesbians as therefore radically other—so different that they are, in effect, not women. She was not the first to seek a way out of the gender binary by positing lesbians as a third term. In her novel *Lover* (1976), Bertha Harris makes a similar claim, though she phrases it more poetically. Flynn, whose periods have just started, is complaining about this new indignity, "*I* had been exchanged for a *woman*." She adds, "I know what you're thinking. You're thinking I am lying, that I was never that. The truth is I got myself back in spite of it. In spite of it, I could become a lover and could stop being a woman. . . . I am a lover not a woman" (102–3). Since Flynn is a lover of women, her claim is tantamount to saying that lesbians are not women, not chained to the heterosexual reproductive cycle as women are. *Lover* was written five years before Wittig made her famous proclamation, and it is reasonable to suppose that Wittig had read Harris's novel.

2. Nouns in French, with the exception of a restricted number that have human referents such as *ambassadeur/ambassadrice*, do not change form in accordance with the gender of the referent. Even when used adjectivally, nouns remain invariable—*une table marron* (a chestnut table)—hence the striking and unusual nature of *Ishtar à la tête/soleille*. Wittig's habit of feminizing has been copied by others. In her fable *Voyages de la grande naine en Androssie* (1993), Michèle Causse describes La Grande Griotte (the Great Storyteller, a character based on Wittig herself), as "la plus hurlevente des Lumineuses" (the most Wuthering of Luminaries). The adjective *hurlevente* is a feminization of the noun *hurlevent*, itself composed of the verb *hurler* (to yell, to roar) and the noun *vent* (wind), from the French translation of Emily Brontë's *Wuthering Heights: Les Hauts de hurlevent*.

Causse echoes Wittig's playful neologizing in the terms she uses for the animal characters of her fable. The male animals are *animaux*$_m$, the female animals *animales*$_f$, and the lesbians *les anomales* (the anomalies$_f$). The husbands of the *animales* are termed their *Saigneurs* (bleeders), a pun on *seigneurs* (lords), with which it is homophonous. The land to which the *grande naine* (great dwarf$_f$) voyages, Androssie, is itself formed from the Greek for man, *andros*. See Armengaud 1994 for further dicussion of Causse's lexical and pronominal innovations. I am grateful to Michèle Causse for drawing my attention to her novel and providing a copy of Armengaud's review.

3. This line has also been parodied, incidentally, by the makers of Valda chewing gum. Their glossy advertisements, which used to grace the walls of Paris métro stations, portrayed a koala bear and the legend "Heureux qui comme Koala a goûté du chewing gum Valda" (Happy [is he] who, like Koala, has tasted the chewing gum Valda). Wittig is scarcely the first to mock the sacred canons of French literature. Indeed, her mockery places her among the French classics.

4. This slogan has an English equivalent in the title of Joanna Russ's science fiction classic *The Female Man*. The title signifies not an effeminate man, like Guy de Maupassant's *homme-fille* (1984, 345–49), but the one in two men who happens to be a woman. The French translation of *The Female Man* is titled *L'Autre moitié de l'homme* (The Other Half of Man), in reference to the Socratic idea of the formerly hermaphroditic being seeking its other half. The translation loses the humor, irony, and implicit feminism of the original.

5. Grammatically feminine generics are much more common in French among smaller animals and insects such as the *grenouille, libellule, coccinelle, araignée, mouche, fourmi, puce,* and *limace* (frog, dragonfly, ladybug, spider, fly, ant, flea, and slug). One might begin to believe in a masculist conspiracy, were it not for the majestic, grammatically feminine *baleine* (whale) and the small, crushable, and grammatically masculine *cafard* (cockroach).

6. In a groundbreaking study of the connections between the writings of theorists such as Lévi-Strauss and Lacan and their implications for women, Gayle Rubin remarks upon Wittig's readings of, and tirades against, Lévi-Strauss. Rubin notes that among French feminists it is particularly *Psychanalyse et Politique* (the group that registered the name *Mouvement de la Libération des Femmes* as their own trade name so that it could not be used by other groups) that is associated with the use and critique of the theories of Lévi-Strauss and Lacan (Rubin 1975, 200). In her fiction, Wittig takes a clearly oppositional stance toward Lévi-Strauss, whereas Psych et Po (as *Psychanalyse et Politique* is familiarly known) develop his theories, as well as those of Lacan, in feminist directions.

7. Unlike most literary versions of Sapir-Whorf, Wittig and Zeig's use of the hypothesis is utopic rather than dystopic. See, e.g., Ayn Rand's *Anthem* (1946), Jack Vance's *The Languages of Pao* (1958), Jean-Luc Godard's film *Alphaville* (1965), and Samuel Delany's *Babel-17* (1967), all of which use the concept of linguistic determinism to show how people may be tyrannized, their very thoughts controlled, by skillful manipulation of the language. It is particularly in feminist reworkings of the hypothesis that its utopic possibilities are brought out. Suzette Haden Elgin's science fiction trilogy—*Native Tongue* (1984), *The Judas Rose* (1987), and *Earthsong* (1994)—involves the introduction of a specifically women's language, Laàdan, to promote women's perceptions and liberate women from men's tyranny. It is also worth noting that the same concept of a causative relationship between language and reality can be seen in the contemporary movement for political correctness. Whatever its actual effects, this movement is in essence utopic. Important studies of the languages of science fiction and fictional uses of the Sapir-Whorf hypothesis may be found in Barnes 1975 and Meyers 1980.

8. It is worth bearing in mind, also, that linguistic and social change does not necessarily go in one direction only, and that almost any linguistic phenomenon may give rise to a range of interpretations. The substitution of *Ms.* for *Miss* or *Mrs.* and the proposed use of *Madelle* in place of *Madame* and *Mademoiselle* (discussed in Graddol and Swann 1989, 97; Yaguello 1979, 190–91; King 1991, 48–50, 88) may be seen as unequivocally feminist moves, eliminating the sexist distinction between married and unmarried women, a distinction not mirrored in the single term *Mr.* or *Monsieur* used to address a man. But as Susan Ehrlich reports, following Frank and Treichler 1989 (216), black women do not necessarily share white middle-class feminists' rejection of the title *Mrs.* since many of them were traditionally denied the right to take their husband's names. Ehrlich adds that some lesbians deliberately use the title *Miss* to signal that they have chosen not to marry men (1990, 49). Clearly, resistance to the social trend that is revising the meaning of *Madame* from "a married woman" to "a mature woman," and of *Mademoiselle* from "an unmarried woman" to "a young woman, a girl," does not necessarily spring from social conservatism.

When I lived in Avignon in 1980, my walk to the university involved crossing the Place de l'Horloge, by the Palais des Pâpes, each morning. Two old women in their seventies would also cross the square, one from the west, the other from the east. They would meet near the middle, and I would often hear them greet each other: "Bonjour, mademoiselle," "Bonjour mademoiselle." I was intrigued. Did they not feel, at the age of seventy, that *mademoiselle* was a little undignified? The owners of the *hôtel particulier* where I rented a room knew one of the women in question and told me firmly that she would not wish to be called *Madame*. She had never married but lived an independent life and wanted her independence noted in the way she was addressed. For these *demoiselles d'Avignon*, the title *mademoiselle* connoted not youth or immaturity, but independence.

5. *French Epicene* on

The chapter title translates as "There are four of us in the same situation."

1. See Rimmon-Kenan 1983 (71–85) for examples of different types of focalization in narrative; I have borrowed the terms *narrator-focalizer* and *internal* and *external narration* from her. Mieke Bal (1977, 39) employs the term narrator-

focalizer in a similar sense to refer to instances where the two functions are combined in one. The examples she gives are, like those of Rimmon-Kenan, also of external narration and external focalization. For readers more used to Genettian terminology, I would point out that Gérard Genette (1972) uses the terms *extradiégétique* and *intradiégétique* to refer to external and internal narration, respectively.

2. The other third person singular pronoun in French, *ça*, in contrast to *on*, is marked for low animacy. Technically an abbreviation of *cela* and thus a demonstrative, either anaphoric or deictic, *ça* is frequently used in colloquial speech to replace the dummy morpheme *il* in descriptions of the weather, as in *ça flotte, ça mouille, ça caille* (it's pissing down, it's wet, it's freezing). When used to designate people, because it presupposes the inanimacy, or at least the low animacy, of the referent, it connotes subhumanity in psychological, social, or mental faculties. Thus *qu'est-ce que ça peut chier* (can that/it ever shit), said of a small baby, would suggest that the baby was not quite human yet.

3. Foreign phrases and quotations are given in italics in the published English translation by Helen Weaver, a procedure that serves to clarify the boundaries between narration and citation. By formally differentiating between the two, however, the translator is making a distinction the author had intentionally blurred. In the episode discussed above, in which three of the girls are playing tennis when a new voice intervenes—"Je suis maître de moi comme de l'univers" (I am master of myself and of the universe)—this last phrase is put in italics in the English text to make clear it is a quotation (1966, 148). This procedure obviates the readers' need to search the text for clues as to its meaning but simultaneously loosens their dependence on the narrator-focalizer. In trying for a colloquial, smooth-flowing translation—and she has done a magnificent job on that score—Helen Weaver sacrifices some of the unique aspects of the novel.

Wittig was disappointed with the translation of *L'Opoponax* into English because the translator did not use the indefinite *one* but the generic *you* (Wittig 1986, 68). In fact, Weaver has a tendency to overinterpret the novel throughout, not just as concerns her translation of the various meanings of *on*, but also in her rendering of quotations, foreign phrases, and the definite article. She uses *you* to translate the plural inclusive *on*, as well as the third person exclusive (i.e., when it refers to Catherine Legrand only), and *they* to translate *on* referring to persons other than Catherine, thus spelling out for the reader who the referents are.

In cases where there may be some ambiguity as to who is meant, she supplies the person's name. In example 5.5, "Brigitte . . . prend Catherine Legrand par le cou. On lui sourit" (Brigitte takes Catherine Legrand by the neck. One/she smiles at her), where there is a risk of confusion as to whether Brigitte smiles at Catherine or Catherine at Brigitte, Weaver translates "on lui sourit" as "Catherine Legrand smiles at her" (1966, 7). In the French original, readers can deduce who is the subject and who is the indirect object, but because these relations are not given formally, they must study the text more carefully than their English counterparts to gain this information.

4. Wittig's experimentation with pronominal forms has been developed by the French novelist Michèle Causse, who introduced the tripartite *ille*, *el*, and *elle*, three distinct third person singular feminine pronouns, two of which are neologisms, into her novel *Voyages de la grande naine en Androssie* (1993). *Ille* indicates the feminine counterpart of *il*, while *el* is used for females who rebel against patriarchal domination but are still enmeshed in the system, and *elle* is reserved for liberated beings who are no longer defined by the masculine. See also chapter 4, note 5, for a discussion of Causse's use of neologistic lexical items.

5. Wittig credits Nathalie Sarraute with bringing *elles* to her attention: "Nathalie Sarraute uses *elles* very often throughout her work . . . I am convinced that without her use, *elles* would never have imposed itself on me with such force." Though she does not specify which of Sarraute's novels she is thinking of, it is in *Tropismes* (first published in 1939) that *elles* most thoroughly pervades the text, while in *Vous les entendez?* the singular *elle* stands out. Although Sarraute's and Wittig's political ideology, style, and literary intentions are markedly different, the feminine pronouns often function in similar ways in their work.

In *Tropismes*, an unspecified *elles* appears in chapters 4, 10, 12, and 20, either as the first word of the chapter or shortly thereafter. "Elles baragouinaient des choses à demi exprimées" (they_f jabbered away about things half expressed) (27); "[d]ans l'après-midi elles sortaient ensemble, menaient la vie des femmes" (in the afternoon they_f went out together, led the life women lead) (63); "[o]n les voyait marcher le long des vitrines . . . elles trottaient le long des boutiques" (one could see them walking along by the shop windows . . . they_f trotted along in front of the shops) (81); and "[q]uand il était petit, la nuit il se dressait sur son lit. Il appelait. Elles accouraient" (when he was little, at night he would sit up in bed. He would call out. They_f came running) (115). Whether all instances of *elles* refer to the same group of females, or to women in general, or to different specific groups, the reader cannot tell. We know that the referents must be animate and assume from the activities involved in the predicates that they are adults, but the information comes only from the verbs. *Elles* are the ones who *baragouinaient, sortaient, trottaient,* and *accouraient.* This is very similar to Wittig's use of *elles* in *Les Guérillères*, where, as explained earlier, this pronoun cannot be said to serve either an anaphoric or a cataphoric function, since no full lexical noun phrases are assigned to it directly. Instances of *elle* used without obvious nominal antecedent or successor may be found on pp. 26–27, 57–58, 67–69, 11, 129, 134, 173–74, and 179 of *Vous les entendez?*

Wittig owes an obvious and admitted debt to the work of the *nouveaux romanciers* (1950–1960) such as Sarraute, Michel Butor, and Alain Robbe-Grillet, all of whom have experimented with pronominal reference to some degree. Sarraute experiments with *elle/s*, Butor with *vous* in *La Modification* (1957), and Robbe-Grillet with a withheld *je* in *La Jalousie* (1957).

6. The feminist novelist Benoîte Groult, who, incidentally, headed the French governmental Commission de terminologie chargée de la féminisation des noms de métiers et de fonction (Commission on Terminology Responsible for Feminizing Job Titles and the Names of Public Offices), entitled one of her works *Ainsi soit-elle* (Let It/Her Be So or Let It Remain So) in ironic criticism of the use of the generic masculine in French as exemplified in the usual *ainsi soit-il*. This title is particularly well chosen for a collection of feminist essays, since at the semantic level it suggests that things should be left as they are in preservation of the status quo, whereas the change in morpheme from *il* to *elle* indicates that in fact everything is to be revolutionized.

6. Epicene Neologisms in English

1. I am grateful to Ursula K. Le Guin, Marge Piercy, Katherine and Roberta Arnold (the daughters of June Arnold), and Dorothy Bryant for providing me with information, references, and opinions about their work and for permission to quote them. They are, of course, in no way responsible for the use I have made of the material they gave me.

2. For an overview of these discussions see, e.g., Dubois and Crouch 1987, Khosroshahi 1989, and Newman 1992. See also the preface to Cameron 1985, for the opposite view: "Most sex-indefinite and generic referents in this book will be *she* and *her*. If there are any men reading who feel uneasy about being excluded, or not addressed, they may care to consider that women get this feeling within minutes of opening the vast majority of books and to reflect on the effect it has." It is instructive to note that whereas early editions (1945–68) of Benjamin Spock's *Child and Baby Care* systematically referred to the baby as *he*, since 1976, in response to feminist criticism, pronominal reference has alternated between the masculine and the feminine. The baby is no longer a generic boy; instead, each situation described presents a different case:

> Every time you pick your baby up . . . every time you change *him*, bathe *him*, feed *him* . . . *he*'s getting a feeling that *he* belongs to you. (1946, 3)

> Every time you pick your baby up—let's assume it's a girl—. . . every time you change *her*, bathe *her* feed *her* . . . *she*'s getting a feeling that *she* belongs to you. (1976, 2; emphasis added)

3. Dennis Baron reports that singular *they* had begun to be attacked by purists as early as the eighteenth century. He quotes the example of the grammarian Lindley Murray, who insisted on correcting "Can anyone, on their entrance into the world, be fully secure that they shall not be deceived?" to "Can anyone, on *his* entrance into the world, be fully secure that *he* shall not be deceived?" (Baron 1986, 194). The nineteenth-century Quaker grammmarian Goold Brown cites the sentence "No person should be censured for being careful of their reputation" as incorrect because "the pronoun *their* is of the plural number, and does not correctly represent its antecedent noun *person*, which is of the third person, singular, masculine" (Baron 1986, 194). Brown gives no reason for interpreting the noun *person* as masculine, except that he wants to justify the use of *he* to anaphorize it. The sentence might more appropriately use the feminine pronoun for women in nineteenth-century England might, arguably, have been more careful of their reputations than men.

The condemnation of singular *they* has continued to the present day, as may be seen in Quirk et al.'s *A Grammar of Contemporary English*, first published in 1972 and still in widespread use in British state schools.

> Everyone thinks they have the answer. (42)
> Has anybody brought their camera? (43)
> No one could have blamed themselves for that. (44)

> The use of *they* in sentences like (42–44) is frowned upon in formal English, where the tendency is to use *he* as the "unmarked" form when the sex of the antecedent is not determined. The formal equivalent of (42) is therefore:

> Everyone thinks he has the answer. (42)

> . . . Although the use of *he* often sounds pedantic, there is no obvious alternative to it, in formal English, except the rather cumbersome device of conjoining both male and female pronouns:

> Every student had to make up *his* or *her* mind. (45a)

Despite feminist concerns about the sexism of the generic *he*, Quirk et al. mention the possibility of sounding pedantic as its only inconvenience. One gets the impression that pedantry is not high on their list of faults to avoid.

4. In order to log on to LambdaMOO, telnet to the following address: <telnet://lambda.moo.mud.org:8888/1>. Once you are on LambaMOO, type "connect Guest" to enter the MOO world. To see the different gender choices for characters in the MOO, type "@gender" and the following text will appear.

Characters & Gender

Your character, as well as every other character in this MOO, has a gender. The choice of gender determines which pronouns will be used when referring to that character. If you type look me, you'll see a phrase about being awake and alert; the pronouns used there are determined by your gender.

Every character is given the default gender when it is created. In this MOO, the default gender is neuter. Spivak is an indeterminate gender (rather than referring to such a person as s/he or he/she, e is the proper pronoun).
@gender
Your gender is currently neuter.
Your pronouns: it, it, its, its, itself, It, It, Its, Its, Itself
Available genders: neuter, male, female, either, Spivak, splat, plural, egotistical, royal, or 2nd
@gender male
Gender set to male.
Your pronouns: he, him, his, his, himself, He, Him, His, His, Himself
@gender female
Gender set to female.
Your pronouns: she, her, her, hers, herself, She, Her, Her, Hers, Herself
@gender either
Gender set to either.
Your pronouns: s/he, him/her, his/her, his/hers, (him/her)self, S/He, Him/Her, His/Her, His/Hers, (Him/Her)self
@gender Spivak
Gender set to Spivak.
Your pronouns: e, em, eir, eirs, emself, E, Em, Eir, Eirs, Emself
@gender splat
Gender set to splat.
Your pronouns: *e, h*, h*, h*s, h*self, *E, H*, H*, H*s, H*self
@gender plural
Gender set to plural.
Your pronouns: they, them, their, theirs, themselves, They, Them, Their, Theirs, Themselves
@gender egotistical
Gender set to egotistical.
Your pronouns: I, me, my, mine, myself, I, Me, My, Mine, Myself
@gender royal
Gender set to royal.
Your pronouns: we, us, our, ours, ourselves, We, Us, Our, Ours, Ourselves
@gender 2nd
Gender set to 2nd.Your pronouns: you, you, your, yours, yourself, You, You, Your, Yours, Yourself
5. In fact, both characters are women, involved in a lovers' quarrel.
6. For feminist renderings of the Sapir-Whorf hypothesis, see, e.g., Spender 1980, 138–62, or Penelope 1990, 202–11.

7. Striking, but not unique in the history of Western literature. In the twelfth-century French "cante-fable" *Aucassin et Nicolete* (author unknown), Aucassin comes across a king lying in childbed: "il gissoit d'enfent" (1977, 30). Upon being asked by Aucassin what he thinks he's doing, the king replies without hesitation, "Je gis d'un fil. / Quant mes mois sera conplis, / Et je sarai bien garis, / Dont irai le messe oïr / Si com mes ancestre fist" (I am lying in childbed. / When my months are completed, / And I am well recovered / Then I will go and hear mass / Just as my ancestors did) (1977, 30). The custom of the father lying in is known as the *couvade*, from the French verb *couver*, meaning to sit on or hatch eggs.

8. Ursula K. Le Guin was kind enough to give me a copy of her unpublished manuscript (MS).

I am pleased to report that when I sent an earlier version of this chapter to the author for comment, she confirmed my analysis of her work, remarking, "I believe you are quite accurate about my various lapses and changes of mind." She notes further, "The most interesting discovery I made was that to get any ungendering effect at all you have to *keep the nouns in the other gender*" (personal communication, 24 July 1994), demonstrating that in order to override the hierarchy of gender markedness, strong tactics, even shock tactics, are needed.

9. Piercy, Le Guin, and Wittig are far from the only authors to invent *lexical* neologisms for feminist ends. In Norway, Gerd Brantenberg's *Egalias Døtre* (1977) introduces a panoply of role reversals in such neologisms as "lordies and gentlewim," "wim and menwim," "wif and housebound," to give the English translations. The German writer Inkae Künkel, in her novel *Auf der Reise nach Avalun* (1982), feminizes grammatically masculine nouns. Thus *der Mond* (the moon$_m$) becomes *die Mondin* (the mooness$_f$); *der Wasserman* (waterman) becomes *die Wasserfrau* (waterwoman). The pronoun *man* (one), derived from the masculine *Mann* (man), is either avoided or underlined. *Niemand* (no one; literally, no man) becomes *niemann-d*, the double *n* emphasizing its masculine connotations (Wiener 1987, 169). Suzette Haden Elgin, an American linguist, has written a science fiction trilogy around Laàdan, the language of women's perceptions: *Native Tongue* (1984), *The Judas Rose* (1986), and *Earthsong* (1994). The novels themselves are written in conventional English, but Elgin has also created *A First Dictionary and Grammar of Laàdan*, which is available from the Society for the Furtherance and Study of Fantasy and Science Fiction, Box 1624, Madison, WI 53701.

10. In popular spoken English, the he/him, she/her, and I/me distinctions have been eroded. Many speakers, including me, say "her and me went to the movies," for example, without conscious solecism.

7. Linguistic Gender and Liminal Identity

The chapter title translates "Before I was a transsexual, now I was a woman."

1. Alison Laing, herself a male-to-female transsexual, offers courses for trans-sexuals in Philadelphia who want to learn more-feminine speech patterns. She has produced a video entitled "Speaking as a Woman with Alison Laing" (1992).

2. There is an extensive body of work on presupposition in linguistics, of which only the most elementary thesis is discussed in this chapter. For more ample information, see, e.g., Strawson 1964; Stalnaker 1973, 1974, 1978; Clark and Haviland 1977; and Ducrot 1984.

3. I use feminine pronouns to refer to male-to-female transsexuals and masculine pronouns to refer to female-to-male transsexuals out of respect for their pronominal preferences.

4. Marina Yaguello describes another grammatical *contretemps* involving the invariable feminine adjective *enceinte* (pregnant$_f$). Captain Prieur, a woman who had been placed under house arrest on a Polynesian island for her part in the sinking of the Greenpeace ship *Rainbow Warrior*, was sent home to France when it was discovered she was pregnant. Because *le capitaine* is grammatically masculine in French, it cannot be anaphorized by the feminine pronoun *elle*. There is, on the other hand, a commonsense objection to this person's being referred to as *il*, especially when the attributive adjective used to qualify the referent is *enceinte*, which only exists in the feminine, for obvious reasons (1988, 73–77).

5. Readers might ask why I have not undertaken a parallel analysis of French (auto)biographies of female-to-male transsexuals. The answer is simple: I have been unable to locate any. I would hypothesize that this is due to the fact that there are fewer female-to-male transsexuals than male-to-female transsexuals, possibly because the operation is so costly as to be out of the reach of most women, whereas men whose earning power is traditionally higher, find it easier to afford.

6. In 1857, Charles Baudelaire and his publisher were tried for affronts against public decency after the publication of *Les Fleurs du mal*, which included poems on lesbian themes. Poet and publisher were found guilty and obliged to pay a hefty fine and remove six poems from the collection.

7. The term "cross-expressing" has been borrowed from Kira Hall (1995, 202). She defines it as "discursive shifting, characterized by the performance of the vocal and verbal garb associated with the other sex."

8. At the same time, the feminist movement, backed by ministerial decree, is hard at work finding and creating suitable feminine terms for women in traditionally male occupations (Moreau 1991, Gervais 1993). It would be an oversimplification to say that gender concord and lexicalized gender distinctions are on the road to extinction. See also chapter 8.

8. Implications

The chapter title translates as "Hung for illicit interventions."

1. I am endebted to Marie-Jo Bonnet (1997) for bringing this passage to my attention. She quotes it in her research into the varying terms for "lesbian" from the sixteenth century to the present day. Her analysis of the passage takes a rather different trajectory than my own. Here is the text in its entirety:

> Sept ou huit **filles** d'autour de Chaumont en Bassigni complotèrent, il y a quelques années, de se vestir en mâle et continuer ainsi leur vie de par le monde. Entre les autres, l'**une** vint en ce lieu de Vitry sous le nom de Mary, gagnant sa vie à être tisserand, **jeune homme** bien conditionné et qui se rendait à un chacun ami. Il fiança audit Vitry une femme qui est encore vivante, mais pour quelque désacord qui survint entre **eux**, leur marché ne passa plus outre. Depuis, etant allé audit Montirandet, gagnant toujours sa vie audit métier, **il** devint amoureux d'une femme laquelle **il** avait épousée et vécu quatre out cinq mois avec elle avec son consentement, à ce qu'on dit, mais ayant été reconn**u** par quelqu'un dudit Chaumont et la chose mise en avant la justice, **elle** avait été condamné**e** à être pendue: ce qu'**elle** disait aimer mieux souffrir

que de se remettre en état de fille. Et fut pendue pour des inventions illicites à suppléer au défaut de son sexe (1955, 44–45).

Several years ago, seven or eight **girls** living near Chaumont in Bassigny plotted to dress in masculine clothes and present themselves in the world thus attired. Of this group, **one woman** bearing the name of Mary came to the town of Vitry, earning **his** living as a weaver$_m$, a young **man** of good condition$_m$ and a friend$_m$ to all. In the said town of Vitry, **he** became engaged to a woman who is still living, but, because of some disagreement that occurred between them$_m$, things did not go any further. After this, having moved$_m$ to Montirandet, still earning **his** living at the said occupation, **he** fell in love$_m$ with a woman whom **he** married and lived with for four or five months, with her consent, according to what people say. But, having been recognized$_m$ by someone from Chaumont, and the affair brought before the courts, **she** was condemned$_f$ to be hanged$_f$: which **she** said **she** preferred to endure rather than resume the status of a girl. And **she** was hanged$_f$ for employing illicit interventions to compensate for the lack inherent in her sex.

Bibliography

Aebischer, Verena (1985). *Les Femmes et le langage: représentations sociales d'une différence*. Paris: Presses Universitaires de France.

Ager, D. E. (1990). *Sociolinguistics and Contemporary French*. Cambridge: Cambridge University Press.

Aldiss, Brian W. and David Wingrove (1986). *Trillion Year Spree: The History of Science Fiction*. London: Gollancz.

Anderson, Kristine (1991). "To Utopia via the Sapir-Whorf Hypothesis." In Michael Cummings and Nicholas Smith, eds., *Utopian Studies III*. New York: University Press of America.

Anscombe, G. E. M. (1957). *Intention*. Oxford: Blackwell.

Armengaud, Françoise (1994). "Michèle Causse: Voyages de la grande naine en Androssie." *Nouvelles questions féministes*, 15, no. 1: 105–10.

Arnold, June (1973). *The Cook and the Carpenter: A novel by the Carpenter*. Plainsfield, Vt.: Daughters, Inc.

Aucassin et Nicolete (1977). Mario Roques, ed. Paris: Honoré Champion.

Audibert-Gibier, Monique (1988). "Etude de l'accord du participe passé sur des corpus de français parlé." Master's thesis, Université de Provence.

Austin, John Langshaw (1961). "A Plea for Excuses." In *Philosophical Papers*. Oxford: Oxford University Press.

Bal, Mieke (1977). *Narratologie: essais sur la signification narrative dans quatre romans modernes*. Paris: Klincksieck.

Balzac, Honoré de (1970). "Sarrasine." In Roland Barthes, *S/Z*. Paris: Editions du Seuil.

Barbin, Herculine ([1868] 1978). "Mes Souvenirs." In Michel Foucault, ed., *Herculine Barbin dite Alexina B*. Paris: Gallimard.

Barnes, Myra (1975). *Linguistics and Languages in Science Fiction–Fantasy*. New York: Arno.

Barney, Natalie Clifford (1930). *The One Who Is Legion, or A. D.'s After-Life*. Orono, Me.: National Poetry Foundation.

Baron, Dennis (1986). *Grammar and Gender*. New Haven, Conn: Yale University Press.

Barrett, Rusty (1997). "The Homo-Genius Speech Community." In Anna Livia and Kira Hall, eds. *Queerly Phrased: Language, Gender, and Sexuality*. New York: Oxford University Press.

Barthes, Roland (1970). *S/Z*. Paris: Editions du Seuil.

Bartlett, John (1995). *Bartlett's Familiar Quotations*, s.v. "pregnant." New York: Time Warner Electronic Publishing.

Bauche, Henri (1928). *Le Langage populaire: grammaire, syntaxe, et dictionnaire du français populaire tel qu'on le parle dans le peuple de Paris*. Vol. 1. Paris: Payot.

Baudelaire, Charles (1972). *Les Fleurs du mal*. Paris: Gallimard.

Bell, Shannon (1993a). "Finding the Male Within and Taking Him Cruising: 'Drag-King-for-a-Day' at the Sprinkle Salon." In Arthur Kroker and Marilouise Kroker, eds., *The Last Sex: Feminism and Outlaw Bodies*. New York: St. Martin's.

——— (1993b). "Kate Bornstein: A Transgender Transsexual Postmodern Tiresias." In Arthur Kroker and Marilouise Kroker, eds., *The Last Sex: Feminism and Outlaw Bodies*. New York: St, Martin's.

Benveniste, Emile (1966a). "La Nature des pronoms." In *Problèmes de linguistique générale*. Paris: Gallimard.

——— (1966b). "Structure des relations de personne dans le verbe." In *Problèmes de linguistique générale*. Paris: Gallimard.

Berlin, Brent, and Paul Kay (1969). *Basic Color Terms: Their Universality and Evolution*. Berkeley: University of California Press.

Blakemore, Diane (1987). *Semantic Constraints on Relevance*. Oxford: Basil Blackwell.

Blanche-Benveniste, Claire (1990). *Le Français parlé: études grammaticales*. Paris: Editions du Centre national de la recherche scientifique.

Bloomfield, Leonard (1933). *Language*. New York: Henry Holt.

Bodine, Ann (1975). "Androcentrism in Prescriptive Grammar: Singular 'They,' Sex-Indefinite 'He,' and 'He or She.' *Language in Society* 4: 129–46.

Bonnet, Marie-Jo (1997). "Sappho, or the Importance of Culture in the Language of Love." In Anna Livia and Kira Hall, eds., *Queerly Phrased: Language, Gender, and Sexuality*. New York: Oxford University Press.

Brantenberg, Gerd ([1977] 1985). *Egalia's Daughters: A Satire of the Sexes*. Translated by Louis Mackay. Seattle: Seal Press.

Bronte, Charlotte [Currer Bell, pseud.] (1891). *Shirley*. London: Frederick Warne.

Brophy, Brigid (1969). *In Transit: An Heroi-Cyclic Novel*. New York: Putnam's.

——— (1987). "He/She/Hesh." In *Baroque-'n'-Roll and Other Essays*. London: Hamish Hamilton.

Brown, Gillian, and George Yukle (1983). *Discourse Analysis*. Cambridge: Cambridge University Press.

Brunot, Ferdinand, and Charles Bruneau (1933). *Précis de grammaire historique de la langue française*. Vol. 1. Paris: Masson.

Bryant, Dorothy (1971). *The Kin of Ata Are Waiting for You*. First published as *The Comforter*. Random House: New York.

Bucholtz, Mary (1999). "Bad Examples: Transgression and Progress in Language and Gender Studies." In Mary Bucholtz, A. C. Liang, and Laurel A. Sutton, eds., *Reinventing Identities: The Gendered Self in Discourse*. New York: Oxford University Press.

Butler, Judith (1990). *Gender Trouble: Feminism and the Subversion of Identity*. London and New York: Routledge, Chapman, Hill.

—— (1993). *Bodies That Matter: On the Discursive Limits of "Sex."* New York: Routledge.

Butor, Michel (1957). *La Modification*. Paris: Editions de Minuit.

—— (1964). "L'Usage des pronoms personnels dans le roman." In *Répertoire II*. Paris: Editions de Minuit.

Cameron, Deborah (1985). *Feminism and Linguistic Theory*. London: Macmillan.

—— ed. (1990). *The Feminist Critique of Language: A Reader*. London: Routledge.

—— (1993). "Language and Gender Studies: How Do We Move Forward? Reflections on the 1993 COSWL and AILA conferences." In *Working Papers on Language, Gender and Sexism*, 3, no. 2, (Dec.). 19–30.

—— (1995). *Verbal Hygiene*. London: Routledge.

Caudwell, Sarah (1981). *Thus Was Adonis Murdered*. London: Penguin.

—— (1984). *The Shortest Way to Hades*. New York: Charles Scribner & Sons.

—— (1989). *The Sirens Sang of Murder*. New York: Bantam, Doubleday, Dell.

Causse, Michèle (1993). *Voyages de la grande naine en Androssie*. Laval, Québec: Editions Trois.

Cellard, Jacques (1978). "Le Caméléon." *Le Monde* (28 February).

Chafe, Wallace, ed. (1980). *The Pear Stories: Cognitive, Cultural, and Linguistic Aspects of Narrative Production*. Norwood, N.J.: Ablex.

Chawaf, Chantal (1976). "La chair linguistique." *Nouvelles littéraires* (26 May): 18.

Cherny, Lynn (1999). *Conversation and Community: Chat in a Virtual World*. Stanford, Ca.: CSLI Publications.

Cixous, Hélène (1975). "Le Rire de la Méduse." *L'Arc*, 61: 39–54.

—— ([1976] 1992). "Le Sexe ou la tête." In Les Cahiers du Grif, eds., *Le langage des femmes*. Paris: Editions Complexe.

Clancy, Patricia (1980). "Referential Choice in English and Japanese Narrative Discourse." In Wallace L. Chafe, ed., *The Pear Stories: Cognitive, Cultural, and Linguistic Aspects of Narrative Production*. Norwood, N.J.: Ablex.

Clark, H., and S. E. Haviland (1977). "Comprehension and the Given–new Contract." In R. Freedle, ed., *Discourse Production and Comprehension*. Hillsdale, N.J.: Lawrence Erlbaum.

Coates, Jennifer, and Mary Ellen Jordan (1997). "Que(e)rying Friendship: Discourses of Resistance and the Construction of Gendered Subjectivity." In Anna Livia and Kira Hall, eds., *Queerly Phrased: Language, Gender, and Sexuality*. New York: Oxford University Press.

Collin, Françoise ([1976] 1992). "Polyglo(u)ssons." In Les Cahiers du Grif, eds., *Le langage des femmes*. Paris: Editions Complexe.

Comrie, Bernard (1976). *Language Universals*. Cambridge: Cambridge University Press.

Conner, Randy (1997). "*Les Molles et les chausses:* Mapping the Isle of Hermaphrodites in Pre-Modern France." In Anna Livia and Kira Hall, eds., *Queerly*

Phrased: Language, Gender, and Sexuality. New York: Oxford University Press.

Conte, Marie-Elisabeth (1988). *Condizioni di coerenza.* Florence: La Nuova Italia Editrice.

Coote, Stephen, ed. (1983). *The Penguin Book of Homosexual Verse.* Harmondsworth: Penguin.

Corbett, Greville (1991). *Gender.* Cambridge: Cambridge University Press.

Crowley, Terry (1992). *An Introduction to Historical Linguistics.* 2d. ed. Oxford: Oxford University Press.

Daly, Mary (1978). *Gyn/Ecology: The Metaethics of Radical Feminism.* London: Women's Press.

——— (1984). *Pure Lust: Elemental Feminist Philosophy.* London: Women's Press.

Daly, Mary, and Jane Caputi (1987). *Webster's First New Intergalactic Wickedary of the English Language.* Boston: Beacon.

Damourette, Jacques, and Edouard Pichon (1911–1927). *Des Mots à la pensée: essai de grammaire de la langue francaise.* Vol. 1. Paris: D'Artrey.

Danès, F., ed. (1974). *Papers on Functional Sentence Perspective.* Mouton: La Haye.

Davies, Bronwyn (1990). "The Problem of Desire." *Social Problems* 37, no. 4. (Nov. 1990): 501–506.

Delany, Samuel (1967). *Babel-17.* London: Victor Gollancz.

Delarue-Mardrus, Lucie (1930). *L'Ange et les pervers.* Paris: Ferenczi et Fils.

Deleuze, Gilles, and Felix Guattari (1987). *A Thousand Plateaus: Capitalism and Schizophrenia.* Minneapolis: University of Minnesota Press.

Derrida, Jacques (1975). "Le Facteur de la vérité." *Poétique* 21:96–147.

——— (1988). *Limited Inc.* Evanston, Il.: Northwestern University Press.

Diane (1987). *Diane par Diane.* Paris: Acropole.

Diaz-Diocaretz, Myriam (1985). *Translating Poetic Discourse: Questions on Feminist Strategies in Adriennne Rich.* Amsterdam: John Benjamins.

La Différence sexuelle dans le langage: Actes du Colloque ADEC-Université Paris III December 1988, Nice: Contrastes.

Dijk, Teun A. van (1972). *Some Aspects of Text Grammars: A Study in Theoretical Linguistics and Poetics.* The Hague: Mouton.

Dijk, Teun A. van, and Walter Kitsch (1983). *Strategies of Discourse Comprehension.* New York: Academic Press.

Dubois, Betty Lou, and Isabel Crouch (1987). "Linguistic Disruption: He/She, S/He, He or She, He-She." In Joyce Penfield, ed., *Women and Language in Transition.* New York: State University of New York Press.

Ducrot, Oswald (1984). *Le Dire et le dit.* Paris: Minuit.

Duffy, Jean (1987). "Women and Language in *Les Guérillères* by Monique Wittig." In *Stanford French Review* 7:399–412.

Duffy, Maureen ([1971] 1994). *Love Child.* London: Virago.

Dullak, Sylvie (1983). *Je serai elle.* Paris: Presses de la Cité.

Durand, Marguerite (1936). *Le Genre grammatical en français parlé à Paris et dans la région parisienne.* Paris: Bibliothèque du français moderne.

Duras, Marguerite (1964). "Une Oeuvre éclatante." *France observateur,* 5 Nov.

Ehrlich, Susan (1990). *Point of View: A Linguistic Analysis of Literary Style.* London: Routledge.

Elgin, Suzette Haden (1984). *Native Tongue.* London: Women's Press.

——— (1987a). *The Judas Rose.* London: Women's Press.

——— (1987b). "Women's Language and Near Future Science Fiction: A Reply." *Women's Studies Interdisciplinary Journal* 14, no. 2:175–181.

——— (1994). *Earthsong*. New York: Daw.

Epstein, Julia (1990). "Either/Or—Neither/Both: Sexual Ambiguity and the Ideology of Gender." *Genders* 7 (spring): 99—142.

Farmer, Ann, and Robert Harnish (1987). "Communicative Reference with Pronouns." In Jef Verschueren and Marcella Bertucelli-Papi, eds., *The Pragmatic Perspective: Selected Papers from the 1985 International Pragmatics Conference*. Amsterdam: John Benjamins.

Farwell, Marilyn (1990). "Heterosexual Plots and Lesbian Subtexts: Toward a Theory of Lesbian Narrative Space." In Karla Jay and Joanne Glasgow, eds., *Lesbian Texts and Contexts: Radical Revisions*. New York: New York University Press.

Fetterley, Judith (1990). "My Ántonia, Jim Burden, and the Dilemma of the Lesbian Writer." In Karla Jay and Joanne Glasgow, eds., *Lesbian Texts and Contexts: Radical Revisions*. New York: New York University Press.

Flaubert, Gustave (1966). "Un Coeur simple." In *Trois Contes*. Paris: Livre de Poche.

——— (1983). *L'Education sentimentale*. Paris: Livre de Poche.

Fleischman, Suzanne (1990). *Tense and Narrativity: From Medical Performance to Modern Fiction*. Austin: University of Texas Press.

Fodor, Istvan (1959). "The Origin of Grammatical Gender," parts 1 and 2. *Lingua* 8:1–41, 186–214.

Foucault, Michel (1966). *Les Mots et les choses*. Paris: Gallimard.

——— (1969). *L'Archéologie du savoir*. Paris: Gallimard.

——— (1970). *The Order of Things: An Archaeology of the Human Sciences*. London: Tavistock.

——— (1972). *The Archeology of Knowledge and the Discourse on Language*. New York: Pantheon.

——— (1978). *Herculine Barbin dite Alexina B*. Paris: Gallimard.

——— (1980). *Herculine Barbin*. New York: Random House.

——— (1990). *The History of Sexuality: An Introduction*. Vol. 1. New York: Random House.

Fornel, Michel de (1987). "Reference to Persons in Conversation." In Jef Verschueren and Marcella Bertucelli-Papi, eds., *The Pragmatic Perspective: Selected Papers from the 1985 International Pragmatics Conference*. Amsterdam: John Benjamins.

Frank, Francine Wattman, and Paula Treichler (1989). *Language, Gender, and Professional Writing: Theoretical Appraoches and Guidelines for Nonsexist Usage*. New York: Commission on the Status of Women in the Profession, Modern Language Association of America.

Freccero, Carla (1986). "The Other and the Same: The Image of the Hermaphrodite in Rabelais." In Margaret Ferguson, Maureen Quilligan, and Nancy J. Vickers. eds., *Rewriting the Renaissance: The Discourses of Sexual Difference in Early Modern Europe*. Chicago: University of Chicago Press.

Frye, Marilyn (1983). *The Politics of Reality: Essays in Feminist Theory*. Trumansberg, N.Y.: Crossing Press.

Fuentes, Carlos (1962). *La muerte de Artemio Cruz*. Mexico City, Mexico: Fondo de cultura Economica.

Garréta, Anne (1986). *Sphinx*. Paris: Grasset.

——— (1987). *Pour en finir avec le genre humain*. Paris: François Bourin.

——— (1989). To Hell with Gender." Unpublished essay.

——— (1990). *Ciels liquides*. Paris: Grasset.

Gaudio, Rudolf (1997). "Not Talking Straight in Hausa." In Anna Livia and Kira Hall, eds., *Queerly Phrased: Language, Gender, and Sexuality*. New York: Oxford University Press.

Gee, James (1991). "A Linguistic Approach to Narrative." *Journal of Narrative and Life History* 1, no. 1: 15–39.

Genette, Gérard (1972). *Figures III*. Paris: Seuil.

George, Ken (1993). "Alternative French." In Carol Sanders. ed., *French Today: Language in Its Social Context*. Cambridge: Cambridge University Press.

Gervais, Marie-Marthe (1993). "Gender and Language in French." In Carol Sanders, ed., *French Today: Language in Its Social Context*. Cambridge: Cambridge University Press.

Goodwin, Marjorie (1990). "Tactical Uses of Stories: Participation Frameworks within Girls' and Boys' Disputes." *Discourse Processes* 13: 33–71.

Gordon, Rebecca (1994). "Delusions of Gender, a review of Kate Bornstein's *Gender Outlaw:* On Men, Women, and the Rest of Us." *Women's Review of Books*, 12, no. 2 (Nov.): 18–19.

Gould, Stephen, and Elizabeth Urba (1982). "Exaptation: A Missing Term in the Science of Form." *Paleobiology* 8: 4–15.

Graddol, David, and Joan Swann (1989). *Gender Voices*. Oxford: Basil Blackwell.

Greenberg, Joseph H. (1978). *Universals of Human Language*. Vol. 3, *Word Structure*. Stanford: Stanford University Press.

Grévisse, Maurice (1970). *Le Bon usage: grammaire française avec des remarques sur la langue française d'aujourd'hui*. 9th ed. Gembloux: Duculot.

Grice, Paul (1990a). "Meaning." In A. P. Martinich, ed., *The Philosophy of Language*. Oxford: Oxford University Press.

——— (1990b). "Logic and Conversation." In A. P. Martinich, ed., *The Philosophy of Language*. Oxford: Oxford University Press.

Groult, Benoîte (1975). *Ainsi soit-elle*. Paris: Grasset.

——— (1981). *La Moitié de la terre*. Paris: Editions Alain Moreau, Collection Presse-Poche.

Gumperz, John J., and Stephen C. Levinson, eds. (1996). *Rethinking Linguistic Relativity*. Cambridge: Cambridge University Press.

Halberstam, Judith (1998). *Female Masculinity*. Durham, N.C.: Duke University Press.

Hall, Kira (1997a). "Shifting Gender Positions among Hindi-Speaking Hijras." In Victoria Bergvall, Janet Bing, and Alice Freed, eds., *Language and Gender Research: Theory and Method*. London: Longman.

——— (1997b). "Go Suck Your Master's Sugar Cane: Hijras and the Use of Sexual Insult." In Anna Livia and Kira Hall. eds., *Queerly Phrased: Language, Gender, and Sexuality*. New York: Oxford University Press.

——— (1995). "Lip Service on the Fantasy Lines." In Kira Hall and Mary Bucholtz, eds., *Gender Articulated: Language and the Socially Constructed Self*. New York: Routledge.

Halliday, Martin, and Ruqaiya Hasan (1976). *Cohesion in English*. London: Longman.

Harris, Bertha (1976). *Lover*. Plainfield, Vt.: Daughers.

Harris, Martin (1978). *The Evolution of French Syntax*. London: Longman.

———— (1988). "French." In Martin Harris and Nigel Vincent eds., *The Romance Languages*. New York: Oxford University Press.

Henley, Nancy (1987). "This New Species That Seeks a New Language: On Sexism in Language and Language Change." In Joyce Penfield, ed., *Women and Language in Transition*. New York: State University of New York Press.

Herder, Johann Gottfried ([1772] 1966). *On the Origin of Language*. Trans. Alexander Gode. New York: Ungar.

Hervé, Jane, and Jeanne Lagier (1992). *Les Transsexuel(le)s*. Paris: Bertoin.

Hill, Jane, and Bruce Mannheim (1992). "Language and World View." *Annual Review of Anthropology* 21: 381–406.

Høeg, Peter (1992). *Miss Smilla's Feeling for Snow*. London: Flamingo.

Hokenson, Jan (1988). "The Pronouns of Gomorrha: A Lesbian Prose Tradition." *Frontiers* 10, no. 1: 62–69.

Houdebine-Gravaud, Anne-Marie (1988). "L'Une n'est pas l'autre (ou genre et sexe en français contemporain)." *Genre et langage*: Actes du colloque tenu à Paris X Nanterre, 14–16 Dec.

Ibrahim, Muhammad Hasan (1973). *Grammatical Gender: Its Origin and Development*. The Hague: Mouton.

Irigaray, Luce (1987). "L'Ordre sexuel du discours." *Langages : le sexe linguistique*, 85 (Mar.): 81–123.

———— (1990). *Sexes et genres à travers les langues: éléments de communication sexuée, français, anglais, italien*. Paris: Grasset.

Jakobson, Roman (1971). *Selected Writings*. Vol. 2, *Word and Language*. The Hague: Mouton.

Jakobson, Roman, and Linda R. Waugh (1987). *The Sound Shape of Language*. 2d ed. Amsterdam: Mouton de Gruyter.

Judge, Anne (1993). "French: A Planned Language?" In Carol Sanders, ed., *French Today: Language in Its Social Context*. Cambridge: Cambridge University Press.

Kay, Paul, and Chad McDaniel (1978). "On the Linguistic Significance of the Meanings of Basic Color Terms." *Language* 54, no. 3: 610–46.

Kay, Paul, and Willett Kempton (1983). "What Is the Sapir-Whorf Hypothesis?" *Berkeley Cognitive Science Report* no. 8, Institute for Human Learning, University of California at Berkeley.

Kessler, Suzanne (1990). "The Medical Construction of Gender: Case Management of Intersexed Infants." *Signs* 16, no. 1 (autumn): 3–26.

Khosroshahi, Fatemeh (1989). "Penguins Don't Care, but Women Do: A Social Identity Analysis of a Whorfian Problem." *Language in Society* 18, no. 4. (Dec.): 505–25.

King, Ruth (1991). *Talking Gender: A Guide to Nonsexist Communication*. Toronto, Ont.: Copp Clark Pitman.

Klein, Kathleen Gregory (1995). *The Woman Detective: Gender and Genre*. Urbana: University of Illinois Press.

Kneip, Nadine (1985). "Quelques réflexions sur l'accord des participes passés en français écrit et en francais parlé." Master's thesis, Université de Provence.

Knight, H. Merle (1992). "Gender Interference in Transsexuals' Speech." In Kira Hall, Mary Bucholtz, and Birch Moonwomon, eds., *Locating Power: Proceedings of the Second Berkeley Women and Language Conference, April 4 and 5, 1992*. Vol. 2. Berkeley: Berkeley Women and Language Group, University of California.

Koskas, Eliane, and Danielle Leeman (1988). *Genre et langage.* Actes du colloque tenu à Paris X Nanterre, 14–16 Dec.

Kramarae, Cheris, and Paula A. Treichler (1985). *A Feminist Dictionary.* London: Pandora Press.

Kristeva, Julia ([1974] 1992). *La Révolution du langage poétique.* Paris: Editions du Seuil.

Künkel, Inkae (1982). *Auf der Reise nach Avalun.* Ahrensbok: Schwarze Mond.

Kuno, Susumu (1987). *Functional Syntax: Anaphora, Discourse, and Empathy.* Chicago: University of Chicago Press.

Kuno, Susumu, and Etsuko Kaburaki (1977). "Empathy and Syntax." *Linguistic Enquiry* 8, no. 4: 627–72.

Labov, William (1972). "The transformation of Experience in Narrative Syntax." In *Language in the Inner City: Studies in the Black English Vernacular.* Philadelphia: University of Pennsylvania Press.

Labov, William, and David Fanshel (1977). *Therapeutic Discourse: Psychotherapy as Conversation.* New York: Academic Press.

Labov William, and Joshua Waletzky (1967). "Narrative Analysis: Oral Versions of Personal Experience." In June Helm, ed., *Essays on the Verbal and Visual Arts.* Seattle: University of Washington Press.

Lacan, Jacques (1966). *Ecrits.* Paris: Seuil.

Laing, Alison (1992). *Speaking as a Woman with Alison Laing.* Philadelphia: CDS, No Frills Video.

Lakoff, Robin (1975). *Language and Woman's Place.* New York: Harper & Row.

Lambrecht, Knud (1987). "On the Status of SVO Sentences in French Discourse." In Russell Tomlin, ed., *Coherence and Grounding in Discourse: Outcome of a Symposium, Eugene, Oregon, June 1984.* Amsterdam: John Benjamins.

Lass, Roger (1990). "How to Do Things with Junk: Exaptation in Language Evolution." *Journal of Linguistics* 26, no. 1 (Mar.): 79–102.

Lautréamont, Comte de (Isidore Ducasse) (1969). *Les Chants de Maldoror.* Paris: Flammarion.

Leclerc, Annie (1976). "Mon écriture d'amour." *Nouvelles littéraires,* 26 May, 18.

Leech, Geoffrey N., and Michael H. Short (1981). *Style in Fiction: A Linguistic Introduction to English Fictional Prose.* Harlow, U.K.: Longman.

Lefanu, Sarah (1988). *In the Chinks of the World Machine: Feminism and Science Fiction.* London: Women's Press.

Le Guin, Ursula K. ([1969] 1973). *The Left Hand of Darkness.* St. Albans: Granada.

——— (1975). "Winter's King." In *The Wind's Twelve Quarters: Short Stories.* New York: Harper & Row.

——— (1976). Introduction to *The Left Hand of Darkness.* New York: Ace.

——— (1978). "Is Gender Necessary?" In *The Languages of the Night: Essays on Fantasy and Science Fiction.* New York: Putnam.

——— (1985). *Always Coming Home.* New York: Harper & Row.

——— (1987). "Is Gender Necessary? Redux." In *Dancing at the Edge of the World: Thoughts on Words, Women, Places.* New York: Grove Press.

——— (1995). Afterword to *The Left Hand of Darkness.* New York: Ace.

Levinson, Stephen (1983). *Pragmatics.* Cambridge: Cambridge University Press.

Lévi-Strauss, Claude ([1949] 1967). *Les Structures élémentaires de la parenté.* Paris: Presses Universitaires de France.

Linde, Charlotte (1993). *Life Stories: The Creation of Coherence*. Oxford: Oxford University Press.

Linguist List (1993a). *Gender-Specific and Gender-neutral Pronouns*. Linguist list Archives, 93/11/23, no. 4.982. http://linguistlist.org.

—— (1993b). *Gender-neutral Pronouns: the Sequel*. Linguist list Archives, 93/12/16, no. 4.1066. http://linguistlist.org.

Livia, Anna (1995a). "I ought to Throw a Buick at You." In Kira Hall and Mary Bucholtz, eds., *Gender Articulated: Language and the Socially Constructed Self*. New York: Routledge.

—— (1995b). "Lucie Delarue-Mardrus and the Phrenetic Harlequinade." Introduction to *The Angel and the Perverts*. New York: New York University Press.

—— (1996a). "The Riddle of the Sphinx: Creating Genderless Characters in French." In Mary Bucholtz, Anita Liang, and Laurel Sutton, eds., *Cultural Performances*. Berkeley: Berkeley Women and Language Group.

—— (1996b). "'She sired six children': Pronominal Gender Play in English." In Mary Bucholtz, Anita Liang, and Laurel Sutton, eds., *Cultural Performances*. Berkeley: Berkeley Women and Language Group.

—— (1997a). "'It's a Girl': Bringing Performativity Back to Linguistics." In Anna Livia and Kira Hall, eds., *Queerly Phrased: Language, Gender, and Sexuality*. New York: Oxford University Press.

—— (1997b). "Disloyal to Masculinity." In Anna Livia and Kira Hall, eds., *Queerly Phrased: Language, Gender, and Sexuality*. New York: Oxford University Press.

—— (1999). *Bruised Fruit: A Novel*. Ithaca, N.Y.: Firebrand Books.

Livia, Anna, and Kira Hall, eds. (1997). *Queerly Phrased: Language, Gender, and Sexuality*. New York: Oxford University Press.

Lodge, R. Anthony (1993). *French: From Dialect to Standard*. London: Routledge.

Maingueneau, Dominique (1986). *Eléments de linguistique pour le texte littéraire*. Paris: Bordas.

Manoliu-Manea, Maria (1990). "French Neuter Demonstratives: Evidence for a Pragma-Semantic Definition of Pronouns." In John N. Green, and Wendy Ayres-Bennett, eds., *Variation and Change in French: Essays presented to Rebecca Posner on the Occasion of her Sixtieth Birthday*. London: Routledge.

Martel, Brigitte (1981). *Né homme, comment je suis devenue femme*. Montreal: Québecor.

Martin of Dacia (1961). *Martini de Dacia opera*. Edited by Henry Roos. Copenhagen: GAD.

Maupassant, Guy de (1984). "L'Homme-fille." In *La Parure et autres contes parisiens*. Paris: Garnier.

Mayrand, Marie (1986). *Combat de la mère d'un transsexuel: l'episode précédant le drame*. Montréal, Quebec: Les Editions: le Cercle International des Gagnants.

McConnell-Ginet, Sally (1979). "Prototypes, Pronouns, and Persons." In Madeleine Mathiot, ed., *Ethnolinguistics: Boas, Sapir, and Whorf Revisited*. The Hague: Mouton.

Mel'cuk, I. A. ([1958] 1971). "Statistics and the Relationship between the Gender of French Nouns and Their Endings." In V. Ju. Rozencvejg, ed., *Essays on Lexical Semantics*. Vol. 1. Stockholm: Skriptor.

Meyers, Walter (1980). *Aliens and Linguists: Language Study and Science Fiction*. Athens: University of Georgia Press.

Michard, Claire (1988). "Les Valeurs sémantiques 'humain' et 'humain mâle': univocité, ambiguité, ou ambivalence?" In Catherine Fuchs, ed., *L'Ambiguité et la paraphrase: opérations linguistiques, processus cognitifs, traitements automatiques*. Caen: Centre de publication de l'université de Caen.

Michard-Marchal, Claire, and Catherine Ribéry (1982). *Sexisme et sciences humaines*. Lille: Presses universitaires de Lille.

Miller, Casey, and Kate Swift (1977). *Words and Women*. London: Gollancz.

Montaigne, Michel de ([1581] 1955). *Journal de voyage en Italie*. Paris: Classiques Garnier.

Moreau, Thérèse (1991). "Langage et sexisme." Introduction to *Dictionnaire masculin féminin des titres et des fonctions*. Geneva: Metropolis.

Morgan, Elaine (1972). *The Descent of Woman*. London: Souvenir Press.

Morton, Donald (1993). "The Politics of Queer Theory." *Genders* 17 (fall): 121–50.

Mühlhäusler, Peter, and Rom Harré (1990). *Pronouns and People: The Linguistic Construction of Social and Personal Identity*. Oxford: Blackwell.

Neuman, Shirley (1991). "Autobiography, Bodies, Manhood." In Shirley Neuman, ed., *Autobiography and Questions of Gender*. London: Frank Cass.

Newman, Michael (1992). "Pronominal Disagreements: The Stubborn Problem of Singular Epicene Antecedents." *Language in Society* 21, no. 3 (Sept.): 447–75.

Niedzwiecki, Patricia (1994). *Au féminin!: code de féminisation à l'usage de la francophonie*. Paris: Nizet.

Noël, Georgine (1994). *Appelez-moi Gina*. Paris: Lattès.

Offord, Malcolm (1990). *Varieties of Contemporary French*. London: Macmillan.

Ostrovsky, Erika (1991). *A Constant Journey: The Fiction of Monique Wittig*. Carbondale: Southern Illinois University Press.

Ovid (1983). *Metamorphoses*. Translated by Rolfe Humphries. Bloomington: Indiana University Press.

Oxford University Press (1999). *Guidelines for Authors: From Manuscript to Bound Book*. New York: Oxford University Press.

Pastre, Geneviève (1997). "Linguistic Gender Play among French Gay Men and Lesbians." In Anna Livia and Kira Hall, eds., *Queerly Phrased: Language, Gender, and Sexuality*. New York: Oxford University Press.

Paul, Robert (1991). *Whatever Happened to Sherlock Holmes: Detective Fiction, Popular Theology, and Society*. Carbondale: Southern Illinois University Press.

Pauwels, Anne (1998). *Women Changing Language*. London: Addison Wesley Longman.

Penelope, Julia (1990). *Speaking Freely: Unlearning the Lies of the Father's Tongues*. New York: Pergamon.

Pettiti, Louis-Edmond (1992). *Les Transsexuels*. Paris: Presses universitaires de France.

Piercy, Marge (1976). *Woman on the Edge of Time*. New York: Ballantine Books.

Pingaud, Bernard (1958). "Je, vous, il." *Esprit* 7–8 (July–Aug.): 91–99.

Pinkster, H. (1991). "Evidence for SVO in Latin." In Roger Wright, ed., *Latin and the Romance Languages in the Early Middle Ages*. London: Routledge.

Porter, Roger (1991). "Figuration and Disfigurement: Herculine Barbin and the Autobiography of the Body." In Shirley Neuman, ed., *Autobiography and Questions of Gender*. London: Frank Cass.

Price, Granville (1971). *The French Language: Present and Past*. London: Arnold.

Priestman, Martin (1990). *Detective Fiction and Literature*. London: MacMillan.

Prince, Ellen (1981). "Toward a Taxonomy of Given-New Information." In Peter Cole, ed., *Radical Pragmatics*. New York: Academic Press.

Pullum, Geoffrey (1991). *The Great Eskimo Vocabulary Hoax and Other Irreverent Essays on the Study of Language*. Chicago: Chicago University Press.

Queneau, Raymond (1959). *Zazie dans le métro*. Paris: Gallimard.

Rand, Ayn (1946). *Anthem*. New York: New American Library.

Raymond, Janice (1979). *The Transsexual Empire: The Making of the She-Male*. Boston: Beacon.

———— (1981). *L'Empire transsexuel*. Translated by Jeanne Wiener-Renucci. Paris: Seuil.

Reinhart, Tanya (1980). "Conditions for text coherence." *Poetics Today* 1, no. 4 (161–180).

Ribeiro, Branca (1994). *Coherence in Psychotic Discourse*. New York: Oxford University Press.

Rickard, Peter (1989). A History of the French Language. London: Unwin Hyman.

Rihoit, Catherine (1980). *Histoire de Jeanne transsexuelle*. Paris: Mazarine.

Rimmon-Kenan, Shlomith (1983). "Text: Focalization." In *Narrative Fiction: Contemporary Poetics*. London: Methuen.

Robbe-Grillet, Alain (1957). *La Jalousie*. Paris: Editions de Minuit.

Rochefort, Christiane (1963). *Les Stances à Sophie*. Paris: Livre de Poche.

Romaine, Suzanne (1999). *Communicating Gender*. Mahwah, NJ: Lawrence Erlbaum.

Rosenfeld, Marthe (1981). "Language and the Vision of a Lesbian-Feminist Utopia in Wittig's *Les Guérillères*." *Frontiers* 6, nos.1–2 (spring–summer).

———— (1984). "The Linguistic Aspect of Sexual Conflict." *Mosaic* 17, no. 2. (spring): 235–41.

Rubin, Gayle (1975). "The Traffic in Women: Notes on the 'Political Economy' of Sex." In Rayna Reiter, ed., *Toward an Anthropology of Women*. New York: Monthly Review Press.

Rudes, Blair, and Bernard Healy Bernard (1979). "Is She for Real? The Concepts of Femaleness and Maleness in the Gay World." In Madeleine Mathiot, ed., *Ethnolinguistics: Boas, Sapir, and Whorf Revisited*. The Hague: Mouton.

Ruwet, Nicolas (1975). "Synecdocques et métonymies." In *Poétique de théorie et d'analyse littéraires* , 23, 1975.

Sapir, Edward ([1929] 1970). "Linguistics as a Science." In D. G. Mandelbaum, ed., *Edward Sapir: Culture, Language, and Personality, Selected Essays*. Berkeley: University of California Press.

Sarraute, Nathalie (1939). *Tropismes*. Paris: Editions de Minuit.

———— (1972). *Vous les entendez?* Paris: Gallimard.

Sartre, Jean-Paul (1949). *Les Chemins de la liberté*. 3 vols. Paris: Gallimard.

Schiffrin, Deborah (1994). *Approaches to Discourse*. Oxford: Blackwell.

Schulz, Muriel (1975). "The Semantic Derogation of Women." In Barrie Thorne and Nancy Henley, eds., *Language and Sex: Difference and Dominance*. Rowley, Mass.: Newbury House.

Searle, John R. (1958). "Proper Names." *Mind* 67, no. 266: 166–217
——— (1979). *Expression and Meaning: Studies in the Theory of Speech Acts.* Cambridge: Cambridge University Press.
——— (1990). *Speech Acts: An Essay in the Philosophy of Language.* 2d ed. Cambridge: Cambridge University Press.
Sedgwick, Eve Kosofsky (1990). *Epistemology of the Closet.* Berkeley: University of California Press.
Shaktini, Namascar (1985). "Le Déplacement du sujet phallique: l'écriture lesbienne de Monique Wittig." Spécial Monique Wittig, *Vlasta* 4: 65–77.
——— (1990). "A Revolutionary Signifier: The Lesbian Body." In Karla Jay and Joanne Glasgow, eds., *Lesbian Texts and Contexts: Radical Revisions.* New York: NewYork University Press.
Sheehan, Susan (1983). *Is There No Place on Earth for Me?* New York: Random House.
Shibamoto-Smith, Janet, and Naoko Ogawa (1997). "The Discursive Gendering of Gay and Japanese Couples." In Anna Livia and Kira Hall, eds., *Queerly Phrased: Language, Gender, and Sexuality.* New York: Oxford University Press.
Silverstein, Michael (1985). "Language and the Culture of Gender: At the Intersection of Structure, Usage, and Ideology." In Elizabeth Mertz and Richard J. Parmentier, eds., *Semiotic Mediation: Sociocultural and Psychological Perspectives.* New York: Academic Press.
Simon, Claude (1964). "Pour Monique Wittig." *L'Express* (30 Nov.–6 Dec.): 70–71.
Smith, Wayne (1990). "Evidence for Auxiliaries in Taiwan Sign Language." In Susan D. Fischer and Patricia Siple, eds., *Theoretical Issues in Sign Language Research.* Vol. 1, *Linguistics.* Chicago: University of Chicago Press.
Soll, L. (1979). "Zur Situierung von on (nous) im neuen Französisch." *Romanische Forschung*, 91.
Spender, Dale (1980), *Man Made Language.* London: Routledge.
Spivak, Gayatri (1976). Translator's preface to Jacques Derrida, *Of Grammatology.* Baltimore: Johns; Hopkins University Press.
Spock, Benjamin ([1957] 1985). *Baby and Child Care.* New York: Pocket Books.
Stalnaker, Robert (1973). "Presuppositions." *Journal of Philosophical Logic* 2: 447–57.
——— (1974). "Pragmatic Presuppositions." In Milton K. Munitz and Peter K. Unger, eds., *Semantics and Philosophy.* New York: New York University Press.
——— (1978). "Assertion." In P. Cole, ed., *Syntax and Semantics* 9: *Pragmatics.* New York: Academic Press.
Stephens, Inge (1983). *Alain Transsexuelle.* Saint-Lambert, Quebec: Les Editions Heritage.
Strawson, Peter F. (1964). "Intention and Convention in Speech Acts." *Philosophical Review*, 73: 439–60.
Stryker, Susan, ed. (1998). *GLQ* 4, no. 2, *The Transgender Issue.*
Tannen, Deborah (1994) *Gender and Discourse.* New York: Oxford University Press [with Robin Lakoff], pp. 137–73.
Thorne, Barrie, and Nancy Henley, eds. (1975). *Language and Sex: Difference and Dominance.* Rowley, Mass: Newbury House.
Trubetzkoy, Nikolaj (1975). *Letters and Notes.* Edited by Roman Jakobson. The Hague: Mouton.
Tukia, Päivi, and Marc Tukia (1988). "Structure linguistique et identification

sexuelle chez les enfants de 16 à 42 mois: analyse psychométrique et linguistique pour tester l'hypothèse Sapir-Whorf." *Contrastes: La différence sexuelle dans le langage*. Actes du colloque ADEC-Université Paris III. December 1988.

Vance, Jack (1958). *The Languages of Pao*. New York: Ace.

Violi, Patrizia (1987). "Les origines du genre grammatical." *Langages* 85 (Mar.): 15–35.

Wagner, Robert-Léon (1968). *La Grammaire française*. Vol. 1. Paris: SEDES.

Waugh, Linda (1982). "Marked and Unmarked: A Choice Between Unequals in Semiotic Structure." *Semiotica* 38, nos. 3–4: 299–318.

Went-Daoust, Y. (1991). "L'Opoponax ou le parcours de *on*." *Neophilologus* 75, no. 3 (July): 358–66.

Wenzel, Hélène (1985). "Le discours radical de Monique Wittig." Special Monique Wittig, *Vlasta* 4: 43–54.

Weston, Kath (1993). "Do Clothes Make the Woman? Gender, Performance Theory, and Lesbian Eroticism." *Genders* 17 (fall): 1– 21.

Whorf, Benjamin (1956a). "Language and Reality." In John B. Carroll, ed., *Language, Thought, and Reality: Selected Writings*. Cambridge, Mass.: MIT Press.

———— (1956b). "Science and Linguistics." In John B. Carroll, ed., *Language, Thought, and Reality: Selected Writings*. Cambridge, Mass.: MIT Press.

———— (1956c). "Languages and Logic." In John B. Carroll, ed., *Language, Thought, and Reality: Selected Writings*. Cambridge, Mass.: MIT Press.

Wiemer, Annegret (1987). "Foreign L(anguish), Mother Tongue: Concepts of Language in Contemporary Feminist Science Fiction." *Women's Studies: Interdisciplinary Journal* 14: 163–73.

Winterson, Jeanette (1992). *Written on the Body*. London: Jonathan Cape.

Wittig, Monique (1964). *L'Opoponax*. Paris: Minuit.

———— (1966). *The Opoponax*. Translated by Helen Weaver. London: Peter Owen.

———— (1969). *Les Guérillères*. Paris: Minuit.

———— (1971). *Les Guérillères*. Translated by David Le Vay. New York: Avon.

———— (1973). *Le corps lesbien*. Paris: Minuit.

———— (1975). *The Lesbian Body*. Translated by David Le Vay. London: Peter Owen.

———— (1985a). *Virgile, non*. Paris: Minuit.

———— (1985b). "Paris-la-Politique." Spécial Monique Wittig, *Vlasta* 4, 8–35.

———— (1986). "The Mark of Gender." In Nancy K. Miller, ed., *The Poetics of Gender*. New York: Columbia University Press.

———— (1987). *Across the Acheron*. London: Peter Owen.

———— (1992a). "The Category of Sex." In *The Straight Mind and Other Essays*. Boston: Beacon Press.

———— (1992b). "The Straight Mind." In *The Straight Mind and Other Essays*. Boston: Beacon Press.

———— (1992c). "The Point of View: Universal or Particular?" In *The Straight Mind and Other Essays*. Boston: Beacon Press.

———— (1992d). "The Site of Action." In *The Straight Mind and Other Essays*. Boston: Beacon Press.

———— (1992e). "On the Social Contract." In *The Straight Mind and Other Essays*. Boston: Beacon Press.

———— (1992f). Preface to *The Straight Mind and Other Essays*. Boston: Beacon Press.

Wittig, Monique, and Sande Zeig (1976). *Brouillon pour un dictionnaire des amantes*. Paris: Grasset et Fasquelle.

——— (1979). *Lesbian Peoples: Materials for a Dictionary*. London: Peter Owen.

Woolf, Virginia ([1928] 1956). *Orlando: a Biography*. New York: Harcourt, Brace, Jovanovich.

——— ([1928] 1977). *A Room of One's Own*. London: Granada.

——— (1990). "Romance and the Heart." In Deborah Cameron, ed., *The Feminist Critique of Language: A Reader*. London: Routledge.

Yaguello, Marina (1978). *Les Mots et les femmes: essai d'approche socio-linguistic de la condition féminine*. Paris: Payot.

——— (1988). "L'elargissement du capitaine Prieur." *Contrastes: la différence sexuelle dans le langage*. Actes du colloque ADEC-Université Paris III. December, 73–77.

Zola, Emile ([1880] 1969). "L'Attaque du moulin." In *Contes choisis*. London: Hodder and Stoughton.

Index